Transformations of the State

The modern state is under threat – its powers increasingly eroded. This series examines the current and future prospects for a traditional conception of the state to provide readers with the 'state of the art' on the 'state of the state'.

More information about this series at
http://www.springer.com/series/14399

Steffen Schneider • Henning Schmidtke • Sebastian Haunss •
Jennifer Gronau
Editors

Capitalism and Its Legitimacy in Times of Crisis

palgrave
macmillan

Editors
Steffen Schneider
SOCIUM Research Center on Inequality and Social Policy
University of Bremen
Bremen, Germany

Henning Schmidtke
Bavarian School of Public Policy, TUM School of Governance
Technical University of Munich
Munich, Germany

Sebastian Haunss
SOCIUM Research Center on Inequality and Social Policy
University of Bremen
Bremen, Germany

Jennifer Gronau
Centre for Global Cooperation Research (Käte-Hamburger-Kolleg)
Duisburg, Germany

Transformations of the State
ISBN 978-3-319-53764-1 ISBN 978-3-319-53765-8 (eBook)
DOI 10.1007/978-3-319-53765-8

Library of Congress Control Number: 2017949269

Cover illustration: The jacket reproduces detail of the annotated version of the etching in Thomas Hobbes's Leviathan (1651) by Lucila Muñoz-Sanchez and Monika Sniegs.

Printed on acid-free paper

This Palgrave Macmillan imprint is published by Springer Nature
The registered company is Springer International Publishing AG
The registered company address is: Gewerbestrasse 11, 6330 Cham, Switzerland

Series Editors' Preface

Over the past four centuries, the national state has emerged as the world's most effective means of organizing society, but its current status and future are decidedly uncertain. Some scholars predict the total demise of the national state as we know it, its powers eroded by a dynamic global economy on the one hand and by the transfer of political decision-making to supranational bodies on the other. Other analysts point out the remarkable resilience of the state's core institutions and assert that even in the age of global markets and politics, the state remains the ultimate guarantor of security, democracy, welfare and the rule of law, and will reassert itself. Does either of these interpretations describe the future of the OECD world's modern, liberal national state? Will the state soon be as obsolete and irrelevant as an outdated computer? Should it be scrapped for some new invention, or can it be overhauled and rejuvenated? Is the state actually thriving and still fit to serve, just in need of a few minor reforms, or is there some paradox involved that allows for no such simple alternatives, as some would have it (Rodrik 2011)?

In an attempt to address these questions, the analyses in the *Transformations of the State* series separate the complex tangle of tasks and functions that comprise the state into four manageable dimensions:

- the monopolization of the means of force;
- the rule of law, as prescribed and safeguarded by the constitution;

- the guarantee of democratic self-governance; and
- the provision of welfare and the assurance of social cohesion.

In the OECD world of the 1960s and 1970s, these four dimensions formed a synergetic constellation that emerged as the central, defining characteristic of the modern state. Books in the series report the results of both empirical and theoretical studies of the transformations experienced in each of these dimensions over the past few decades.

Stephan Leibfried and Michael Zürn (2005), Achim Hurrelmann et al. (2007), Heinz Rothgang and Steffen Schneider (2015) and Leibfried et al. (2015) define the basic concepts of state transformation employed in all of these studies and provide an overview of the issues addressed. Written by political scientists, lawyers, economists and sociologists, the series tracks the development of the post-World War II OECD state. Here, at last, is an up-to-date series of reports on the state of the state and a crystal-ball glimpse into its future.

References

Hurrelmann, Achim, Stephan Leibfried, Kerstin Martens and Peter Mayer, eds. 2007. *Transforming the Golden-Age National State*. Basingstoke: Palgrave Macmillan.

Leibfried, Stephan, Evelyne Huber, Matthew Lange, Jonah D. Levy, Frank Nullmeier and John D. Stephens, eds. 2015. *The Oxford Handbook of Transformations of the State*. Oxford: Oxford University Press.

Leibfried, Stephan and Michael Zürn, eds. 2005. *Transformations of the State?* Cambridge: Cambridge University Press.

Rodrik, Dani, 2011. *The Globalization Paradox. Why Global Markets, States, and Democracy Can't Co-exist*. Oxford: Oxford University Press.

Rothgang, Heinz and Steffen Schneider, eds. 2015. *State Transformations in OECD Countries. Dimensions, Driving Forces and Trajectories*. Basingstoke: Palgrave Macmillan.

Preface and Acknowledgements

This book concludes a research project on the legitimation of democratic nation states (Germany, Switzerland, the United Kingdom, the United States), international organizations (EU, G8, UN) and capitalism as an economic regime. The project was directed by Frank Nullmeier, carried out at the Collaborative Research Centre 'Transformations of the State' (University of Bremen, Germany) and generously funded by the German Research Council (DFG) in the years 2003–2014. The findings of the project have been published in a number of joint articles and books by the contributors to the present volume and previous members of the research team; these publications notably include an edited volume and a monograph published with Palgrave (Hurrelmann, Schneider and Steffek 2007; Schneider et al. 2010; see also Hurrelmann et al. 2009; Nullmeier et al. 2010).

The editors of the present volume wish to use the opportunity to thank Achim Hurrelmann, Zuzana Krell-Laluhová, Roland Lhotta, Martin Nonhoff and Achim Wiesner, who were collaborators of the project at different points in time. We also thank a number of student research assistants who assisted us in retrieving and coding the text corpus on which the volume is based, and in managing data: Wiebke Anton, Anna Braam, Clara Friedrich, Wolfgang Geißler, Kristen Isherwood, Isabelle Kim, Klara Kopperschmidt, Katja Lamich, Nora Sinner, Sebastian Streb and Christoph Uhl. Dieter Wolf, the Collaborative Research Centre's managing director, greatly assisted the research team in solving administrative and funding issues. Particular thanks go to our former colleagues at the Collaborative Research Centre – especially its speaker, Stephan Leibfried – for many valuable discussions about problems of legitimacy research, and to the DFG for funding this endeavour. Finally, we would like to thank our anonymous reviewer for the close reading of the manuscript and excellent comments which greatly improved the volume, and our editors at Palgrave – Judith Allan and Beth Farrow – for their patience and support.

Steffen Schneider, Henning Schmidtke,
Sebastian Haunss and Jennifer Gronau
Bremen, August 2016

References

Hurrelmann, Achim, Zuzana Krell-Laluhová, Frank Nullmeier, Steffen Schneider and Achim Wiesner. 2009. 'Why the Democratic Nation-state is Still Legitimate: A Study of Media Discourses'. *European Journal of Political Research* 48(4): 483–515.

Hurrelmann, Achim, Steffen Schneider and Jens Steffek, eds. 2007. *Legitimacy in an Age of Global Politics*. Basingstoke: Palgrave Macmillan.

Nullmeier, Frank, Dominika Biegoń, Jennifer Gronau, Martin Nonhoff, Henning Schmidtke and Steffen Schneider. 2010. *Prekäre Legitimitäten. Rechtfertigung von Herrschaft in der postnationalen Konstellation*. Frankfurt am Main: Campus.

Schneider, Steffen, Achim Hurrelmann, Frank Nullmeier, Achim Wiesner and Zuzana Krell-Laluhová. 2010. *Democracy's Deep Roots. Why the Nation State Remains Legitimate*. Basingstoke: Palgrave Macmillan.

Contents

Notes on Contributors

Dominika Biegoń is Political Advisor for European Politics at the *Friedrich-Ebert-Stiftung*, Berlin, Germany.

Jennifer Gronau is a Postdoctoral Fellow at the Centre for Global Cooperation Research (*Käte-Hamburger-Kolleg*), Duisburg, Germany.

Sebastian Haunss is a Senior Research Fellow at the Research Centre on Inequality and Social Policy (SOCIUM), University of Bremen, Germany.

Falk Lenke is a doctoral student at the University of Bremen, Bremen, Germany.

Frank Nullmeier is Professor of Political Science at the Research Centre on Inequality and Social Policy (SOCIUM), University of Bremen, Germany.

Henning Schmidtke is a Senior Research Fellow at the Bavarian School of Public Policy, TUM School of Governance, Technical University of Munich, Germany.

Steffen Schneider is a Senior Research Fellow at the Research Centre on Inequality and Social Policy (SOCIUM), University of Bremen, Germany.

List of Figures

List of Tables

1

A Legitimation Crisis of the Capitalist Market Economy?

Steffen Schneider and Henning Schmidtke

The severity of the 2008 global financial crisis has frequently been compared with the Great Depression (Almunia et al. 2010; Claessens et al. 2010). For a moment, the global financial system, international trade and whole national economies appeared to be on the verge of collapse. For many observers, no less than the future of capitalism as an economic *regime* was at stake (Schneider et al. 2010: Chapter 6). Thus, the financial crisis with the ensuing Great Recession (Grusky et al. 2011) was arguably a *critical juncture* – a potentially transformative moment of uncertainty about capitalism's ideational and, especially, normative

S. Schneider (✉)
Research Centre on Inequality and Social Policy (SOCIUM), University of Bremen, Bremen, Germany
e-mail: stschnei@uni-bremen.de

H. Schmidtke
Bavarian School of Public Policy, TUM School of Governance, Technical University of Munich, Munich, Germany
e-mail: henning.schmidtke@hfp.tum.de

S. Schneider et al. (eds.), *Capitalism and Its Legitimacy in Times of Crisis*, Transformations of the State,
DOI 10.1007/978-3-319-53765-8_1

foundations comparable to the 1920s/30s and 1970s/80s (Blyth 2002; Capoccia and Kelemen 2007).

However, as Kahler and Lake (2013: 9) point out in their discussion of the 2008 critical juncture and its impact, economic crises frequently remain undertheorized, 'an undifferentiated deus ex machina, a convenient explanation for otherwise unexplained changes'. The present volume and its contributions posit that the capitalist market economy as a regime is underpinned by *ideas* that relate, for instance, to its constitutive elements, their functioning and relationships, and their proper roles (Hall 1989; Blyth 2002: 11). What is more, as 'part of an overall sequence of institutional change', ideas – on the causes, nature and scope of an economic crisis, on responsibilities and culprits, and on viable solutions – have a crucial impact on the *outcomes* of critical junctures: They either 'reduce uncertainty, act as coalition-building resources, empower agents to contest existing institutions, act as resources in the construction of new institutions, and finally coordinate agents' expectations, thereby reproducing institutional stability' (Blyth 2002: 15), or they fail to do so. Not every critical juncture, in other words, turns out to be a Great Transformation (Polanyi 2001) that ushers in new institutional arrangements based on a new set of factual and normative ideas such as Keynesianism in the 1920s/30s and neoliberalism in the 1970s/80s (Blyth 2002: 36).

Recent work in historical institutionalism has begun to explore the role of *discourse* in the social construction of ideas (Campbell 1998; Hay 2008; Schmidt 2008). The volume moves beyond this literature and also extends the purview of legitimation research in political science by putting the crucial aspect of an economic regime's *legitimacy* front and centre, and by highlighting the crucial role of discourse in the (re-) production or transformation of legitimation ideas. Public debate on the problems that caused major economic crises is likely to foster the contestation of existing institutional arrangements – a legitimation crisis of the regime in place (Blyth 2002: 5, 39). Yet transformative – that is, abrupt and wholesale – institutional change should only be expected where the ideational resources of the old regime lose traction, exposing it to massive delegitimation while legitimating new arrangements.

In the wake of the 2008 financial crisis, many proponents of the capitalist market economy feared that it might trigger institutional change of precisely this kind while some of its critics saw a window of opportunity for outright *alternatives* to capitalism (Elster and Moene 1989): The question 'When, if not now?' has presumably motivated the latest cyclical peak of highly critical literature (Posner 2009; Streeck 2014, 2016). Yet with hindsight, the ideational foundations and institutional arrangements of the regime proved surprisingly robust (Mayntz 2012; Drezner 2014).

By focusing on the (de-)legitimation of the capitalist market economy, a regime that is essentially ubiquitous in the world of today, our volume contributes to the explanation of this puzzling outcome: Why were the challengers of the regime unable to use their window of opportunity more effectively? The volume also makes the case for *text-analytical* research on the legitimacy of the capitalist market economy: All the chapters treat public spheres and discourse – more precisely, media discourse – as the key arenas of (de-)legitimation processes; drawing on the same original, jointly gathered corpus of pertinent articles from the quality press of four OECD countries, they zero in on the discursive processing of the 2008 financial crisis and examine the contours of the legitimation crisis triggered by it.

Individually, the chapters examine different aspects of this discursive legitimation crisis. Together, they indicate that the uncertainty surrounding the financial crisis indeed translated into a spike of public debate on the ideational foundations of the capitalist market economy and growing contestation of its legitimacy after 2008. However, a closer look at various aspects of discourse – and notably at the discursive strategies of the regime's challengers and defenders – reveals that the legitimation crisis was not only short-lived; its delegitimating character was also remarkably limited. The regime managed to shield itself to a surprising extent against attributions of responsibility for the financial crisis and Great Recession. Whereas the challengers of the regime failed to make a much stronger case for alternatives to the capitalist market economy and the ideas that underpin it, the rhetorical devices of its defenders proved quite effective. Finally, critical voices do not appear to have galvanized into a powerful delegitimating coalition. These findings go a long way towards explaining why a more profound delegitimation of the capitalist market economy has not occurred, let alone a Great Transformation of the regime or its replacement with an alternative system.

The Legitimacy of Economic Regimes: Conceptual Foundations

Some readers might question the claim that legitimacy is a pertinent concept for the study of economic regimes – or, in any case, for the regime examined here: the capitalist market economy.[1] In this section, we therefore begin by discussing the meaning and pertinence of the term legitimacy in the context of a study on the capitalist market economy. Secondly, we justify our focus on legitimacy-related communication and media discourse. Thirdly, we explain how the analysis of legitimation discourse in the context of the post-2008 critical juncture can help us to understand why the Great Recession did not result in a Great Transformation.

Is the Capitalist Market Economy A-Legitimate?

The most prominent strand of research on legitimacy ties the concept to the notions of political authority and coercive powers (Weber 1922: 122–4; Gilley 2013). Hence, one might argue that the term legitimacy should be reserved for political systems narrowly conceived and that only regimes with authority and coercive powers are in need of legitimation. This is in fact the position taken by economists such as Nobel Prize winner Buchanan (1995: 20):

> The categorical difference between market and political interaction lies in the continuing presence of an effective exit option in market relationships and in its absence in politics. To the extent that the individual participant in market exchange has available effective alternatives that may be chosen at relatively low cost, any exchange is necessarily voluntary. In its stylized

form, the market involves no coercion, no extraction of value from any participant without consent. In dramatic contrast, politics is inherently coercive, independently of the effective decision rules that may operate.

Here, the market as a spontaneous, voluntary and non-hierarchical coordination mechanism in which nobody is forced to participate or act in a specific way is viewed as essentially 'a-legitimate' (Steffek 2007: 190). To evaluate the validity of this a-legitimacy claim, we need to distinguish between a normative and an empirical understanding of legitimacy. While the former relates to the acceptability of a regime from an external observer's point of view and based on the normative standards she puts forward, the latter considers the acceptance of a regime by those who are subject to its authority, and their underlying legitimacy beliefs, as *social facts* (Barker 2001: 22–5).

Even from a normative point of view, the a-legitimacy claim has not gone undisputed. Ever since the development of industrial capitalism in the nineteenth century, the capitalist market economy has been faced with waves of severe criticism – most prominently by Karl Marx and Friedrich Engels, and in the entire tradition of anticapitalist thought spawned by their writings. This anticapitalist literature – which includes literature proposing alternatives to the capitalist regime – has not limited itself to questioning the regime's *functionality*. Instead, it has contested its acceptability – and thus its *legitimacy* – on the basis of a broad array of normative ideas (as demonstrated in Chapter 2 of this volume; see also Mueller 2012: Chapter 1; Jaeggi 2013).

The a-legitimacy claim may be questioned on several grounds. Firstly, even social arrangements that are *prima facie* voluntary and non-hierarchical may require prior justification and consent from a normative point of view. Secondly, it is questionable that the 'organized' (Hilferding 1968) or 'late' (Habermas 1973) stage of the capitalist market economy which has provided the backdrop of neo-Marxist theorizing and anticapitalist critique since the twentieth century, or today's financial capitalism, is as voluntary and non-hierarchical as the cited view suggests: There is no doubt that ideal-typical market competition – if it ever was a reality – has given way to more business concentration and oligopolistic structures, and that market arrangements have been reshaped by (welfare) state intervention. Thirdly, a number of market actors and institutions have *themselves* acquired genuinely political authority and coercive powers. In short, the acceptability of the capitalist market economy has become a normative issue and legitimacy a relevant concept. In the wake of globalization and the neoliberally inspired privatization and deregulation wave since the 1970s, the actors and institutions of the capitalist market economy have taken over even more genuine state functions (Genschel and Zangl 2014: 344–7). This development further undermines the a-legitimacy claim from a normative point of view.

Such normative considerations are, however, only partially relevant – and therefore need not be pursued further – if legitimacy is understood as an empirical concept, as is the case in this volume. From such an empirical perspective and in the tradition of David Easton (1965, 1975), legitimacy is a pertinent category once it can be shown, first, that the capitalist market economy is perceived as a regime that bears authority by at least some of those who are affected by its decisions and outcomes, and secondly, that the acceptability of that regime at least occasionally becomes an issue of public consideration and debate in much the same way as the acceptability of political systems and institutions (North 1981; Fligstein 2002). Our volume builds on Easton's definition of legitimacy as the major source of diffuse support for authoritative regimes – be they political or economic – by their constituencies. The empirical reality may often correspond to the a-legitimacy scenario in which the capitalist market economy is taken for granted and thus enjoys *latent* support (Suchman 1995: 582). But the legitimacy of all types and stages of the capitalist market economy can also become an issue and be publicly debated by its constituencies, using a range of normative standards. Where the acceptance of the regime is grounded in such normative foundations, it is empirically legitimate. Where normative ideas are used to contest legitimacy and withdraw diffuse support, the regime becomes illegitimate. As for political systems, one may hypothesize a link between legitimacy and compliance or regime stability (Weber 1922: 122–4; Lipset 1959). The revolutionary breakdown of the capitalist market economy in Russia and other parts of the world throughout the twentieth century as well as the collapse of the socialist regime towards its end provide *ex negativo* evidence for the importance of this kind of support for both political and economic regimes.

From the Social Construction of Legitimacy to the Role of Public Discourse

An empirical understanding of legitimacy and the notion that the capitalist market economy at least potentially requires legitimation underpins all the chapters of the volume. But how can we gauge the legitimacy of the regime? There is definitely a dearth of empirical work on the legitimacy of the capitalist market economy. The chapters of this volume are a pioneering effort to correct this oversight. All of the contributions show that the concepts and methods of empirical legitimacy research in political science can be plausibly adapted to investigate the (de-)legitimation of economic regimes.

The study of attitudes, behaviour and discourse provides three complementary access points to regime legitimacy (Schmidtke and Schneider 2012). Max Weber's legitimacy beliefs (1922: 122) or related concepts such as Easton's diffuse support (Easton 1965: Chapter 17, 1975: 436–7) are traditionally measured with the help of public opinion research, which captures the dimension of political *attitudes* (Weatherford 1992; Norris 1999, 2011; Dalton 2004; Torcal and Montero 2006; Booth and Seligson 2009). Alternatively, researchers observe political *behaviour* (participation and protest) to derive indicators of compliance and legitimacy (Levi 1997; Norris 2002; Haunss 2007; Rucht 2007; Tarrow 2011; Tilly and Tarrow 2015). Both perspectives and sets of indicators may also be combined (as in Gilley 2006).

Thus, surveys may plausibly be used to measure trust in or satisfaction with economic regimes. The literature describing and explaining attitudes related to free trade is already extensive (Scheve and Slaughter 2001; Hainmueller and Hiscox 2006; Mansfield and Mutz 2009); other aspects of the capitalist market economy might be tackled by public opinion research in a similar fashion. It is also feasible to observe forms of (consumer) behaviour and use the data as indicators of legitimacy.

In line with the interpretation of voting and other conventional forms of participation as indicators of support for *political* systems, merely participating in market activities and consuming brand-name products may be interpreted as expressions of general support for the capitalist regime and its protagonists, while consumer boycotts and similar protest activities presumably indicate that its legitimacy is contested (Baker 2005; Tarrow 2011: Chapter 4; Urbatsch 2013).

There is no doubt that each of these perspectives has comparative advantages in the study of legitimacy and (de-)legitimation processes (Schneider et al. 2010: 16–44; Schmidtke and Nullmeier 2011). In research on *political* systems, the traditions of public opinion and participation research are well established. However, unresolved problems stand in the way of a simple transfer of these methods to the study of *economic* regimes. Suitable question items in surveys and participation-based indicators are often not available, at least not for more than a single country or point in time. Moreover, it is often unclear how attitudinal and behavioural data should be interpreted. The habitual acceptance of market rules and activities is arguably an important source of compliance with the capitalist market economy, and thus the reactive character of survey research might be even more problematic in the economic context than in measuring political attitudes: The stimuli provided by questionnaires are likely to generate a large number of 'non-responses' – assessments of the regime *not* grounded in the firm normative positions that the concepts of legitimacy beliefs and diffuse support imply. Similar problems with the interpretation of data might arise when various types of behaviour are employed as indicators of legitimacy without firm knowledge about their underlying motivations: For instance, one might doubt that merely participating in market activities really indicates support for the capitalist economic regime as such.

Most importantly, both perspectives tend to ignore that the nature of regimes – for instance, the voluntary and non-hierarchical character of the capitalist market economy or its levels of authority – as well as their legitimacy or, for that matter, their perceived a-legitimacy have to be understood as *socially constructed* rather than 'objective' features (Luckmann 1987; Raufer 2005; Offe 2006: 26). Hence, legitimacy is the temporary, precarious outcome of legitimation processes in which the acceptability of a regime and its normative foundations are established (Nullmeier et al. 2010). These processes – the focus of our analysis of (de-)legitimation and (the absence of) institutional change in response to the 2008 financial crisis – are essentially *communicative*. Hence, unlike the traditional approaches in the field of empirical legitimacy research, the contributions to this volume focus on the role of public spheres and discourse – or more precisely, of discursive practices, strategies and struggles – in the (re-)production or contestation of legitimacy and the ideas that underpin it. A regime's legitimacy is (re-) produced successfully where the legitimacy claims of a political or economic regime's incumbents and supporters are accepted by the wider public; where this is no longer the case, we are faced with the contestation of legitimacy or its normative foundations.

All of the contributions, moreover, highlight the role of public spheres, which to date largely remain *national* public spheres (Wessler et al. 2008: 5; Risse 2010: Part II), in legitimation processes. With Jürgen Habermas (2008: 138–91) and Bernhard Peters (2005), we consider democratic public spheres to be characterized by three aspects: Firstly, they consist of various discursive arenas, ranging from national parliamentary debates to private conversations among 'ordinary' citizens. Secondly, the *media* are key players in the (re-)production of public spheres; they serve as 'conveyor belts' and 'gatekeepers' between the 'centre' (political and economic power holders) and the 'periphery' (individual citizens and society as a whole), and also contribute their own agendas and evaluations to public debates (Peters 2008: Chapter 2). Thirdly, the *quality press* continues to play an important role as opinion-leader and mediator between arenas, despite growing competition by other print and digital media and the relatively low circulation of quality newspapers (Koopmans and Statham 2010a: 47–51).

Finally, the volume – whose empirical contributions draw on a corpus of articles from the quality press – highlights the role of *elite discourse* (as opposed to mass public opinion) in legitimation processes. Thus, unlike the traditional 'bottom-up' perspective, it takes up Easton's observation that 'an active political elite, a military cadre, or an organized intelligentsia' tend to be more important legitimacy constituencies of a regime such as the capitalist market economy than 'ordinary' citizens, as they 'may be able to make their positive or negative support count more than high levels of support from unorganized millions' (1965: 167). There is no doubt that elite actors broadly conceived dominate public debates on the legitimacy of political or economic regimes from which citizens take their cues. Hence, their legitimacy-related attitudes and behaviour are heavily influenced by elite (de-)legitimation practices and strategies, including the self-legitimation practices of a regime's incumbents (Barker 2001: 35; Zaum 2013: 16–19; Gronau and Schmidtke 2016). In an attempt to understand when critical junctures result in institutional change, a focus on elite legitimation discourse is even more apposite. Where the incumbents of a regime – business elites in the case of the capitalist market economy – as well as the political actors whose support would be required for major reforms continue to affirm the regime's legitimacy and do not question its ideational foundations, transformative change is unlikely. Conversely, change is most likely where even the regime's incumbents and traditional supporters begin to contest its legitimacy and ideational foundations, coalescing around reform coalitions underpinned by a different set of economic and legitimation ideas (Palazzo and Scherer 2006).

From Legitimation Crises to Institutional Change

Why do some critical junctures – such as the Great Depression of the 1920s and 1930s or the economic turmoil of the 1970s and 1980s – result in massive change of the capitalist market economy, transforming both its ideational foundations and its institutional arrangements, while others do not? How can we explain the puzzle that the economic regime has weathered the 'perfect storm' of the 2008 financial crisis largely – and surprisingly – unaltered?

In the vein of the cited historical-institutional literature on such questions, the contributors to this volume build on the notions of path dependence and punctuated equilibria (Thelen 1999, 2003; Mahoney 2001). They argue, first, that critical junctures are moments of *uncertainty* in which established ideas about a regime are reconsidered and sometimes replaced with new ones. By offering 'an interpretative framework, which describes and accounts for the workings of the economy by defining its constitutive elements and proper (and therefore "improper") interrelations' (Blyth 2002: 11), ideas guide the responses of key economic and political actors to moments of economic crisis, thus potentially helping to establish a new path of institutional development or, in other words, a new regime.

Secondly, the volume takes up and expands on the notion that critical junctures are essentially *legitimation crises* of the capitalist market economy: Beyond public debate about the nature and severity of the problems that triggered an economic crisis or about viable solutions, we expect critical junctures to be accompanied by the contestation of the regime itself and its legitimacy. Put differently, a shift from the a-legitimacy scenario of taken-for-grantedness (Suchman 1995: 582) or latent support to explicit public debate on the legitimacy of the capitalist market economy and its foundations is not only the strongest indicator but, in fact, a key feature of a critical juncture. Where the intensity of such legitimation discourse remains low and the tone of legitimacy assessments largely positive, we should presumably not diagnose a critical juncture, because a necessary precondition for transformative change – a discursive window of opportunity that enables challengers of the economic regime to make their case – is not given. By contrast, a discursive legitimation crisis may, in the words of Douglass North (1981: 65),

> lead to a reassessment of the legitimacy of an existing economic order. Opportunities will be offered the ideological entrepreneur to build on [. . .] alienation [. . .] to construct a counter ideology. [. . .]. Just as the rise of a political-economic unit is associated historically with a consensus on values, the decline is associated with a disintegration of a common value system.

Thirdly, in line with Capoccia and Kelemen (2007; see also Capoccia 2015: 165–6), the contributions view critical junctures as *open-ended*: They may or may not be transformative. Hence, a tautological definition that uses the transformative outcome of a critical juncture as its defining criterion is avoided (but see, for instance, Pierson 2004: 51). In a similar vein, and very much in line with the traditional meaning given to the term crisis in medicine or economics (Habermas 1973: 9–19), a legitimation crisis is conceptualized as a turning point: It may be linked with weak symptoms and subside quickly, or it may be more serious and reach a point of no return followed by transformative change of the dominant interpretive framework, the normative foundations and the institutional arrangements of an economic regime. Put differently, a legitimation crisis is a necessary but not sufficient precondition for institutional change. How legitimation discourse unfolds during critical junctures is thus crucial in explaining institutional stability or development.

Anything other than growing intensity and a more critical tone of media discourse after 2008 – a shift away from the a-legitimacy scenario towards a legitimation crisis – would in fact be surprising. The alternative regime of a state-planned economy had collapsed in the early 1990s and was thoroughly discredited; liberal democracy and the capitalist market economy were touted as the triumphant couple of the modern social order in the post-Cold War years (Fukuyama 1992). The occasional cyclical downturns and stock market crashes of the following two decades paled in comparison with the post-2008 financial crisis. If the legitimacy of the capitalist market economy was indeed not on the public agenda in the first years of the twenty-first century, then the events in the wake of the financial crisis must have come as a shock.

The chapters of the present volume document that these events triggered the expected legitimation crisis. However, they also indicate the temporary nature and limited scope of this crisis. Evidently, critics of the capitalist economy were unable to seize the opportunity for a more radical and consequential shake-up of the regime's ideational foundations. The legitimacy of the regime did become an issue, but the scope and nature of delegitimation efforts ultimately proved insufficient to destabilize its institutional arrangements and to foster transformative change. The chapters unfold Blyth's (2002) notion of a 'sequence' of institutional stability or development to make this point. They show that ideas and arguments about the legitimacy of the capitalist market economy – and about the necessity or possibility of reforming or replacing it – are encapsulated in two types of contributions to legitimation discourse: Firstly, there are attributions of responsibility for an economic crisis and for solving it. To solve a crisis, it takes ideas about the actors or structures responsible for a crisis, on the one hand, and about the actors or institutions that might be able to respond to it effectively, on the other. These responsibility attributions entail ideas about the functional mechanisms and problems of the economic regime and also about the role of the state in regulating market arrangements. Moreover, they proffer an implicit *delegitimation* of the culprits identified or, by assigning responsibility for solving a crisis, implicitly *legitimate* the actors or institutions trusted to handle it. A second type of proposition makes such legitimacy evaluations explicit by tapping into the normative foundations of a regime and assessing it – or some element of it – in light of related normative standards.

These responsibility attributions and legitimacy evaluations may refer to the capitalist market economy as a whole or to some of its core principles, varieties and major actor groups. Responsibility attributions and evaluations can, in other words, be very general or highly specific; they can also be deflected to other, political regimes such as the (nation or welfare) state. A legitimation crisis of the capitalist market economy is unlikely to usher in transformative institutional change if elite discourse remains focused on a few, perhaps marginal institutions and actors or is deflected to the political sphere.

Two types of ideas are linked with responsibility attributions and legitimacy evaluations in the context of a legitimation crisis: firstly, the causal ideas that underpin problem diagnoses and proposed solutions such as enhanced regulation or institutional transformation of the capitalist market economy, and secondly, normative ideas used to justify responsibility attributions or legitimacy evaluations (a similar distinction is made by Goldstein and Keohane 1993: 10; see also Blyth 2002: 24–5). Thus, we may find that the economic regime or some of its principles, varieties and actors have been targeted as responsible for the economic turmoil in the wake of the 2008 financial crisis and also explicitly criticized on the basis of normative benchmarks. However, transformative change is only likely where the participants of legitimation discourse 'delegitimate [the capitalist market economy] by contesting the ideas that underlie them', as '[e]conomic ideas are effectual weapons for transforming existing institutions precisely because *existing* economic institutions are the result of *past* economic ideas' about the (proper) functioning of the regime; a new set of causal and normative ideas thus provides a blueprint and legitimacy for genuine institutional transformation (Blyth 2002: 39).

There is obviously a range of linguistic forms to express the content of responsibility attributions and legitimacy evaluations, and successful ideas are likely to be combined into larger units such as 'frames', 'repertoires' or – Goldstein's and Keohane's term – 'worldviews'. The *packaging* of regime evaluations in rhetorical tropes may itself be a legitimation resource. Conversely, the success of a regime's delegitimizers in calling for institutional change is likely to be fostered by the availability of such a convincing packaging.

Finally, to gauge the transformative potential of a legitimation crisis, the arenas and participants of legitimation discourse need to be considered. The legitimacy of a regime such as the capitalist market economy is stable where the legitimating ideas (self-legitimations; Gronau and Schmidtke 2016) of its representatives are taken up by other key discourse participants, and hence where a solid *legitimating* discourse coalition drawing on an established set of normative benchmarks as resources emerges. Conversely, the success and scope of calls for an institutional transformation of the capitalist market economy hinges on the emergence of a sufficiently broad and powerful *delegitimating* 'advocacy' coalition whose critique of the regime is underpinned by a coherent and convincing set of ideas (Hall 2010: 207, 212; Jenkins-Smith et al. 2014).

Studying the (De-)Legitimation of the Capitalist Market Economy: Overview of the Book

This section describes the comparative research design that underpins the empirical Chapters 3–7 of the volume as well as the procedure used to collect and code the corpus of legitimacy-related articles and statements that is the textual basis of these chapters. We then give an overview of the specific aspects of legitimation discourse each of the chapters examines, the text-analytical method used and key findings.

A Comparative Perspective on Legitimation Discourse in Four Countries, Before and After 2008

All of the contributions draw on a corpus of articles from the quality press that documents public legitimation discourse on the capitalist market economy over a 14-year period (1998–2011) in four countries and eight newspapers. The four advanced industrial economies considered in the book – Germany, Switzerland, the United Kingdom and the United States – are all established liberal democracies, but characterized by marked differences in terms of their political systems and cultures. The sample notably includes cases of Westminster democracy (the United Kingdom) and consensus democracy (Germany, Switzerland) as well as the *sui generis* case of the United States (Lijphart 1999). While all four countries are highly developed, they also display marked differences in economic characteristics – differences that should be particularly relevant for the (de-)legitimation of the capitalist market economy as a regime. The four countries represent different 'varieties of capitalism' (Hall and Soskice 2001) which are arguably grounded in different sets of economic and legitimation ideas – a liberal market economy in the United States and the United Kingdom (King and Wood 1999), a coordinated market economy (or 'Rhenish capitalism') in Germany and Switzerland (Albert and Gonenc 1996). The size, relative openness and vulnerability of the four national economies vary considerably, with Switzerland at one end of the spectrum and the United States at the other (Katzenstein 1985; Berger and Dore 1996). The international financial sector has more weight in the British, Swiss and US economies than in Germany (on the United Kingdom, see Johal et al. 2012: 68–73; on Switzerland, Steinlin and Trampusch 2012: 146–7; on the United States, Woolley and Ziegler 2012: 34–5; on Germany, Handke and Zimmermann 2012: 119–20).

Two quality newspapers per country (one centre-left and one centre-right) were examined: *Süddeutsche Zeitung*, *Frankfurter Allgemeine*

Zeitung (Germany); *Tagesanzeiger, Neue Zürcher Zeitung* (Switzerland); *The Guardian, The Times* (the United Kingdom); *The New York Times, The Washington Post* (the United States). This sample is not meant to 'represent' the ideological spectrum or regional media landscapes of the four countries. Instead, we focus on the opinion-leaders at the national level (the same or similar samples are, for instance, used in Wessler et al. 2008; Koopmans and Statham 2010b; Kriesi et al. 2012).

Finally, our study covers a relatively long time period (from 1998 to 2011) and therefore allows a comparison of national discursive structures before and after the onset of the 2008 financial crisis. The pre-crisis observation period (1998–2007) comprises 10 years and hence reaches back to the (end of the) 'roaring nineties' (Stiglitz 2004) and the IT bubble bursting in 2001; the post-crisis observation period (2008–2011) covers four years. For most observers, the financial crisis began in earnest with the collapse of Lehman Brothers on 15 September 2008 (Reinhart and Rogoff 2009: Chapter 15; Woolley and Ziegler 2012: 29). In the wake of this event, the US mortgage and real-estate crisis turned into a global and, especially, a European crisis:

> The collapse of the investment bank Lehman Brothers [. . .] opened the black box of modern financial markets to the world. It exposed finance's vast and complex machine, until then largely invisible to the wider public and poorly mastered by even its most skilled practitioners. (Fourcade et al. 2013: 601–2)

The contributions to this volume (with the exception of Chapter 4), however, use 1 January 2008 as the temporal cut-off point between the pre- and post-crisis portions of the observation period. They follow Helleiner (2011) and Kahler and Lake (2013: 1), who date the beginning of the crisis as far back as December 2007: In at least two of the countries examined – the United States and the United Kingdom – the burst of the real-estate bubble was already looming on the horizon in 2006 and 2007. The events that aggravated the crisis and turned it into a global one included the forced sale of Bear Stearns and the Federal Housing Finance Agency taking over control at Fannie Mae and Freddie Mac in late March and early September

2008, respectively, together with the bailouts of other major US and European financial institutions. Through its impact on global demand and trade, the financial crisis also turned into a crisis of the real economy: the Great Recession. A range of 'liberal Keynesian' (Crouch 2009) emergency measures – including stimulus packages and tax cuts, bank rescue operations and (partial) nationalizations – prevented the feared global economic collapse and led to a temporary recovery in mid-2009, but only in 2011 (the final year of the period examined here) global economic output and trade returned to pre-recession levels (Kahler and Lake 2013: 4; see also Pontusson and Raes 2012).

While all four countries examined in this volume undoubtedly experienced 'an unstable situation of extreme danger or difficulty' (Kahler and Lake 2013: 10) after 2008, they nevertheless belong to three groups in terms of the timing, duration and severity of the financial crisis (Claessens et al. 2010: 276–7, 279–80, 282). The crisis began and was arguably most severe in the United States but expanded quickly to countries whose financial sectors are strongly interwoven with their US counterpart, such as the United Kingdom and Germany (although the 'sick man of Europe' proved unexpectedly resilient, see Kitschelt and Streeck 2004; Dustmann et al. 2014). The impact of the crisis was felt later and was milder in Switzerland (Armingeon 2011: 166; Mach and Trampusch 2011: 20; Steinlin and Trampusch 2012: 143). The varying impact of the financial crisis in the four countries leads us to expect differences in the scope of the discursive legitimation crisis that the moment of economic uncertainty and political upheaval after 2008 triggered.

The Grammar of Discursive Legitimation

How can we identify pertinent text material for a study of public and mediated legitimation discourse? The empirical analyses of the following chapters all draw on the same, jointly gathered corpus of newspaper articles. The point of departure in the selection of pertinent articles was the notion that a specific type of proposition – *legitimation statements* – may be viewed as the most elementary discursive *practice* of legitimation and delegitimation.

What, then, characterizes relevant propositions? The volume draws inspiration from the literature on political 'claims-making'. To identify and examine legitimation statements, we use a stylized grammar (Koopmans and Statham 1999, 2010a; Franzosi 2004; Kriesi et al. 2012: Chapter 2). As illustrated by Table 1.1, legitimation statements are propositions that *evaluate* the capitalist market economy as a whole or its regime principles, varieties and key actors. These semantic units are defined by four variables: their legitimating (positive) or delegitimating (negative) *tone*, the *legitimation object* assessed, the evaluation standard or *legitimation criterion* used to make the assessment and the author (*speaker*) of the proposition.

The first variable, tone, is dichotomous: The capitalist market economy or one of its elements is either supported or criticized, that is, legitimated or delegitimated; we do not consider the intensity of an evaluation and ignore neutral, descriptive statements altogether. There may be more complex and balanced legitimacy assessments, yet these can be interpreted and dealt with as a *combination* of positive and negative evaluations, decomposing them into affirmative and critical statements on the basis of the legitimation grammar.

Secondly, who or what exactly is being assessed in legitimating or delegitimating statements? The contributions to this volume share an understanding of economic regimes that is narrower than, for instance, Karl Polanyi's concept of capitalism as a social system (2001: 78) or Wolfgang Streeck's (2012, 2014) notion of a capitalist society, which also includes related aspects of the social system and the state beyond the economic system proper (in a similar vein, Jessop 2002; Schimank 2015). Instead, we draw inspiration from David Easton's (1965, 1975) regime concept, thus distinguishing regimes both from policies (or their equivalents in the economic sphere, such as individual corporate decisions) and from 'authorities' (the incumbents of leadership roles, such as Apple's Steve Jobs or Goldman Sachs's Lloyd C. Blankfein). We concede that assessments of policies and authorities are frequently made in the quality press and relevant in the legitimation context. However, our understanding of legitimation does not include these reference objects.

Table 1.1 Legitimation grammar with examples

Example 1	'[F]ree market capitalism is the best system to allocate resources and create innovation, growth and jobs' (*New York Times*, 'Why Wall St. Is Deserting Obama', 31 August 2010).			
Daniel S. Loeb (hedge fund manager) says:	The free market economy…	is legitimate…	because it…	• is efficient, • fosters innovation and • creates wealth
Speaker	*Legitimation object*	*Tone*		*Legitimation criterion*
Example 2	'The capitalist model has clearly broken down when shareholders get so little and the managers grab so much' (*The Guardian*, 'Well They Did Say the Time for Remorse Was Over', 8 March 2011).			
Lord Oakeshott (Liberal Democrat peer) says:	Capitalism…	is illegitimate…	because it …	is unjust.
Speaker	*Legitimation object*	*Tone*		*Legitimation criterion*

With Easton, we argue that the legitimacy of regimes as a whole and their core elements is more consequential than the acceptance of incumbents (who may be replaced through standard procedures of a regime) or their decisions (which may be revised through standard procedures; for a more detailed explanation of our coding scheme for legitimation objects, see Chapter 3).

Thirdly, as also illustrated by the examples, legitimation statements may use different normative benchmarks – *legitimation criteria* – to justify the evaluations that they contain. As Chapter 2 and the empirical contributions to the volume show, a plethora of benchmarks plays a role in academic literature and public discourse in addition to standards deemed pertinent by economists, such as efficiency. With Fourcade et al. (2013: 604), we argue that '[a]ll too often, policy-makers and intellectuals delude themselves into believing that moral judgments can be safely separated from "objective" benchmarks of economic action' (for a more detailed explanation of our coding scheme for legitimation criteria, see Chapter 3).

Finally, we are interested in the *authors* of legitimation statements: Do journalists themselves contribute them or do they cite the positions of others? The 'authenticity' of statements ascribed to speakers in direct or indirect citations is irrelevant; journalists may put statements into the mouth of certain speakers – and even a direct quote represents a deliberate choice by the media, which thus have the power to give more or less 'voice' to different individuals and groups in public legitimation discourse. Other than journalists' own legitimacy evaluations, we distinguish statements made by economic, political and a range of civil society actors (for a more detailed explanation of our coding scheme for speakers, see Chapter 3).

Each of the articles in the corpus thus evaluates the legitimacy of the capitalist market economy or one of its elements at least once. For each newspaper and year, the articles published in four 'constructed' weeks were browsed with the help of the described content-analytical procedure – 'political valuation analysis' (Schmidtke and Nullmeier 2011) – to identify legitimation statements (see Appendix for details). The procedure yielded a corpus of 1026 articles and a data set of 2514 statements (Table 1.2).

Table 1.2 Number of pertinent articles and statements, by country and year

	CH		DE	
Year	Articles	Statements	Articles	Statements
1998	30	17	30	75
1999	18	9	18	31
2000	27	8	27	81
2001	34	36	34	79
2002	30	43	30	48
2003	27	29	27	61
2004	24	18	24	56
2005	45	20	45	107
2006	27	26	27	56
2007	32	28	32	68
2008	44	39	44	137
2009	58	30	58	169
2010	26	7	26	62
2011	43	74	43	131
Σ	465	384	465	1161
	UK		US	
Year	Articles	Statements	Articles	Statements
1998	12	22	13	30
1999	17	41	5	13
2000	24	42	8	22
2001	24	46	10	16
2002	20	37	6	11
2003	12	20	3	3
2004	16	26	6	9
2005	20	27	3	4
2006	7	11	5	14
2007	21	58	4	6
2008	24	95	10	33
2009	37	106	18	48
2010	20	76	4	9
2011	45	102	17	42
Σ	299	709	112	260

A Mixed-Method Perspective on Legitimation Discourse

The social construction or contestation of legitimacy and its normative foundations in public discourse is a multifaceted phenomenon. This volume makes the case that methodological eclecticism is required to adequately capture legitimation processes. After a theoretical contribution that develops a typology of the normative standards used to justify or criticize the capitalist market economy (Chapter 2), the empirical contributions (Chapters 3–7) therefore run the gamut of text-analytical methods – from descriptive statistical analysis to discourse network analysis via the interpretive methods of metaphor and narrative analysis – to probe the nature and trajectories of legitimation discourse in Germany, Switzerland, the United Kingdom and the United States before and after the 2008 financial crisis. In doing so, they draw on the entire text corpus and data set introduced above or parts of it, and they focus on different elements of the legitimation grammar or move beyond it to examine the rhetorical tropes and larger semantic or discursive units in which legitimation statements are embedded. Together, then, the contributions bridge the alleged divide between high and low case numbers, metric and categorical data, statistical and non-statistical forms of text analysis (Bennett 2015). Such distinctions notwithstanding, the chapters are all essentially in the interpretive camp even where they use statistical forms of analysis. A classical distinction in content analysis – between manifest and latent content (Krippendorff 2004: Chapter 2; Neuendorf 2012) – is therefore largely irrelevant: Identifying and coding legitimation statements and responsibility attributions or metaphors and narratives required an interpretive approach throughout the book, that is, the discovery of latent concepts and the reconstruction of *meaning* (Bauer and Gaskell 2000; Bergman 2010).

Based on a review and extension of extant classifications, Chapter 2 by Frank Nullmeier and Dominika Biegoń develops a typology of arguments for the justification and criticism of the capitalist market economy in economic and social science writing. Nullmeier and Biegoń show that four groups of legitimation criteria – 'classical' criteria going back to Adam Smith and Karl Marx as well as justice-, democracy- and culture-centred arguments and normative ideas – may be distinguished both in procapitalist and in anticapitalist thought and discourse. Their typology of criteria underpins the analyses in the empirical chapters.

Chapter 3 by Henning Schmidtke and Steffen Schneider uses descriptive statistical methods of content analysis for a bird's eye view on the 2514 statements in our text corpus. It draws on the legitimation grammar introduced above to demonstrate that the events of 2008 triggered a discursive legitimation crisis – a moment of uncertainty and politicization characterized by rising intensity and a more critical tone of media discourse. However, Schmidtke and Schneider also present evidence for the limited scope of the legitimation crisis: The legitimacy of the capitalist market economy hardly became an issue for business and political elites. Delegitimation focused on specific actors and institutions, not on the regime as a whole, and no radical shift in the normative ideas that underpin it occurred.

The second type of legitimacy-related propositions introduced above, responsibility attributions, is examined in Chapter 4 by Falk Lenke and Henning Schmidtke, using a similar type of grammar as Chapter 3 and a combination of quantitative and interpretive methods to analyse these propositions. Who is *blamed* for the crisis, the capitalist market economy or the state (which would indicate a deflection of criticism from the economic to the political sphere)? Who is entrusted with the task of *solving* the problems induced by the financial crisis, the state or market actors themselves (where the latter scenario would amount to a form of relegitimation)? Lenke and Schmidtke show that the discursive attribution of 'causal' and 'treatment' responsibility has helped to stabilize the economic regime: Discourse participants mostly blamed specific actor groups and did not call for strong intervention by other than economic actors; public debate on institutional responses to the crisis was dominated by regulatory reform proposals, not ideas for a radical transformation of the capitalist market economy.

Instead of 'translating' natural language into the categories of the grammars of legitimation and responsibility attribution, and of moving 'from words to numbers' (Franzosi 2004), the next two chapters return to the subtleties of natural language and examine the linguistic forms of legitimation discourse, the use of rhetorical tropes – metaphors and narratives – on its anticapitalist and procapitalist sides. Chapter 5 by Jennifer Gronau is devoted to metaphors in *delegitimating* statements on the capitalist market economy. She shows that metaphors help speakers to deal with complex phenomena – including economic regimes – and imply, or entail, specific ideas about their nature and potential for change. A combination of quantitative and interpretive methods is again used to establish which metaphors are most prominent and which ideas about the necessity or possibility to reform or replace the capitalist market economy they entail. Gronau's analysis reveals that the metaphors of anticapitalist discourse raise high cognitive hurdles to thinking about and mobilizing support for a genuine institutional transformation of the regime. Instead, dominant metaphors – like the responsibility attributions examined in Chapter 4 – tend to imply that only regulatory reform of the regime is required or possible.

Chapter 6 by Dominika Biegoń uses an interpretive approach to uncover the narratives that underpin procapitalist discourse. She demonstrates that such narratives are another rhetorical instrument to reduce complexity and to tie different legitimation ideas into a coherent and stable whole. Thus, narratives are an important resource of the capitalist market economy's supporters, who manage to stabilize the regime and its legitimacy foundations by successfully keeping a number of convincing procapitalist story lines in the public eye. In the wake of the financial crisis, not even a substantially new *procapitalist* narrative – which might have fostered calls for at least some institutional change – has emerged.

Chapter 7 by Sebastian Haunss uses the data set of Chapter 3 and the innovative method of discourse network analysis (Leifeld and Haunss 2012) to examine the use of legitimation criteria by the legitimizers and delegitimizers of the capitalist market economy. His analysis of the relational structures linking discourse participants and their repertoires of arguments indicates that characteristic sets of normative ideas and legitimation criteria underpin the pro- and anticapitalist discourse coalitions that have voice in media discourse. Yet, closer inspection reveals that no powerful coalition delegitimating the capitalist market economy and laying the groundwork for transformative institutional change emerged in the wake of the financial crisis. Instead, the speakers on the delegitimating side were largely 'peripheral'; their argumentation remained incoherent and failed to catch on in the wider public.

Finally, Chapter 8 by Jennifer Gronau and Sebastian Haunss draws on social movement literature and the concept of diagnostic, prognostic and motivational framing to summarize the findings of the individual chapters and to provide an answer to the volume's key question: Why has there not been a Great Transformation of the capitalist market economy in the wake of the 2008 financial crisis? Gronau and Haunss conclude that viewed through the lens of these three framing types, the post-2008 discursive legitimation crisis did not bring about radically new ideas about the capitalist market economy and did not mobilize sufficiently widespread support for its institutional transformation or replacement. In short, the discursive treatment of the financial crisis helped to stabilize the current institutional design of the capitalist market economy instead of radically challenging it.

Appendix: Description of Text Retrieval and Data Collection Procedure

Our text material was retrieved from electronic newspaper data bases in a two-step procedure. Firstly, we developed routines for automated searches that enabled us to focus on articles that were *likely* to contain evaluations of the capitalist market economy's legitimacy.[2] These routines used search words related to the economic regime as whole (level I of the legitimation object hierarchy presented in Chapter 3). The lists of search words were based on extensive pretests which confirmed that including search terms related to other types of legitimation objects (specific principles, varieties or actors of the regime – that is, levels II to IV of the legitimation object hierarchy) would have been inefficient: If these additional terms had been added, the searches would have yielded exceedingly large numbers of articles, but a very low share of ultimately relevant ones.[3]

The searches were not conducted for the complete calendar years 1998 through 2011, but on the basis of four randomly 'constructed' weeks per newspaper and year. This sampling strategy ensures a representative sample from an extensive 'population' of articles, without limiting the article searches to the front pages or politics sections of the newspapers examined. Therefore, we are able to make plausible inferences for entire countries and years on the basis of the sample (Lacy et al. 2001). For each year in the period examined, one constructed week per newspaper and quarter – one Monday, one Tuesday, one Wednesday, one Thursday, one Friday and one Saturday – was randomly selected. This procedure ensured that all weekdays (with the exception of Sundays) are equally represented in the sample, without any bias due to the preponderance of particular weekdays (which may differ from other days in terms of volume or content). The procedure was performed for each newspaper independently.

To date, there is no reliable automated procedure for identifying the complex semantic relationships and structures underpinning legitimation statements. Hence, our automated search routines were designed to minimize the number of relevant articles *not* found by the routines ('false negatives'); as a trade-off, the number of ultimately irrelevant articles produced by the search routines ('false positives') was still considerable. Therefore, a second, manual step of selecting pertinent articles was necessary. All articles in the corpus contain at least one legitimation statement evaluating a level I legitimation object. Hence, the procedure undoubtedly creates a certain bias in favour of legitimation statements evaluating this type of object. Yet, this seems unproblematic because assessments of the capitalist market economy as a whole are also particularly *relevant* for the legitimation of that regime and hence for the key research question of our book.

Six members of the research team participated in the manual selection of relevant articles and in the identification and coding of legitimation statements. Reliability was tested for the article selection procedure, for the identification of legitimation statements in articles and for coding each of the legitimation grammar variables. A random sample of approximately 10 per cent of the corpus was used for these tests. For all steps of the selection and coding process, we achieved high levels of pairwise intercoder reliability (90 per cent and more agreement) and a Krippendorff's α of 0.7 or higher. Next, a random sample of articles was assigned to each member of the coding team for identifying and coding statements; each statement considered relevant by the first coder was checked by a second coder and any discrepancies between first and second coder were resolved by two other members of the team who were not involved in the first and second steps – this departs from the standard content-analytical procedure of reliability testing and coding (Lombard et al. 2002: 600–2) but, in our view, greatly improves data quality.

Notes

1. Throughout the book, we use the encompassing label 'capitalist market economy' to refer to all varieties of a capitalist, market-based economic regime. Thus, we do not follow authors who distinguish between 'capitalism' and the 'market economy' or give them distinct – negative and positive – connotations. However, such 'elective affinities' between the label 'capitalism' and criticism, on the one hand, and the label 'market economy' and support, on the other, are very pronounced in public legitimation discourse (see Chapter 3).
2. Wherever possible, electronic versions of articles available in the Factiva data base (global.factiva.com) were used. For the FAZ, we relied on FAZ-BiblioNet; text material from the 1998 *Tagesanzeiger* – which is not available electronically – could not be included.
3. The search routines are documented in our codebook at http://www.sfb597.uni-bremen.de/download/en/forschung/B1_Codebook.pdf.

References

Albert, Michel and Rauf Gonenc. 1996. 'The Future of Rhenish Capitalism'. *Political Quarterly* 67(3): 184–93.

Almunia, Miguel, Agustín Bénétrix, Barry Eichengreen, Kevin H. O'Rourke, Gisela Rua, Silvana Tenreyro and Fabrizio Perri. 2010. 'From Great Depression to Great Credit Crisis: Similarities, Differences and Lessons'. *Economic Policy* 62: 219–65.

Armingeon, Klaus. 2011. 'A Prematurely Announced Death? Swiss Corporatism in Comparative Perspective'. In *Switzerland in Europe. Continuity and Change in the Swiss Political Economy*, eds. Christine Trampusch and André Mach. London: Routledge, 165–85.

Baker, Andy. 2005. 'Who Wants to Globalize? Consumer Tastes and Labor Markets in a Theory of Trade Policy Beliefs'. *American Journal of Political Science* 49(4): 924–38.

Barker, Rodney. 2001. *Legitimating Identities. The Self-Presentation of Rulers and Subjects*. Cambridge: Cambridge University Press.

Bauer, Martin W. and George Gaskell, eds. 2000. *Qualitative Researching with Text, Image and Sound. A Practical Handbook*. London: Sage.

Bennett, Andrew. 2015. 'Found in Translation: Combining Discourse Analysis with Computer Assisted Content Analysis'. *Millennium – Journal of International Studies* 43(3): 984–97.

Berger, Suzanne and Ronald Dore, eds. 1996. *National Diversity and Global Capitalism*. Ithaca: Cornell University Press.

Bergman, Manfred M. 2010. 'Hermeneutic Content Analysis: Textual and Audiovisual Analyses within a Mixed Methods Framework'. In *Sage Handbook of Mixed Methods in Social & Behavioral Research*, eds. Abbas Tashakkori and Charles Teddlie. Los Angeles: Sage, 379–96.

Blyth, Mark. 2002. *Great Transformations. Economic Ideas and Institutional Change in the Twentieth Century*. Cambridge: Cambridge University Press.

Booth, John A. and Mitchell A. Seligson. 2009. *The Legitimacy Puzzle in Latin America. Political Support and Democracy in Eight Nations*. Cambridge: Cambridge University Press.

Buchanan, James M. 1995. 'Federalism as an Ideal Political Order and an Objective for Constitutional Reform'. *Publius* 25(2): 19–27.

Campbell, John L. 1998. 'Institutional Analysis and the Role of Ideas in Political Economy'. *Theory and Society* 27(3): 377–409.

Capoccia, Giovanni. 2015. 'Critical Junctures and Institutional Change'. In *Advances in Comparative-Historical Analysis*, eds. James Mahoney and Kathleen Thelen. Cambridge: Cambridge University Press, 147–79.

Capoccia, Giovanni and R. Daniel Kelemen. 2007. 'The Study of Critical Junctures: Theory, Narrative, and Counterfactuals in Historical Institutionalism'. *World Politics* 59(3): 341–69.

Claessens, Stijn, Giovanni Dell'Ariccia, Deniz Igan and Luc Laeven. 2010. 'Cross-Country Experiences and Policy Implications from the Global Financial Crisis'. *Economic Policy* 62: 267–93.

Crouch, Colin. 2009. 'Privatised Keynesianism: An Unacknowledged Policy Regime'. *British Journal of Politics and International Relations* 11(3): 382–99.

Dalton, Russell J. 2004. *Democratic Challenges, Democratic Choices. The Erosion of Political Support in Advanced Industrial Democracies*. Oxford: Oxford University Press.

Drezner, Daniel W. 2014. *The System Worked. How the World Stopped Another Great Depression*. Oxford: Oxford University Press.

Dustmann, Christian, Bernd Fitzenberger, Uta Schönberg and Alexandra Spitz-Oener. 2014. 'From Sick Man of Europe to Economic Superstar: Germany's Resurgent Economy'. *Journal of Economic Perspectives* 28(1): 167–88.

Easton, David. 1965. *A Systems Analysis of Political Life*. New York: Wiley.

Easton, David. 1975. 'A Re-Assessment of the Concept of Political Support'. *British Journal of Political Science* 5(4): 435–57.

Elster, Jon and Karl Ove Moene, eds. 1989. *Alternatives to Capitalism*. Cambridge: Cambridge University Press.

Fligstein, Neil. 2002. *The Architecture of Markets. An Economic Sociology of Twenty-First-Century Capitalist Societies*. Princeton: Princeton University Press.

Fourcade, Marion, Philippe Steiner, Wolfgang Streeck and Cornelia Woll. 2013. 'Moral Categories in the Financial Crisis'. *Socio-Economic Review* 11(3): 601–27.

Franzosi, Robert. 2004. *From Words to Numbers. Narrative, Data, and Social Science*. Cambridge: Cambridge University Press.

Fukuyama, Francis. 1992. *The End of History and the Last Man*. New York: Free Press.

Genschel, Philipp and Bernhard Zangl. 2014. 'State Transformations in OECD Countries'. *Annual Review of Political Science* 17: 337–54.

Gilley, Bruce. 2006. 'The Meaning and Measure of State Legitimacy: Results for 72 Countries'. *European Journal of Political Research* 45(3): 499–525.

Gilley, Bruce. 2013. *The Right to Rule. How States Win and Lose Legitimacy*. New York: Columbia University Press.

Goldstein, Judith and Robert O. Keohane. 1993. 'Ideas and Foreign Policy: An Analytical Framework'. In *Ideas and Foreign Policy. Beliefs, Institutions, and Political Change*, eds. Judith Goldstein and Robert O. Keohane. Ithaca: Cornell University Press, 3–30.

Gronau, Jennifer and Henning Schmidtke. 2016. 'The Quest for Legitimacy in World Politics – International Institutions' Legitimation Strategies'. *Review of International Studies* 42(3): 535–57.

Grusky, David B., Bruce Western and Christopher Wimer, eds. 2011. *The Great Recession*. New York: Russell Sage Foundation.

Habermas, Jürgen. 1973. *Legitimationsprobleme im Spätkapitalismus*. Frankfurt am Main: Suhrkamp.

Habermas, Jürgen. 2008. 'Hat die Demokratie noch eine epistemische Funktion? Empirische Forschung und normative Theorie'. In *Ach Europa. Kleine Politische Schriften XI*. Frankfurt am Main: Suhrkamp.

Hainmueller, Jens and Michael J. Hiscox. 2006. 'Learning to Love Globalization: Education and Individual Attitudes towards International Trade'. *International Organization* 60(2): 469–98.

Hall, Peter A. 1989. *The Political Power of Economic Ideas. Keynesianism across Nations*. Princeton: Princeton University Press.
Hall, Peter A. 2010. 'Historical Institutionalism in Rationalist and Sociological Perspective'. In *Explaining Institutional Change. Ambiguity, Agency, and Power*, eds. James Mahoney and Kathleen Thelen. Cambridge: Cambridge University Press, 204–23.
Hall, Peter A. and David Soskice. 2001. 'An Introduction to Varieties of Capitalism'. In *Varieties of Capitalism. The Institutional Foundations of Comparative Advantage*, eds. Peter A. Hall and David Soskice. Oxford: Oxford University Press, 1–68.
Handke, Stefan and Hubert Zimmermann. 2012. 'Institutional Change in German Financial Regulation'. In *Crisis and Control. Institutional Change in Financial Market Regulation*, ed. Renate Mayntz. Frankfurt am Main: Campus, 119–42.
Haunss, Sebastian. 2007. 'Challenging Legitimacy: Repertoires of Contention, Political Claims Making, and Collective Action Frames'. In *Legitimacy in an Age of Global Politics*, eds. Achim Hurrelmann, Steffen Schneider and Jens Steffek. Basingstoke: Palgrave Macmillan, 156–72.
Hay, Colin. 2008. 'Constructivist Institutionalism'. In *Oxford Handbook of Political Institutions*, eds. R.A.W. Rhodes, Sarah A. Binder and Bert A. Rockman. Oxford: Oxford University Press, 56–74.
Helleiner, Eric. 2011. 'Understanding the 2007-2008 Global Financial Crisis: Lessons for Scholars of International Political Economy'. *Annual Review of Political Science* 14: 67–87.
Hilferding, Rudolf. 1968. *Das Finanzkapital*. Frankfurt am Main: Europäische Verlagsanstalt.
Jaeggi, Rahel. 2013. 'Was (wenn überhaupt etwas) ist falsch am Kapitalismus? Drei Wege der Kapitalismuskritik'. In *Nach Marx. Philosophie, Kritik, Praxis*, eds. Rahel Jaeggi and Daniel Loick. Berlin: Suhrkamp, 321–49.
Jenkins-Smith, Hank C., Daniel Nohrstedt, Christopher M. Weible and Paul A. Sabatier. 2014. 'The Advocacy Coalition Framework: Foundations, Evolutions, and Ongoing Research'. In *Theories of the Policy Process*, eds. Paul A. Sabatier and Christopher M. Weible. Boulder: Westview Press, 183–224.
Jessop, Bob. 2002. *The Future of the Capitalist State*. Cambridge: Polity Press.
Johal, Sukhdev, Michael Moran and Karel Williams. 2012. 'Post-Crisis Financial Regulation in Britain'. In *Crisis and Control. Institutional Change*

in Financial Market Regulation, ed. Renate Mayntz. Frankfurt am Main: Campus, 67–96.

Kahler, Miles and David A. Lake. 2013. 'Introduction: Anatomy of Crisis. The Great Recession and Political Change'. In *Politics in the New Hard Times. The Great Recession in Comparative Perspective*, eds. Miles Kahler and David A. Lake. Ithaca: Cornell University Press, 1–26.

Katzenstein, Peter J. 1985. *Small States in World Markets. Industrial Policy in Europe*. Ithaca: Cornell University Press.

King, Desmond and Stewart Wood. 1999. 'The Political Economy of Neoliberalism: Britain and the United States in the 1980s'. In *Continuity and Change in Contemporary Capitalism*, eds. Herbert Kitschelt, Peter Lange, Gary Marks and John D. Stephens. Cambridge: Cambridge University Press, 371–97.

Kitschelt, Herbert and Wolfgang Streeck. 2004. *Germany. Beyond the Stable State*. London: Psychology Press.

Koopmans, Ruud and Paul Statham. 1999. 'Political Claims Analysis: Integrating Protest Event and Political Discourse Approaches'. *Mobilization* 4(2): 203–21.

Koopmans, Ruud and Paul Statham. 2010a. 'Theoretical Framework, Research Design, and Methods'. In *The Making of a European Public Sphere. Media Discourse and Political Contention*, eds. Ruud Koopmans and Paul Statham. Cambridge: Cambridge University Press, 34–59.

Koopmans, Ruud and Paul Statham, eds. 2010b. *The Making of a European Public Sphere. Media Discourse and Political Contention*. Cambridge: Cambridge University Press.

Kriesi, Hanspeter, Edgar Grande, Martin Dolezal, Marc Helbling, Dominic Höglinger, Swen Hutter and Bruno Wüest. 2012. *Political Conflict in Western Europe*. Cambridge: Cambridge University Press.

Krippendorff, Klaus. 2004. *Content Analysis. An Introduction to Its Methodology*. Second Edition. Thousand Oaks: Sage.

Lacy, Stephen, Daniel Riffe, Staci Stoddard, Hugh Martin and Chang Kuang-Kuo. 2001. 'Sample Size for Newspaper Analysis in Multi-Year Studies'. *Journalism and Mass Communication Quarterly* 78(4): 836–45.

Leifeld, Philip and Sebastian Haunss. 2012. 'Political Discourse Networks and the Conflict over Software Patents in Europe'. *European Journal of Political Research* 51(3): 382–409.

Levi, Margaret. 1997. *Consent, Dissent and Patriotism*. Cambridge: Cambridge University Press.

Lijphart, Arend. 1999. *Patterns of Democracy. Government Forms and Performance in Thirty-six Countries*. New Haven: Yale University Press.

Lipset, Seymour Martin. 1959. 'Some Social Requisites of Democracy: Economic Development and Political Legitimacy'. *American Political Science Review* 53(1): 69–105.

Lombard, Matthew, Jennifer Snyder-Duch and Cheryl Campanella-Bracken. 2002. 'Content Analysis in Mass Communication: Assessment and Reporting of Intercoder Reliability'. *Human Communication Research* 28(4): 587–604.

Luckmann, Thomas. 1987. 'Comments on Legitimation'. *Current Sociology* 35(2): 109–17.

Mach, André and Christine Trampusch. 2011. 'The Swiss Political Economy in Comparative Perspective'. In *Switzerland in Europe. Continuity and Change in the Swiss Political Economy*, eds. André March and Christine Trampusch. London: Routledge, 11–26.

Mahoney, James. 2001. *The Legacies of Liberalism. Path Dependence and Political Regimes in Central America*. Baltimore: Johns Hopkins University Press.

Mansfield, Edward D. and Diana C. Mutz. 2009. 'Support for Free Trade: Self-Interest, Sociotropic Politics, and Out-Group Anxiety'. *International Organization* 63(3): 425–57.

Mayntz, Renate, ed. 2012. *Crisis and Control. Institutional Change in Financial Market Regulation*. Frankfurt am Main: Campus.

Mueller, Dennis C., ed. 2012. *Oxford Handbook of Capitalism*. Oxford: Oxford University Press.

Neuendorf, Kimberly A. 2012. *The Content Analysis Guidebook*. Thousand Oaks: Sage.

Norris, Pippa. 1999. *Critical Citizens. Global Support for Democratic Government*. Oxford: Oxford University Press.

Norris, Pippa. 2002. *Democratic Phoenix. Reinventing Political Activism*. Cambridge: Cambridge University Press.

Norris, Pippa. 2011. *Democratic Deficit. Critical Citizens Revisited*. Cambridge: Cambridge University Press.

North, Douglass. 1981. *Structure and Change in Economic History*. New York: W. W. Norton & Company.

Nullmeier, Frank, Dominika Biegoń, Jennifer Gronau, Martin Nonhoff, Henning Schmidtke and Steffen Schneider. 2010. *Prekäre Legitimitäten. Rechtfertigung von Herrschaft in der postnationalen Konstellation*. Frankfurt am Main: Campus.

Offe, Claus. 2006. 'Political Disaffection as an Outcome of Institutional Practices? Some Post-Tocquevillean Speculations'. In *Political Disaffection in Contemporary Democracies. Social Capital, Institutions, and Politics*, eds. Mariano Torcal and José Ramón Montero. London: Routledge, 23–45.

Palazzo, Guido and Andreas Georg Scherer. 2006. 'Corporate Legitimacy as Deliberation: A Communicative Framework'. *Journal of Business Ethics* 66(1): 71–88.

Peters, Bernhard. 2005. 'Public Discourse, Identity and the Problem of Democratic Legitimacy'. In *Making the European Polity. Reflexive Integration in the EU*, ed. Erik Oddvar Eriksen. London: Routledge, 84–123.

Peters, Bernhard. 2008. *Public Deliberation and Public Culture. The Writings of Bernhard Peters, 1993-2005*. Basingstoke: Palgrave Macmillan.

Pierson, Paul. 2004. *Politics in Time. History, Institutions, and Social Analysis.* Princeton: Princeton University Press.

Polanyi, Karl. 2001. *The Great Transformation. The Political and Economic Origins of Our Time.* Boston: Beacon Press.

Pontusson, Jonas and Damian Raess. 2012. 'How (and Why) Is This Time Different? The Politics of Economic Crisis in Western Europe and the United States'. *Annual Review of Political Science* 15: 13–33.

Posner, Richard A. 2009. *A Failure of Capitalism. The Crisis of '08 and the Descent into Depression.* Cambridge, MA: Harvard University Press.

Raufer, Thilo. 2005. *Die legitime Demokratie. Zur Begründung politischer Ordnung in der Bundesrepublik.* Frankfurt am Main: Campus.

Reinhart, Carmen M. and Kenneth S. Rogoff. 2009. *This Time Is Different. Eight Centuries of Financial Folly.* Princeton: Princeton University Press.

Risse, Thomas. 2010. *A Community of Europeans? Transnational Identities and Public Spheres.* Ithaca: Cornell University Press.

Rucht, Dieter. 2007. 'The Spread of Protest Politics'. In *Oxford Handbook of Political Behavior*, eds. Russell J. Dalton and Hans-Dieter Klingemann. Oxford: Oxford University Press, 708–22.

Scheve, Kenneth F. and Matthew J. Slaughter. 2001. 'What Determines Individual Trade-policy Preferences?' *Journal of International Economics* 54(2): 267–92.

Schimank, Uwe. 2015. 'Modernity as a Functionally Differentiated Capitalist Society: A General Theoretical Model'. *European Journal of Social Theory* 18(4): 413–30.

Schmidt, Vivien A. 2008. 'Discursive Institutionalism: The Explanatory Power of Ideas and Discourse'. *Annual Review of Political Science* 11: 303–26.

Schmidtke, Henning and Frank Nullmeier. 2011. 'Political Valuation Analysis and the Legitimacy of International Organizations'. *German Policy Studies* 7(3): 117–53.

Schmidtke, Henning and Steffen Schneider. 2012. 'Methoden der empirischen Legitimationsforschung: Legitimität als mehrdimensionales Konzept'. In *Der Aufstieg der Legitimitätspolitik. Rechtfertigung und Kritik politisch-ökonomischer Ordnungen*, eds. Anna Geis, Frank Nullmeier and Christopher Daase. Baden-Baden: Nomos, 225–44.

Schneider, Steffen, Achim Hurrelmann, Frank Nullmeier, Achim Wiesner and Zuzana Krell-Laluhová. 2010. *Democracy's Deep Roots. Why the Nation State Remains Legitimate*. Basingstoke: Palgrave Macmillan.

Steffek, Jens. 2007. 'Legitimacy in International Relations: From State Compliance to Citizen Consensus'. In *Legitimacy in an Age of Global Politics*, eds. Achim Hurrelmann, Steffen Schneider and Jens Steffek. Basingstoke: Palgrave Macmillan, 175–92.

Steinlin, Simon and Christine Trampusch. 2012. 'Increasing Vulnerability. Financial Regulation in Switzerland'. In *Crisis and Control. Institutional Change in Financial Market Regulation*, ed. Renate Mayntz. Frankfurt am Main: Campus, 143–70.

Stiglitz, Joseph E. 2004. *The Roaring Nineties. A New History of the World's Most Prosperous Decade*. New York: W.W. Norton & Company.

Streeck, Wolfgang. 2012. 'How to Study Contemporary Capitalism?' *European Journal of Sociology* 53(1): 1–28.

Streeck, Wolfgang. 2014. 'How Will Capitalism End?' *New Left Review* 87: 35–64.

Streeck, Wolfgang. 2016. 'On the Dismal Future of Capitalism'. *Socio-Economic Review* 14(1): 163–70.

Suchman, Mark C. 1995. 'Managing Legitimacy: Strategic and Institutional Approaches'. *Academy of Management Review* 20(3): 571–610.

Tarrow, Sidney. 2011. *Power in Movement. Social Movements and Contentious Politics*. Revised and Updated Edition. Cambridge: Cambridge University Press.

Thelen, Kathleen. 1999. 'Historical Institutionalism in Comparative Politics'. *Annual Review of Political Science* 2: 369–404.

Thelen, Kathleen. 2003. 'How Institutions Evolve: Insights from Comparative-Historical Analysis'. In *Comparative Historical Analysis in the Social Sciences*, eds. James Mahoney and Dietrich Rueschemeyer. Cambridge: Cambridge University Press, 208–40.

Tilly, Charles and Sidney G. Tarrow. 2015. *Contentious Politics*. Second Edition. Oxford: Oxford University Press.

Torcal, Mariano and José Ramón Montero. 2006. *Political Disaffection in Contemporary Democracies. Social Capital, Institutions, and Politics*. London: Routledge.

Urbatsch, Robert. 2013. 'A Referendum on Trade Theory. Voting on Free Trade in Costa Rica'. *International Organization* 67(1): 197–214.

Weatherford, M. Stephen. 1992. 'Measuring Political Legitimacy'. *American Political Science Review* 86(1): 149–66.

Weber, Max. 1922. *Wirtschaft und Gesellschaft*. Tübingen: Mohr Siebeck.

Wessler, Hartmut, Bernhard Peters, Michael Brüggemann, Katharina Kleinen-von Königslöw and Stefanie Sifft. 2008. *Transnationalization of Public Spheres*. Basingstoke: Palgrave Macmillan.

Woolley, John T. and J. Nicholas Ziegler. 2012. 'The Two-Tiered Politics of Financial Reform in the United States'. In *Crisis and Control. Institutional Change in Financial Market Regulation*, ed. Renate Mayntz. Frankfurt am Main: Campus, 29–65.

Zaum, Dominik. 2013. 'International Organizations, Legitimacy, and Legitimation'. In *Legitimating International Organizations*, ed. Dominik Zaum. Oxford: Oxford University Press, 3–25.

Cited Newspaper Articles

The Guardian 8 March 2011. 'Well They Did Say the Time for Remorse Was Over'.

New York Times 31 August 2010. 'Why Wall St. Is Deserting Obama'.

2

Justifying and Criticizing the Capitalist Market Economy: A Typology of Legitimation Criteria

Frank Nullmeier and Dominika Biegoń

In this chapter, we review arguments and normative ideas used in economic and social science literature to defend or attack the capitalist market economy. Which normative criteria may underpin legitimating or delegitimating evaluations of the regime? To what extent do justifications and criticism of the capitalist market economy differ in their normative foundations? Do legitimizers and delegitimizers use the *same* normative benchmarks and merely end up with different (positive or negative) *assessments* of the extent to which the regime lives up to them, or do justifications and criticism of the capitalist market economy rely on different sets of ideas altogether?

F. Nullmeier (✉)
Department of Political Science, Research Centre on Inequality and Social Policy (SOCIUM), University of Bremen, Bremen, Germany
e-mail: frank.nullmeier@gmx.de

D. Biegoń
Friedrich-Ebert-Stiftung, Berlin, Germany
e-mail: dominika.biegon@fes.de

S. Schneider et al. (eds.), *Capitalism and Its Legitimacy in Times of Crisis*, Transformations of the State,
DOI 10.1007/978-3-319-53765-8_2

A vast array of legitimation criteria plays a role both in the academic literature and – as will be shown in Chapters 3 and 7 – in public discourse on the capitalist market economy. A classification of legitimating and delegitimating arguments into broader categories is required to provide some orientation for empirical analyses of legitimation discourse. The following typology of (de-)legitimation criteria was developed on the basis of our own text material, supplemented by a close reading of perspectives on the capitalist market economy in the history of economic thought (Schumpeter 1954; Pribram 1998) and in the broader social science literature on the market economy and capitalism. Our typology may be used for a comparative analysis of different types of capitalism (Hall and Soskice 2001) and – as in the empirical contributions to this volume – for comparing justifications and criticism of the economic regime before and after the financial crisis in 2008 (Posner 2009, 2010; Bermeo and Pontusson 2012; Kahler and Lake 2013; Bermeo and Bartels 2014).

The chapter proceeds in three steps. Firstly, we review literature on the history of economic thought which classifies arguments used over the course of time to justify or criticize the capitalist market economy. Secondly, we introduce our own typology of legitimation criteria based on the distinction of classical, justice-centred, democracy-centred and culture-centred criteria. This typology guides the empirical analyses of the subsequent chapters. The chapter closes with a discussion of current ideas about alternatives to the capitalist market economy.

Classifying (De-)Legitimation Criteria for the Capitalist Market Economy

Arguments for and against capitalism can be found in almost every social science book on the basic structures of modern societies. There are also a few systematic and detailed discussions of the comparative advantages of socialism and capitalism (Parijs 1993; as a *locus classicus*: von Mises 1951). Some authors provide fairly exhaustive lists of core arguments – for instance, Erik Olin Wright with a list of reasons *against* capitalism (2010: 37–85). However, such discussions and lists are hardly ever brought together in *typologies* which may inform empirical research on the changing ideational foundations of the capitalist market economy. In this section, we review the noteworthy exceptions and develop a set of requirements that a typology suitable for empirical research has to meet.

The most developed approach is Luc Boltanski's and Ève Chiapello's *New Spirit of Capitalism* (2007). The authors examine dominant motivations for active participation in the capitalist regime during particular historical phases. They concentrate on management literature to reconstruct foundations of legitimacy and ideological driving forces which they consider decisive for personal identification – especially of mid-level managers – with the economic regime. In an earlier contribution, Boltanski and Thévenot (1991) discern seven fundamental justificatory regimes ('Cités' in the French original) for different phases of economic development and present a historical sequence of these justifications. Until 1930, the 'commercial justification' complemented the 'domestic justification', later the 'civic' and 'industrial' justifications came to the fore. In the 1980s, this constellation was replaced by a 'projects-oriented justification'.

In Boltanski's and Chiapello's view, historically specific and predominant forms of criticism also shape the dynamics of critique. They subsume criticism that evaluates capitalism as unjust, inequality- and egoism-enhancing under the category 'social critique'. In marked contrast, the label 'artistic critique' denotes arguments according to which capitalism is alienating, oppressive and destructive for authentic ways of life. Following the two authors, the rise of artistic critique in the wake of the student movements of the 1960s triggered the transition to projects-oriented justifications of the capitalist market economy. It is important to underline that Boltanski's and Chiapello's inquiry into the spirit of capitalism does not focus on traditional justifications of the capitalist market economy based on material wealth, productivity, efficiency and performance, and grounded in economic freedom. Their analysis of management literature considers those arguments to some extent but primarily aims to reconstruct *additional* motivations and the strength of underlying arguments. The two authors are particularly interested in motivations facilitating managers' identification with capitalism and their adaptation to capitalist working conditions (Boltanski and Chiapello 2007: 15).

Rahel Jaeggi has recently (2013) suggested a different typology, limited to forms of *criticizing* the capitalist economic regime. According to Jaeggi, voices questioning capitalism can be divided into three groups: Functional criticism draws on arguments that depict capitalism as dysfunctional, necessarily crisis-prone and self-destructive. Secondly, moral criticism focuses on forms of injustice that the capitalist system produces. Finally, arguments emphasizing the alienating and destructive power of capitalism with regard to authentic ways of life – the type of criticism that Boltanski and Chiapello call artistic critique – are subsumed under the category of ethical criticism. Jaeggi's typology is useful but leaves open the question whether *justifications* of the capitalist market economy can also be categorized into these three groups and hence whether arguments justifying and criticizing this regime are symmetric.

Political science research might also provide us with categories for analysing public legitimation discourse on the capitalist market economy. The widely used dichotomy of input and output legitimation comes to mind (Scharpf 1999, 2009). This division indeed appears suitable for analysing legitimation discourse. Preconditions for an efficient market (private property, no access restrictions, rule of law, free bargaining about prices, consumer and producer freedom) can be regarded as inputs – and effects of a market system (such as growth, wealth, distributional outcomes, the satisfaction of social and economic needs, innovation and democracy promotion) as outputs. Thus, positions attacking, for instance, the inequality that capitalism produces would count as forms of output delegitimation; a positive evaluation of the freedom that capitalism guarantees would qualify as input legitimation. However, prominent theoretical justifications of the market economy (such as Adam Smith's 'invisible hand') rely on a close link between inputs – freedom of choice for all participants in the market – and outputs – the highest achievable level of wealth for all (Smith 1999; Herzog 2013). In sum, based on existing categorizations and our own considerations, a typology of criteria for legitimating or delegitimating the capitalist market economy should meet the following requirements; it should

- provide a categorization scheme for both everyday legitimation criteria and theoretical contributions from the social sciences and economics;
- be broad enough to encompass legitimation criteria from different historical phases of capitalist development;
- cover both justifications and criticism of the capitalist market economy in one and the same categorization scheme;
- offer a limited number of basic types enabling us to classify the abundance of individual arguments in favour of or against the capitalist market economy.

A Typology of Economic Legitimation Criteria

In order to meet these requirements, we differentiate, in a first step, between *classical* and *non-classical* forms of justification and criticism. In a second step, we introduce three subtypes of non-classical criteria – justice-centred, democracy-centred and culture-centred – to bring order to this diverse set of ideas in a parsimonious but encompassing typology.

Classical criteria are most important, because they represent the basic ideology of the capitalist market economy. A classical justification of the capitalist market economy in the tradition of Adam Smith (1999) credits this regime with the highest degree of economic coordination and productivity growth. According to the classical line of reasoning, economic coordination and productivity are the results of a system of voluntary, coercion-free economic exchange between utility-maximizing actors. The market is self-regulating – it operates effectively precisely because it is based on individual freedom. This freedom is not only compatible with social coordination but also produces the highest possible level of growth, wealth and welfare for all participants. Market freedom is highly productive. This is the core of the classical justification.

There is a corresponding classical form of criticism in the tradition of Karl Marx according to which the capitalist market economy invariably leads to self-destruction and to the collapse of the economic regime. This form of criticism acknowledges that capitalism might initially foster economic progress. Yet, in the long run, the system will destroy itself because of inherent crisis tendencies. In addition, criticism in the classical tradition highlights that economic freedom for some (owners of capital) results in a lack of freedom for many (workers). And even the freedom companies enjoy is an illusion in the light of the economic constraints that force them to meet ever-increasing productivity demands. Instead of guaranteeing a growing level of wealth, this development results in the massive impoverishment of a large share of the global population: This is the essence of classical *criticism* of capitalism, which considers self-destruction, impoverishment and the lack of freedom as different facets of a process that ultimately leads to the breakdown of capitalism. Like their positive counterparts, these critical arguments address the effectiveness of the capitalist market economy and the freedom it ensures, but instead of conceding that the free market is the best possible arrangement for the efficient economic allocation of resources, the critics of capitalism emphasize the limits and inherent self-destructive tendencies of self-regulation, which are the result of employers' freedom to invest and to force those who do not own capital to sell their labour.

In contrast to classical (de-)legitimation criteria, *non-classical* criteria do not remain within the realm of functional and freedom-based ideas, and thus do not refer to allocative efficiency, productivity, levels of growth, utility or profit maximization, economic equilibria and the freedom of economic actors. This group of arguments is heterogeneous. In a second step, we therefore differentiate between three subtypes of non-classical justifications and criticism. Taking up the distinctions made by Rahel Jaeggi, Luc Boltanski and Ève Chiapello, and adding considerations from political science, we discern three groups of criteria within the non-classical category.

Justice-centred criteria: This group – which corresponds to Jaeggi's moral arguments and Boltanski's and Chiapello's social critique – encompasses arguments that draw on the terminology of just/unjust or equal/unequal. These justice-centred criteria focus on the distributive effects of an economic regime and on the general conditions of (in-) justice resulting from market transactions and market processes.

Democracy-centred criteria: This group is missing in the lists provided by the referenced authors. Yet, it plays a considerable role for both criticizing and justifying the capitalist market economy in public discourse (see Chapter 3). Proponents of the regime argue that market freedom is a central precondition for democracy. The economic and the political regime are not only viewed as highly compatible but as depending on each other. In contrast, critics argue that the capitalist market economy undermines political equality and democracy; political participation turns into a farce in the face of fundamental global market constraints. In this view, only a transition to economic democracy can safeguard political democracy in the long run.

Culture-centred criteria: We call references to non-classical criteria that roughly correspond to Jaeggi's category of ethical criticism culture-centred criteria. This group comprises arguments referring to the value (or lack of value) of cultural practices, lifestyles and individual patterns of behaviour. Arguments referring to vices and virtues (honesty, respectability or integrity v. greed) and ethical ideas about social and communicative (leadership) competence are part of this category together with arguments about ways of life in a society and their quality. Against the background of these criteria, the capitalist market economy is legitimate because it facilitates a higher level of civility or because it ensures individual lifestyles, attitudes and manners that are superior to those in other economic regimes. Culture-centred *criticism* claims the opposite: The capitalist market economy destroys the cultural foundation of communities and creates a merciless culture corroded by vices, corruption and egoism, where people only concentrate on their own benefit. The following sections discuss in more detail justifications and criticism of the capitalist market economy underpinned by classical, justice-centred, democracy-centred and culture-centred criteria.

Classical Forms of Justification and Criticism

The *classical* legitimation of the capitalist market economy goes back to Adam Smith in *The Wealth of Nations* (1999). It has remained the core justification of the regime up to this day. Its most distinctive concepts are the 'invisible hand' and the 'spontaneous order': The classical legitimation of the capitalist market economy is based on the argument that in a decentred system of economic coordination through market exchange the self-interest of producers and consumers will lead to a general increase of welfare. The freedom of individuals to follow their self-interest produces overall wealth and thus advances the common good most effectively. Individual self-interest and the absence of a hierarchical instance purposefully establishing order lead to economic prosperity, which is produced without humans intending it, merely as a result of the coordinative power of the price formation mechanism and of cutting back state intervention. The 'invisible hand' and the 'spontaneous order' are crucial concepts, because they give a name to the 'miracles' made possible by the market, that is, the market's ability to enhance common welfare on the basis of individual self-interest without authority or coercive powers. This combination of freedom from arbitrariness, self-regulation and the increase of the material common good is the core of the classical justification of the market economy. The argumentation is neither purely input- nor purely output-based. Its strength lies in the fact that a particular constellation of inputs (voluntary character of market exchanges, freedom, property rights, self-interest, utility maximization and individual opportunities for action) is linked to particular outputs (prosperity, welfare, common good, economic growth and increase of productivity). In a market-based order, freedom is a necessary precondition for the increase of wealth, and welfare is the ultimate consequence of self-interest on all sides.

In the history of economic theory and in public debates on economic issues, these basic ideas have witnessed numerous modifications. The mathematization and micro-theoretical foundation of economics facilitated a line of argument emphasizing the market's equilibrium tendencies. Evidence for the claim that a general balance is possible was strategically important in the field of economic theory (Pribram 1998: 535–41). The disadvantage of this theoretical development was, however, that it did not sufficiently map the competitive dynamics of market processes. The model was too rigid, with competition serving a normalizing function, and lacked elements of risk and collapse or change and development. The dynamics of market processes were first highlighted by Joseph Schumpeter in *The Theory of Economic Development* (1934), and his insights led to a modification of the classical legitimation of the capitalist market economy. 'Creative destruction' and the innovative power of risky entrepreneurial action were now viewed as central elements of market processes.

Such market dynamics, understood as the permanent increase of the level of wealth in a society and among market participants, also dominate arguments from welfare economics (Pribram 1998: 572–5). The invention of the gross domestic product, a measurement construct that has become a key indicator of market performance, is the practical result of this line of reasoning. An increase of this indicator has become the major yardstick for the success of the capitalist market economy. Competition-driven technical change, rising income and welfare levels, improving consumer opportunities and rising productivity through innovation are the focus of a growth-centred variant of the classical justification.

Libertarian thinkers downplay the classical link between self-interest, the market and an increase of wealth in favour of an accent on the input side of economic processes. The libertarian justification of the market radically emphasizes freedom. Representatives of this approach attempt to construct a political philosophy that is primarily based on the right to freedom but not on the capitalist market economy's superior allocative efficiency. Justifications for state intervention, which still existed in Adam Smith's classical version, are further reduced in the libertarian tradition. The most prominent and influential academic representative of libertarianism is Robert Nozick with *Anarchy, State and Utopia* (1974). According to Nozick, more than minimal state intervention collides with the right to freedom. Taxes – just like an array of other policy measures – are interpreted as a violation of personal freedom limiting the scope of action of individuals.

An even more radical libertarian position culminates in an extreme version of *anarcho-capitalism*. One of the main representatives of this position is Ayn Rand. Her defence of egoism has acquired cult status in the United States (Rand 1964, 1967, 1992). In her theory, ownership and self-interest become normatively laden categories leading to a strict rejection of social concepts such as community, solidarity and common good, which had still played a major role as background concepts in Adam Smith's work, in particular in his *Theory of Moral Sentiments* (2002). In Rand's hyper-liberalism, everything belongs to the individual and nothing to the community. All forms of socialization except voluntary market transactions are denounced as a means of disempowering and expropriating the individual, because individual rights are considered to be identical with the right to private property. Private ownership is the primary concept and has a human rights status in Rand's theory (1967). Such a line of reasoning rigorously undermines an output-based legitimation of the capitalist market economy. While the libertarian position acknowledges that the capitalist market economy leads to an increase in welfare for all, that it facilitates technical progress and high productivity and that everyone profits from a flourishing market, it rejects founding the justification of the regime on these building blocks. According to Rand's school of thought, these outputs are only second-order effects. The capitalist market economy should primarily be defended and admired because of its freedom-enhancing nature. As such, the justification of the regime is disconnected from the consequentialist mode that is typical for economic thought and focuses on the results that a regime provides.

We treat arguments asserting that a system of individual freedom and decentred coordination is not stable, sustainable or effective as classical forms of *criticizing* the capitalist market economy. According to these positions, market-based self-regulation ultimately leads to self-destruction. The work of Karl Marx and Friedrich Engels (1956) best represents socialist writing asserting that there are economic laws that inevitably lead to the breakdown of the capitalist market economy. Marxist criticism offers a crisis and collapse theory of the capitalist market economy and attacks every element of the Adam Smith tradition of market legitimation. According to the Marxist account, wage slavery and the economic laws of capital accumulation dominate the regime, and not the individual freedom of consumers, workers and employers. Capitalism leads to a loss of freedom even on the side of capitalists, who find themselves forced to choose between economic failure and compliance with market laws. According to this line of criticism, the capitalist market economy does not give rise to a general increase of wealth but inevitably leads to the impoverishment of the mass of workers, resulting in an extremely top-heavy distribution of wealth. The capitalist economy does not stabilize itself in market equilibrium. Instead, it forges ahead on a path of ever-intensifying crises inevitably leading to collapse and, ultimately, to a new and superior economic system.

This historical-philosophical account has always been highly controversial and is now considered to be untenable (see, for instance, Parijs 1993; Wright 2010: 89–109). Therefore, the idea of an inevitable revolutionary transformation into an alternative economic regime should not be seen as a core element of this form of criticism. However, current variants of the collapse theorem can, for instance, be found in the work of David Graeber, the most prominent representative of the Occupy Movement. He attacks the classical justification of the capitalist market economy on the grounds that it makes thinking about alternatives impossible. According to him, the classical justification depicts capitalism as the possibly worst but also as the only functioning economic regime. The fight against alternatives seems to be more important than safeguarding the capitalist regime's own long-term survival. This presumably turns capitalism into a form of 'kamikaze capitalism' (Graeber 2010) moving towards its own collapse and thus committing suicide. Similarly, work that calls the regime 'disaster capitalism' (Klein 2007) revives older collapse theories while milder forms of this type of criticism are at least sceptical about the future of capitalism.

The impoverishment thesis, which has long been a weak spot of Marxist-inspired criticism, has nevertheless found an indirect successor in current discussions on wealth and poverty. The impact of Thomas Piketty's (2014) study can partly be attributed to the fact that it depicts the ever-widening gap between rich and poor as a law-like phenomenon that will ultimately lead to the failure of the capitalist market economy. However, one can also interpret Piketty's studies as mere criticism of the injustices of the current economic regime. Regarding the output of the capitalist market economy, there are points of contact and even overlaps with justice-based forms of criticism. Yet, we interpret only arguments that connect the unequal distribution of wealth with the instability of markets and their inability to regulate themselves as instances of the classical type of criticism.

Justice-Centred Forms of Justification and Criticism

Applying categories of justice to the justification of the capitalist market economy seems difficult. The standard approach of economists is to differentiate between questions of allocation and distribution. In doing so, they admit that superior forms of allocation produce unequal distributions which, according to them, have to be accepted even though they appear unjust. This makes it impossible to justify the capitalist market economy on the grounds of (distributive) justice. Such a path was taken most consistently by Friedrich August von Hayek (1998). In his view, the term distributive or social justice is meaningless if applied to spontaneous orders such as the market. Moreover, markets do not achieve results that could be justified in terms of merit or desert. Market competition is a mechanism for the coordination of decentralized information. Rewards in this system are dependent on coincidental supply-and-demand equilibria, and not on skills, effort or contributions to the common good. In a market economy, only market success is rewarded. Thus, a merit-based justification of market outcomes does not work, and the concept of equal opportunity is often used to reclaim or preserve the idea of social justice for the capitalist market economy (Miller 1999). In this context, equality of opportunity means that there is only a selective guarantee of equal starting positions by means of legally protected equal access to all social institutions. Another version of this line of reasoning presents the general increase of wealth, conceptualized as a rise in the absolute level of overall wealth, as a central effect of justice. Productivity effects are believed to be so high that all parts of the population – despite unequal distribution – will reach higher levels of welfare than in any other economic regime. This 'elevator effect' of the capitalist market economy presumably makes the system as a whole just, and not a reduction of the gap between the socially disadvantaged and the wealthier members of the population.

An explicit justice-centred theory of the capitalist market economy can be found in the writings of John Locke (1988) and Robert Nozick (1974). Their point of departure is a theoretical situation in which resources are equally distributed. A sequence of transactions that are all inherently just because they are nonviolent and voluntary will then presumably lead to social conditions that may themselves be considered just or legitimate as long as every single step in the chain of action is just. Thus, no specific distributive condition is described as just. Any kind of distribution may be considered just as long as it can be shown to have resulted from fair transactions and fair initial positions. The basis of this argument is the single transaction. Voluntary contracts, understood as exchanges without coercion, threats, deception and information asymmetries, are the smallest building blocks of a theory of just economic and social constitutions. An economic regime that is founded on these building blocks is just, regardless of the distributive impacts it might have.

Arguably the best-known way of criticizing the capitalist market economy attacks the lack of justice in this regime, suggesting that market processes invariably or typically lead to an unjust distribution of income, wealth, prosperity and opportunities. This type of criticism accuses capitalism of producing a market that divides societies into rich and poor people, and therefore of raising *inequality*. According to this argument, capitalism cements and even increases divisions (Stiglitz 2012). Although this criticism is not necessarily as far-reaching as the Marxist impoverishment theory, it is based on an attempt to corroborate the claim that the distribution of income and wealth achieved by the capitalist regime is highly unequal and is becoming more unequal over time (Piketty 2014). The measure employed is not necessarily strict equality in the sense of a fully equal distribution of economic resources; a degree of inequality that is justifiable because it has advantageous effects for everyone, corresponding to the difference principle elaborated by John Rawls (1971, 2001), may be acceptable.

From the viewpoint of *needs-based* justice (Miller 1999), the relevant standard is merely whether the economic regime is able to satisfy basic needs or rather causing starvation and poverty. The failure to satisfy basic needs is the prime bone of contention for this form of criticism. An economic regime as productive as the market economy, which generates a high level of wealth at least in some regions of the world, is fundamentally deficient from the perspective of global justice if it does not ensure that the basic needs of all people (on all continents) are met (Pogge 2008;

Pogge and Moellendorf 2008; Jaggar 2010; see also Brock 2009; Sen 2009; Miller 2010). Von Hayek's proposition that the market is not able to ensure merit-based justice is a weak spot of his argumentation that is taken up by critics of the capitalist market economy. Sociological evidence that capitalism only rewards market success instead of performance, effort or skills is then used to condemn it as a regime that rewards market success simply for being market success. As indicated by research on the 'winner-takes-all society' (Frank and Cook 2010) or 'winner-takes-all politics' (Hacker and Pierson 2010), top managers are rewarded with exorbitant incomes and profits, creating a new class, the super-rich (Freeland 2012), while other forms of work, presumably deserving similar appreciation, no longer guarantee a living wage.

Democracy-Centred Forms of Justification and Criticism

An explicitly democratic justification of the capitalist market economy is rare in the academic literature (for an exception, see Tomasi's 2012 concept of 'market democracy'). It is evident that the basic democratic principle ('one person, one vote') clashes with the fundamental practices of the capitalist market economy, where financial means and their distribution are crucial. As a consequence, authors justifying the regime on the basis of democracy only stress the *compatibility* of a capitalist market economy with liberal-democratic political systems. It is not the capitalist market economy itself that is presented as democratic. Instead, democratization processes are regarded as an indirect effect of the market economy. The claim is that the market economy contributes to politics becoming and remaining democratic. The close link between economic and political freedom lies at the heart of arguments put forward by von Hayek (1960) and Friedman (1962), who maintain that a free society is premised on free markets. However, the misfit between the capitalist market economy as a *global* economy and the lack of democratic processes such as elections at the international level above the EU is not addressed.

The application of political and democratic evaluation criteria to the economic regime typically leads to severe criticism of the capitalist market economy. The regime does not meet the normative requirements of democratic decision-making; investment decisions are taken according to the will of individual investors or financially potent elites and thus do not reflect the will of the people. Economic action is founded on unequal power resources and not on political equality. In addition, market processes and business decisions do not comply with standards of transparency and public deliberation. The transfer of normative ideas from the political realm to the economic sphere implies that an economic regime is only considered legitimate if economic decisions are made via collectively binding decisions on the basis of political equality and the majority rule. Nonetheless, the implicit counter-model of this democratic form of criticism is not a dictatorial, state-planned economy. Instead, an economic regime may be considered democratic if it has successfully transformed itself into an 'economic democracy' (Naphtali 1966).

In addition to the direct application of democratic norms to the capitalist market economy, there is a line of reasoning that acknowledges the division between the political and the economic sphere, yet at the same time contests the view that the capitalist market economy is conducive to democracy. This argument comes in two variants. In the weaker variant, authors merely argue that the capitalist market economy does not *necessarily* contribute to democracy. Proponents of the stronger variant, by contrast, emphasize that one has to choose between the capitalist market economy and democracy because these two orders have become incompatible, or they expect growing conflict between democracy and the capitalist market economy, each striving to become the dominant regime on a global scale (Rodrik 2011; Schäfer and Streeck 2013; Streeck 2014).

Culture-Centred Forms of Justification and Criticism

Cultural justifications emphasize that capitalism has a character-forming effect and contributes to a more civilized society. Albert O. Hirschman (1997) traces this argument back to the eighteenth century, when philosophers such as Adam Smith and David Hume claimed that there was a connection between the expansion of trade and good manners. Following this line of reasoning, capitalism strengthens or fosters virtues such as diligence, honesty, empathy, fairness and moderation (Maitland 1997). In addition to the character-forming effects of the market economy, Hirschman (1982, 1997) subsumes a range of positive effects on social relations and a civilizing impact on society as a whole under the 'doux commerce' label. The proponents of the 'doux commerce' thesis welcome capitalism because it creates a new form of social relations that has a primarily voluntary nature. Categories such as tradition, family, culture and race do not play a role in the market (Maitland 1997: 26; Berger 2001: 22). Under favourable conditions, market interactions can build trust, which has a civilizing and integrative effect on society and turns market participants into norm-following actors. In line with Max Weber (1922) and other classical authors, current economic sociology has demonstrated that shared convictions, virtuous market actors and routine life forms need to be in place to ensure self-regulation in the capitalist market economy. Without trust, a set of respected norms and shared cognitive frameworks that create shared expectations, the market economy can hardly be effective (Beckert 1997, 2007; Fligstein 2002; Aspers 2011).

Cultural criticism of capitalism emphasizes that the market regime destroys the ethical foundations of society and that it corrupts people because it erodes the link between the economy and normatively founded social conditions. As such, it facilitates egoism and greed, and makes social cohesion and solidarity impossible (Polanyi 2001). According to this argument, pure greed dominates 'turbo capitalism', and the virtues of respectable merchants are replaced by unreasonable forms of generating income as an end in itself. This criticism focuses on actors of the capitalist market economy such as managers, shareholders, 'financial jugglers', entrepreneurs and bankers. The capitalist market economy is criticized because it facilitates vices and thus leads to an ethically inacceptable social order. The regime makes it impossible for people to live a good – that is, an authentic, non-alienated – life or to achieve a good society. In the capitalist market economy, there is no progress towards a decent human society; the market prevents lifestyles and even the development of authentic desires that are not geared towards growth (Skidelsky and Skidelsky 2012).

Some authors claim that the loss of social cohesion that capitalism provokes will ultimately lead to social collapse. The capitalist market economy is attacked because it fosters the economization of all aspects of life, all social relationships such as the family, partnerships and friendships, or culture, science and the public sphere at large. Hence, the expansion of the market logic into spheres beyond the economy is deplored. The capitalist market economy is considered legitimate to the extent that it concentrates on the exchange of goods and remains circumscribed by an overarching normative order. As soon as it transgresses its functional sphere and normative principles, its legitimacy is questioned. As soon as society is infused with the capitalist logic through marketing campaigns (Klein 2000), the market transcends the limits of the economic sphere. Similar positions acknowledge that the economic regime can usefully fulfil certain tasks and coordinate the exchange of goods, while other tasks should remain beyond the purview of the market in order to safeguard the social integrity of society (Satz 2010; Sandel 2012). From this perspective, the capitalist market economy only becomes the object of criticism if the dividing line between these two social spheres is crossed (Walzer 1983). The notion of clear boundaries, of a strict division of spheres and the plea to limit the expansion of the capitalist logic are key elements of this line of reasoning.

Alternatives to the Capitalist Market Economy?

For all types of argumentation, especially for criticism of the capitalist market economy, the intellectual availability of alternative economic models is crucial. Does capitalism have to be defended against opposing economic models? Does the critique of capitalism inform these alternative models? The availability of such blueprints is crucial for a wholesale transformation of the current economic regime. This section therefore briefly turns to alternative models.

Since the collapse of socialism in the 1990s, political debates and theorizing on fundamental alternatives to the capitalist market economy have abated; competing models have almost disappeared, and hence the regime has lost its 'other'. There is presumably no longer a normatively attractive alternative to the capitalist market economy – just as there is none to democracy in the political sphere. Ever since democracy prevailed over (constitutional) monarchy and various forms of authoritarianism, no other regime type has been credibly presented as superior. In contrast, the capitalist market economy had faced potentially viable alternatives or utopias, known under the name of socialism or communism, since the era of industrialization. However, the conspicuous inefficiency and, ultimately, collapse of planned economies in the Soviet Union and its sphere of influence clearly demonstrated the failure of the socialist economic regime and discredited the once powerful idea of socialism. As a consequence, fundamental criticism of capitalism became much more difficult. Non-dogmatic observers were forced to either deny that the collapsed systems had ever been socialist in any meaningful sense or to concede that socialism had indeed failed as an economic regime. To be taken seriously, any newly formulated alternative to capitalism had to repudiate this pedigree. This certainly weakens the voice of critics whose goal remains to construct such an alternative.

Some alternative economic models and concepts have nevertheless been proposed, following older models such as 'industrial democracy', 'economic democracy' or 'workplace democracy' (Naphtali 1966; Dahl 1985; Martens 2010), or postulating new blueprints such as the 'democratization of wealth' (Alperovitz 2011) or the model of a 'property-owning democracy' propagated by John Rawls (1971; see also Krouse and McPherson 1988; Jackson 2012; O'Neill and Williamson 2012). Despite the prominence of its proponent, John Rawls's concept of a property-owning democracy has not been taken up beyond philosophical circles. The term 'economic democracy' (Naphtali 1966) as a socialist alternative to 'organized capitalism' (Hilferding 1968) has been used since 1928, but it has rarely been the object of further conceptual development. John E. Roemer's (1994) 'market socialism' is one of the few theoretical models that have bucked the trend since the 1990s (see also Elster and Moene 1989; Schweickart 1993, 2002). In other contributions, the market is sidelined completely, for instance, in *Why Not Socialism?* (Cohen 2009), which develops an ideal community scenario that seems only viable in small groups (see also Cohen 2008; Ronzoni 2012). Michael Albert's and Robin Hahnel's work on 'participatory economics' (1991; see also Albert 2006, 2014; Wright 2010) is perhaps the most interesting attempt to formulate a democratic alternative to the capitalist market economy (Wright 2010: 252–62). Most recent contributions concentrate on the topicality of socialism (Honneth 2016) or the potential rise of 'post-capitalism' as a consequence of the revolution in information technology (Mason 2015). The intellectual availability or real-world existence of alternative economic regimes does not force us to modify the proposed typology of legitimating and delegitimating criteria, but it enables a more dualistic argumentation by the critics of capitalism in legitimation discourse.

Conclusion

The aim of this chapter was to present a typology of legitimating and delegitimating criteria. Following and modifying classifications by Rahel Jaeggi, Luc Boltanski and Ève Chiapello, we focused on the differentiation between classical and non-classical forms of justification and criticism. Classical criteria refer to the idea of economic coordination via markets as a system of voluntary, coercion-free economic exchange between utility-maximizing actors. Classical justification sees self-regulating markets based on individual freedom as producers of the highest possible level of growth, wealth and welfare for all participants. Classical criticism of the capitalist market economy denies some or all elements of this legitimation of the capitalist market economy: the self-regulating capacity of the market, the freedom of the individual in the market, the coordination without any form of coercion, the productive potential of the regime and its contribution to the wealth of all participants. Non-classical criteria do not address links between freedom, self-regulation and the production of wealth. We define as non-classical all other arguments for or against the capitalist market economy. These non-classical forms of justification and criticism are diverse. We identified three subtypes: justice-centred, democracy-centred and culture-centred criteria, using arguments about distributive justice, popular sovereignty and participation or moral integration as core ideas. With these differentiations, we provide a theoretically informed instrument for the detailed empirical study of legitimation discourse.

References

Albert, Michael. 2006. *Parecon. Leben nach dem Kapitalismus*. Frankfurt am Main: Trotzdem.

Albert, Michael. 2014. *Realizing Hope. Life Beyond Capitalism*. London: Zed Books.

Albert, Michael and Robin Hahnel. 1991. *The Political Economy of Participatory Economics*. Princeton: Princeton University Press.

Alperovitz, Gar. 2011. *America Beyond Capitalism. Reclaiming Our Wealth, Our Liberty, and Our Democracy*. Second Edition. Takoma Park: Democracy Collaborative Press.

Aspers, Patrik. 2011. *Markets*. Cambridge: Polity Press.

Beckert, Jens. 1997. *Grenzen des Marktes. Die sozialen Grundlagen wirtschaftlicher Effizienz*. Frankfurt am Main: Campus.

Beckert, Jens. 2007. 'Die soziale Ordnung von Märkten'. In *Märkte als soziale Strukturen*, eds. Jens Beckert, Rainer Diaz-Bone and Heiner Ganßmann. Frankfurt am Main: Campus, 43–62.

Berger, Johannes. 2001. 'Der diskrete Charme des Markts'. In *Die beste aller Welten? Marktliberalismus versus Wohlfahrtsstaat*, ed. Karl Ulrich Mayer. Frankfurt am Main: Campus, 13–34.

Bermeo, Nancy and Larry M. Bartels, eds. 2014. *Mass Politics in Tough Times. Opinions, Votes, and Protest in the Great Recession*. Oxford: Oxford University Press.

Bermeo, Nancy and Jonas Pontusson, eds. 2012. *Coping with Crisis. Government Reactions to the Great Recession*. New York: Russell Sage Foundation.

Boltanski, Luc and Ève Chiapello. 2007. *The New Spirit of Capitalism*. London: Verso.

Boltanski, Luc and Laurent Thévenot. 1991. *De la justification. Les économies de la grandeur*. Paris: Gallimard.

Brock, Gillian. 2009. *Global Justice. A Cosmopolitan Account*. Oxford: Oxford University Press.

Cohen, Gerald A. 2008. *Rescuing Justice and Equality*. Cambridge, MA: Harvard University Press.

Cohen, Gerald A. 2009. *Why Not Socialism?* Princeton: Princeton University Press.

Dahl, Robert A. 1985. *A Preface to Economic Democracy*. Berkeley: University of California Press.

Elster, Jon and Karl Ove Moene, eds. 1989. *Alternatives to Capitalism*. Cambridge: Cambridge University Press.

Fligstein, Neil. 2002. *The Architecture of Markets. An Economic Sociology of Twenty-First-Century Capitalist Societies*. Princeton: Princeton University Press.

Frank, Robert H. and Philip J. Cook. 2010. *The Winner-Take-All Society. Why the Few at the Top Get So Much More Than the Rest of Us*. London: Virgin Books.

Freeland, Chrystia. 2012. *Plutocrats. The Rise of the New Global Super-Rich and the Fall of Everyone Else*. New York: Penguin.

Friedman, Milton. 1962. *Capitalism and Freedom*. Chicago: University of Chicago Press.

Graeber, David. 2010. 'Against Kamikaze Capitalism: Oil, Climate Change and the French Refinery Blockades'. *Shift Magazine* (November).

Hacker, Jacob S. and Paul Pierson. 2010. *Winner-Take-All Politics. How Washington Made the Rich Richer – And Turned Its Back on the Middle Class*. New York: Simon & Schuster.

Hall, Peter A. and David Soskice, eds. 2001. *Varieties of Capitalism. The Institutional Foundations of Comparative Advantage*. Oxford: Oxford University Press.

Hayek, Friedrich A. von. 1960. *The Constitution of Liberty*. Chicago: University of Chicago Press.

Hayek, Friedrich A. von. 1998. *Law, Legislation and Liberty. A New Statement on the Liberal Principles of Justice and Political Economy*. London: Routledge.

Herzog, Lisa. 2013. *Freiheit gehört nicht nur den Reichen. Plädoyer für einen zeitgemäßen Liberalismus*. Munich: Beck.

Hilferding, Rudolf. 1968. *Das Finanzkapital*. Frankfurt am Main: Europäische Verlagsanstalt.

Hirschman, Albert O. 1982. 'Rival Interpretations of Market Society: Civilizing, Destructive, or Feeble?' *Journal of Economic Literature* 20(4): 1463–84.

Hirschman, Albert O. 1997. *The Passions and the Interests. Political Arguments for Capitalism before Its Triumph*. Princeton: Princeton University Press.

Honneth, Axel. 2016. *The Idea of Socialism*. Cambridge: Polity Press.

Jackson, Ben. 2012. 'Property-Owning Democracy: A Short History'. In *Property-Owning Democracy. Rawls and Beyond*, eds. Martin O'Neill and Thad Williamson. Malden: Wiley-Blackwell, 33–52.

Jaeggi, Rahel. 2013. 'Was (wenn überhaupt etwas) ist falsch am Kapitalismus? Drei Wege der Kapitalismuskritik'. In *Nach Marx. Philosophie, Kritik, Praxis*, eds. Rahel Jaeggi and Daniel Loick. Berlin: Suhrkamp, 321–49.

Jaggar, Alison M., ed. 2010. *Thomas Pogge and His Critics*. Cambridge: Polity Press.
Kahler, Miles and David A. Lake, eds. 2013. *Politics in the New Hard Times. The Great Recession in Comparative Perspective*. Ithaca: Cornell University Press.
Klein, Naomi. 2000. *No Logo. Taking Aim at the Brand Bullies*. Toronto: Alfred A. Knopf.
Klein, Naomi. 2007. *The Shock Doctrine. The Rise of Disaster Capitalism*. New York: Metropolitan Books.
Krouse, Richard and Michael McPherson. 1988. 'Capitalism, "Property-Owning Democracy" and the Welfare State'. In *Democracy and the Welfare State*, ed. Amy Gutmann. Princeton: Princeton University Press, 157–85.
Locke, John. 1988. *Two Treatises of Government. Edited with an Introduction by Peter Laslett*. Cambridge: Cambridge University Press.
Maitland, Ian. 1997. 'Virtuous Markets: The Market as School of the Virtues'. *Business Ethics Quarterly* 7(1): 17–31.
Martens, Helmut. 2010. *Neue Wirtschaftsdemokratie. Anknüpfungspunkte im Zeichen der Krise von Ökonomie, Ökologie und Politik*. Hamburg: VSA.
Marx, Karl and Friedrich Engels. 1956. *Karl Marx, Friedrich Engels. Werke*, 43 Volumes. Berlin: Institut für Marxismus-Leninismus beim ZK der SED, Dietz.
Mason, Paul. 2015. *Postcapitalism. A Guide to Our Future*. London: Allen Lane.
Miller, David. 1999. *Principles of Social Justice*. Cambridge, MA: Harvard University Press.
Miller, Richard W. 2010. *Globalizing Justice. The Ethics of Poverty and Power*. Oxford: Oxford University Press.
Mises, Ludwig von. 1951. *Socialism*. New Haven: Yale University Press.
Naphtali, Fritz. 1966. *Wirtschaftsdemokratie. Ihr Wesen, Weg und Ziel*. Frankfurt am Main: Europäische Verlagsanstalt.
Nozick, Robert. 1974. *Anarchy, State, and Utopia*. New York: Basic Books.
O'Neill, Martin and Thad Williamson, eds. 2012. *Property-Owning Democracy. Rawls and Beyond*. Malden: Wiley-Blackwell.
Parijs, Philippe Van. 1993. *Marxism Recycled*. Cambridge: Cambridge University Press.
Piketty, Thomas. 2014. *Capital in the Twenty-First Century*. Cambridge, MA: Belknap Press.
Pogge, Thomas. 2008. *World Poverty and Human Rights. Cosmopolitan Responsibilities and Reforms*. Second Edition. Cambridge: Polity Press.

Pogge, Thomas and Darrel Moellendorf, eds. 2008. *Global Justice. Seminal Essays*. Saint Paul: Paragon House.
Polanyi, Karl. 2001. *The Great Transformation. The Political and Economic Origins of Our Time*. Boston: Beacon Press.
Posner, Richard A. 2009. *A Failure of Capitalism. The Crisis of '08 and the Descent into Depression*. Cambridge, MA: Harvard University Press.
Posner, Richard A. 2010. *The Crisis of Capitalist Democracy*. Cambridge, MA: Harvard University Press.
Pribram, Karl. 1998. *Geschichte des ökonomischen Denkens*. Frankfurt am Main: Suhrkamp.
Rand, Ayn. 1964. *The Virtue of Selfishness*. New York: Penguin.
Rand, Ayn. 1967. *Capitalism. The Unknown Ideal*. New York: Penguin.
Rand, Ayn. 1992. *Atlas Shrugged*. New York: Penguin.
Rawls, John. 1971. *A Theory of Justice*. Cambridge, MA: Belknap Press.
Rawls, John. 2001. *Justice as Fairness. A Restatement. Edited by Erin Kelly*. Cambridge, MA: Belknap Press.
Rodrik, Dani. 2011. *The Globalization Paradox. Democracy and the Future of the World Economy*. New York: W. W. Norton & Company.
Roemer, John E. 1994. *A Future for Socialism*. Cambridge, MA: Harvard University Press.
Ronzoni, Miriam. 2012. 'Life is not a Camping Trip – On the Desirability of Cohenite Socialism'. *Politics, Philosophy & Economics* 11(2): 171–85.
Sandel, Michael J. 2012. *What Money Can't Buy. The Moral Limits of Markets*. New York: Farrar, Straus and Giroux.
Satz, Debra. 2010. *Why Some Things Should Not Be for Sale. The Moral Limits of Markets*. Oxford: Oxford University Press.
Schäfer, Armin and Wolfgang Streeck, eds. 2013. *Politics in the Age of Austerity*. Cambridge: Polity Press.
Scharpf, Fritz W. 1999. *Governing in Europe. Effective and Democratic?* Oxford: Oxford University Press.
Scharpf, Fritz W. 2009. 'Legitimacy in the Multilevel European Polity'. *European Political Science Review* 1(2): 173–204.
Schumpeter, Joseph A. 1934. *The Theory of Economic Development. An Inquiry into Profits, Capital, Credit, Interest, and the Business Cycle. With a New Introduction by John E. Elliott*. New Brunswick: Transaction Publishers.
Schumpeter, Joseph A. 1954. *History of Economic Analysis*. New York: Oxford University Press.

Schweickart, David. 1993. *Against Capitalism*. Cambridge: Cambridge University Press.
Schweickart, David. 2002. *After Capitalism*. Lanham: Rowman & Littlefield.
Sen, Amartya. 2009. *The Idea of Justice*. Cambridge, MA: Belknap Press.
Skidelsky, Robert and Edward Skidelsky. 2012. *How Much is Enough? Money and the Good Life*. New York: Other Press.
Smith, Adam. 1999. *The Wealth of Nations. Books I-III*. London: Penguin.
Smith, Adam. 2002. *The Theory of Moral Sentiments*. Cambridge: Cambridge University Press.
Stiglitz, Joseph E. 2012. *The Price of Inequality. How Today's Divided Society Endangers Our Future*. New York: W. W. Norton & Company.
Streeck, Wolfgang. 2014. *Buying Time. The Delayed Crisis of Democratic Capitalism*. London: Verso.
Tomasi, John. 2012. *Free Market Fairness*. Princeton: Princeton University Press.
Walzer, Michael. 1983. *Spheres of Justice. A Defense of Pluralism and Equality*. New York: Basic Books.
Weber, Max. 1922. *Wirtschaft und Gesellschaft*. Tübingen: Mohr Siebeck.
Wright, Erik Olin. 2010. *Envisioning Real Utopias*. London: Verso.

3

Legitimation Discourse before and after the Financial Crisis: Contours and Trajectories

Henning Schmidtke and Steffen Schneider

What were the contours of British, German, Swiss and US media communication on the legitimacy of the capitalist market economy before and after the 2008 financial crisis? How close to the a-legitimacy scenario was legitimation discourse in the years between 1998 and 2007 (the first part of our observation period)? Was the financial crisis the expected critical juncture, as evidenced by a discursive *legitimation crisis* of the capitalist market economy after 2008? Are there characteristic national differences in the way the legitimacy of the regime has been addressed in the wake of the financial crisis? Finally, does a look at

H. Schmidtke (✉)
Bavarian School of Public Policy, TUM School of Governance, Technical University of Munich, Munich, Germany
e-mail: henning.schmidtke@hfp.tum.de

S. Schneider
Research Centre on Inequality and Social Policy (SOCIUM), University of Bremen, Bremen, Germany
e-mail: stschnei@uni-bremen.de

S. Schneider et al. (eds.), *Capitalism and Its Legitimacy in Times of Crisis*, Transformations of the State,
DOI 10.1007/978-3-319-53765-8_3

discursive patterns contribute to explaining the surprising absence of transformative institutional change?

Against the backdrop of these questions and drawing on the legitimation grammar introduced in Chapter 1, the present contribution examines the contours and trajectories of legitimation discourse in our corpus of newspaper articles. On the basis of a quantitative content analysis of legitimation statements, the first section of the chapter probes shifts after 2008 in levels of attention to the legitimacy issue (legitimation intensity) and in the tone of legitimation discourse (legitimacy levels) – our indicators of a legitimation crisis; we show that its varying severity in the four countries is not fully explained by differences in economic problem pressure induced by the financial crisis. The second section considers three additional elements of the legitimation grammar that are decisive for the transformative potential of a legitimation crisis: the voice of different actor types in legitimation discourse (speakers), the principles, varieties and actors of the capitalist market economy they address and the normative standards they use to evaluate them (legitimation objects and criteria).

The content analysis reveals the existence of genuine legitimation discourse even before the financial crisis. Since 2008, however, discourse in all four national public spheres has indeed been characterized by the shifts in intensity and tone that we qualify as signs of a legitimation crisis – continued differences across countries in the discursive treatment of the legitimacy issue notwithstanding. A closer look at the discursive reactions to the financial crisis in light of the speakers, objects and criteria variables, for its part, reveals the temporary and limited nature of the capitalist market economy's financial crisis-induced delegitimation – an issue that will be explored in greater detail in Chapters 4–7.

Intensity, Tone and Scenarios of (De-) Legitimation

In this section, we begin by probing the intensity and tone of legitimation discourse in Germany, Switzerland, the United Kingdom and the United States before and after 2008.[1] Considering intensity and tone together enables us to gauge how close to the a-legitimacy scenario media communication was before the financial crisis and to what extent it has moved towards the scenario of a legitimation crisis since 2008.

Legitimation Intensity and Tone

We diagnose a legitimation crisis where the legitimacy issue is particularly salient and the overall tone of evaluations highly critical. Our indicator in the dimension of salience – *legitimation intensity* – is simply the number of (positive and negative) legitimation statements identified in each of the four countries and 14 years – or 56 country-years – examined (see Table 1.2, Chapter 1). This indicator has a theoretically meaningful absolute minimum (zero) that corresponds to the a-legitimacy scenario outlined in the introduction to the volume: A regime's legitimacy is not explicitly discussed because it is accepted 'as necessary or inevitable based on some taken-for-granted cultural account' (Suchman 1995: 582). As it turns out, however, the figures suggest a modicum of legitimation discourse in all country-years – especially when taking into account that our corpus is based on only four constructed weeks per year and hence that a comprehensive survey of annual press coverage would presumably have yielded about 13 times as many legitimation statements in each case (see Appendix, Chapter 1).

As there is no readily available and theoretically plausible *a priori* threshold value for qualifying the legitimation intensity of a given country-year as low or high, our further interpretation relies on averages and measures of dispersion gleaned from the data. The *overall* mean of legitimation statements per country-year is 44.9 – a total of 2514 statements divided by 56. Using this benchmark, we may qualify the intensity of legitimation discourse in the United States and Switzerland – with *national* 14-year averages of 18.6 and 27.4 – as comparatively low. British (50.6) and, especially, German discourse (82.9) is considerably more intense. Thus, US discourse is closest to the a-legitimacy scenario – the taken-for-grantedness of the capitalist market economy – while German discourse is farthest away. One might suspect that varying legitimation intensity is an effect of differences in national media cultures (Hallin and Mancini 2004) or, trivially, of differences in the volume of the newspapers in our sample. However, an alternative measure of legitimation intensity – the number of pertinent articles in a given country-year divided by the total number of articles – yields very similar results, and the two measures of intensity are highly correlated (Pearson's $r = 0.86$). What is more, a parallel study examining media communication on the legitimacy of national *political* systems (Schneider forthcoming, 2010a: 71) reveals, first, that legitimation discourse on the capitalist market economy is much less intense across the board. Secondly, US discourse has the highest intensity and German discourse the second-lowest when the democratic nation state, its institutions and actors are evaluated. Thus, the varying salience of capitalism's legitimacy in the four public spheres is unlikely to be the mere effect of journalists' greater or lesser propensity to make evaluative propositions of the legitimation statement type *per se*.

Finally, as suggested in the introductory chapter to this volume, critical junctures presumably foster uncertainty and, as a consequence, more intense public debate on the legitimacy of political or economic regimes and their normative foundations. Has this been the case in the wake of the 2008 financial crisis? Has the legitimacy of the capitalist market economy become a more salient issue – perhaps even for national publics that tend to take it for granted? Figure 3.1 – which contrasts mean annual legitimation intensity before (1998–2007) and after the financial crisis (2008–2011) – suggests as much: The intensity of legitimation discourse has grown everywhere – almost threefold in the United Kingdom and twofold in Germany. In the low intensity countries – Switzerland and United States – the rise is similarly pronounced, but intensity values stay below the 56 country-year average indicated by the horizontal line.

This shift away from a relative 'depoliticisation of the economic' (Swanson 2008) towards growing awareness of the legitimacy issue – both in the United States, where the financial crisis began, and in three European countries – is evidence for the international character of the crisis and confirms the expectation formulated in Chapter 1: The normative foundations of the capitalist market economy have clearly become more problematic – and therefore the subject of explicit public debate – since 2008.

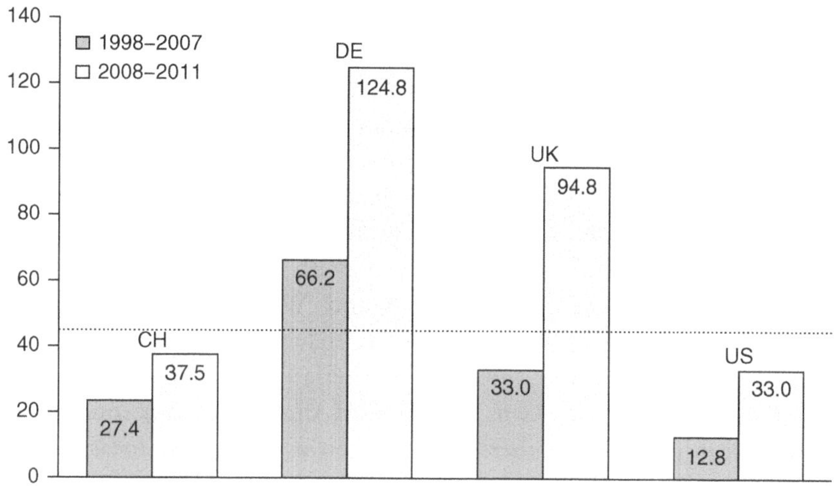

Fig. 3.1 Legitimation intensity (number of legitimation statements), 10-year pre-financial crisis and four-year post-crisis average, by country

But has the financial crisis also led to more contestation of the regime's legitimacy? Our indicator for the more or less critical tone of discourse – *legitimacy levels* – is the percentage share of positive legitimation statements. This indicator is thus bounded between 0 and 100 per cent, but like the extreme a-legitimacy scenario – the complete absence of legitimation discourse – the 'full' withdrawal of discursive support is empirically unlikely. Only a single one of the 56 country-years – Swiss discourse in 2010 – has a legitimacy level of 0 per cent (accompanied by very low legitimation intensity). The opposite, a legitimacy level of 100 per cent and hence a kind of public acclamation scenario, does not occur at all (the highest value is 64.3 per cent in 2006 US discourse – also in a low intensity context).

Again, we are faced with the challenge that an *a priori* threshold between high and critically low values of our legitimacy level measure is difficult to justify (a problem we share with other strands of empirical legitimacy research; see, for instance, Gilley 2006). A threshold of 50 per cent – the dividing line between a surplus and a deficit of positive evaluations – has some plausibility, but its meaning should not be overstated: A critical public that regularly assesses political systems and their economic foundations ('critical citizenship') is not only normatively desirable but also very likely to be an empirically observable feature of democratic societies such as the ones examined in this book (Barker 2007: 28–31; Norris 2011). Hence, we may safely assume the existence of a negative media bias in legitimacy assessments of political and economic regimes, even if the strength of this bias remains disputed and is likely to vary with differences in national media cultures (Norris 2000; Hepp and Wessler 2009). What is more, the meaning of legitimacy levels may depend on the precise objects evaluated and the legitimation criteria used – a topic we return to later in this chapter. As in the intensity dimension, our interpretation of legitimacy levels therefore relies on averages and measures of dispersion gleaned from the data. The average legitimacy level of the 56 country-years is a mere 27.9 per cent and thus far below the 50 per cent threshold; only five country-years – all before the financial crisis – have legitimacy levels of 50 per cent or higher. Drawing on the 27.9 per cent benchmark instead, the 14-year averages of legitimacy levels in the United States, Switzerland and Germany turn out to be slightly above the overall mean and highly similar (31.0, 29.9 and 29.9 per cent) while the British value (20.8 per cent) is lower. Even in the US quality press, then, the capitalist market economy tends to be assessed critically when its legitimacy is made the subject of explicit discussion. This critical thrust is even more pronounced in the British press. Another glance at corresponding values for legitimacy assessments of national *political* systems (Schneider forthcoming, 2010a: 71) shows, first, that these are evaluated more positively – much more positively in the case of Switzerland (with a 14-year average of 53.5 per cent) and the United States (47.0 per cent) – than the capitalist market economy. Secondly, the gap is quite small in the British press, where the negative media bias is most pronounced and even the regime of Westminster democracy and its institutions have a legitimacy level of only 25.0 per cent. Here, then, national media cultures and journalistic styles appear to play a considerable role.

Finally, we examine the impact of the financial crisis on legitimacy levels. Have legitimacy levels suffered in the wake of the events of 2008?

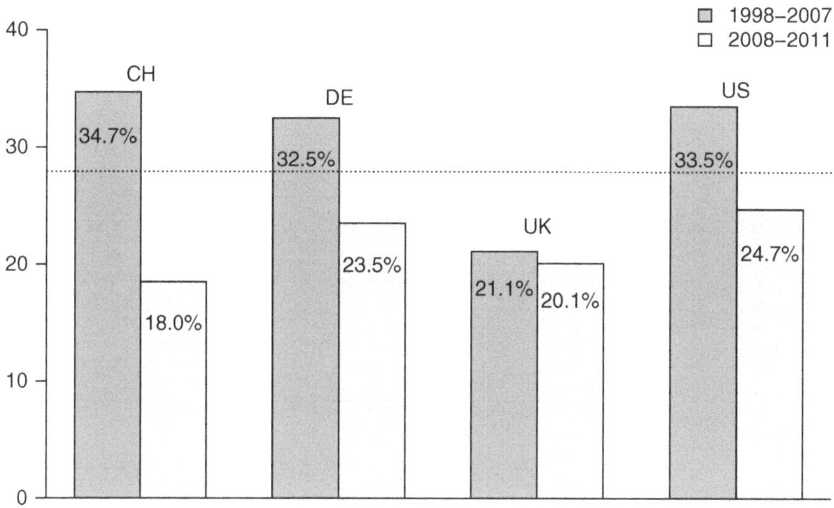

Fig. 3.2 Legitimacy levels (% positive statements), 10-year pre-financial crisis and four-year post-crisis average, by country

Anything else would be a surprise, but Fig. 3.2 documents a decline in all four national publics. It is most pronounced in Switzerland (16.7 percentage points) and least so in the United Kingdom, where discursive support for the capitalist market economy was considerably below the 56 country-year average (the horizontal line) even *before* the onset of the financial crisis.

Scenarios of (De-)Legitimation

We are now in a position to gauge the extent to which the financial crisis triggered a legitimation crisis of the capitalist market economy characterized by growing salience of the legitimacy issue and a more critical tone of legitimation discourse. Figure 3.3 displays tone on the x-axis and intensity on the y-axis. The coordinates of the 56 data points are the legitimacy levels and numbers of statements for the 56 country-years, transformed into z-scores.[2] Hence, the x-axis depicts average legitimation intensity (44.9 statements, z-score = 0) and

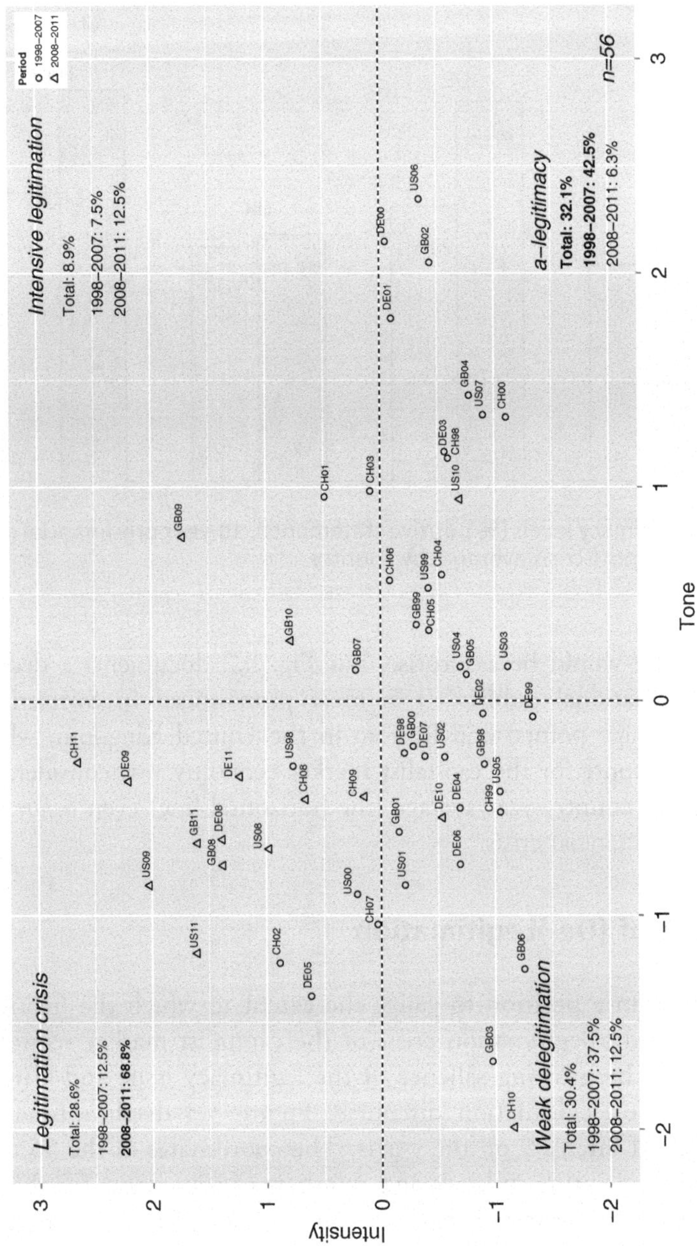

Fig. 3.3 Legitimation scenarios, country-years

separates high intensity scenarios (above) from low intensity scenarios (below); the y-axis depicts the mean legitimacy level (27.9 per cent, z-score = 0) and separates low level scenarios (left) from high level scenarios (right).

The bottom-right quadrant – or more precisely, its bottom-right *corner* – represents the a-legitimacy scenario and the top-left quadrant the scenario of a legitimation crisis. The discursive effect of the financial crisis stands out quite dramatically: Up to 2007, 42.5 per cent of the country-years – a clear plurality – were in the low legitimation intensity and high legitimacy level category, followed by the weak delegitimation scenario (low intensity and low legitimacy level). Only five country-years before the financial crisis have the features of a legitimation crisis: US discourse in 1998 and 2000, Swiss discourse in 2002 and 2007, and German discourse in 2005. Yet, these isolated country-years hardly indicate critical junctures. Firstly, all five instances of a discursive legitimation crisis were short-lived. Secondly, as closer inspection of our text material for these years suggests, they were triggered by nationally specific events and discursive contexts. In the United States, discourse was dominated by public debate on the 1997 and 1998 Asian financial crisis and its impact on the global financial architecture, notably including the Washington-based International Monetary Fund and World Bank; the IT ('dot.com') bubble of the late 1990s – which had been largely driven by the US 'new' economy – burst in March 2000. Swiss discourse reflects particularly weak growth of the national economy in 2002 and the first signs of the looming global financial crisis in 2007. German discourse in 2005 was also marked by domestic politics: In a federal election year, the merger of the Party of Democratic Socialism (PDS) with the *Wahlalternative Arbeit und soziale Gerechtigkeit* (WASG) into a new left-wing party (*Die Linke*) forced the Social Democrats (SPD) to vigorously defend their political home turf. The highly publicized attack of SPD leader Franz Müntefering on the 'locusts' of the financial industry and his critique of neoliberal globalization fostered intensive and highly critical legitimation discourse which, however, faded out quickly after the election.

In the post-2008 portion of the observation period, more than two thirds of the country-years shift into the legitimation crisis category, followed by the scenarios of weak delegitimation and intensive legitimation (high intensity and high legitimacy level). A single country-year (US discourse in 2010) is now in the a-legitimacy category. Moreover, there are two Swiss and German cases of weak delegitimation (also in 2010) and two British cases of intensive legitimation (in 2009 and 2010). This finding suggests that media attention was briefly distracted from the legitimacy issue in the United States, Switzerland and Germany while relegitimation efforts proved temporarily successful in the United Kingdom. However, the overall picture is a shift towards the legitimation crisis scenario.

Finally, we draw on the z-scores in the dimensions of intensity and tone to construct an indicator for the size of this shift and to examine where the post-2008 legitimation crisis was most severe. The formula (z-score LI – z-score LL)/2 was used to calculate the value of the indicator for each country-year. Thus, a value greater than zero indicates higher-than-average legitimation intensity, a lower-than-average legitimacy level or a shift from 'normalcy' towards the legitimation crisis scenario in both dimensions; *mutatis mutandis*, a value below zero indicates closeness to the a-legitimacy scenario in one or both dimensions. Moreover, a one-unit – that is, a one-standard deviation – difference across countries or a one-unit change over time in the values taken by the indicator may be considered sizeable. Table 3.1 shows that the mean values for both the 1998–2007 and the 2008–2011 portion of our observation period are remarkably similar across countries. The negative sign in the first time period (t_1) reflects the dominance of the low legitimation intensity and high legitimacy level scenario described above. Conversely, the positive sign in the second time period (t_2) and

Table 3.1 Legitimation crisis indicator pre/-post-financial crisis, by country

	Mean 1998–2007	Mean 2008–2011	Δ t_2–t_1
CH	-0.27	0.68	0.95
DE	-0.31	0.77	1.08
UK	-0.29	0.73	1.02
US	-0.31	0.71	1.02
Overall	-0.29	0.73	1.02

Table 3.2 Severity of legitimation crisis and economic problem pressure, country ranking

	GDP	Unemployment	Debt	Economic problem pressure overall	Legitimation crisis ranking
CH	4	4	4	4	4
DE	2	3	3	3	1
UK	1	2	1	1	2
US	3	1	2	2	3

Note: The indicators of economic problem pressure are ranked from highest (= 1) to lowest (= 4), as is the indicator of the severity of the post-2008 legitimation crisis. The indicator of overall economic problem pressure is based on the sum of the GDP, unemployment and debt rankings.

the roughly one-unit change between t_1 and t_2 underline the strong discursive effect of the financial crisis and the severity of the legitimation crisis it triggered: The economic problem pressure visibly translated into growing attention to and contestation of the capitalist market economy's legitimacy (Table 3.2).

However, one might ask whether economic problem pressure is the sole driver of legitimation intensity and legitimacy levels in the wake of the financial crisis. If so, the severity of the legitimation crisis – as measured by our crisis indicator – should vary across countries with the length and depth of the post-2008 recession. We use the four-year (2008–2011) means of economic growth and unemployment rates as well as debt levels to rank our country cases by problem pressure, which was strongest where the mean growth rate was lowest and the unemployment rate and debt levels were highest.[3]

To what extent were the 'cues' provided by standard measures of economic and fiscal performance (or hardship) taken up in mediated legitimation discourse (Zaller 1992; Soroka 2006; Singer 2011)? Table 3.2 shows a fairly consistent rank order of the four countries across all three measures of problem pressure; it indicates that the United Kingdom was affected most negatively by the financial crisis, followed by the United States and Germany. Switzerland was least affected – while the unemployment rate essentially stagnated, debt levels even shrank – and also experienced the least pronounced legitimation crisis. Moreover, recession hit all four countries in 2009, but the various (inter-)national emergency measures and stimulation packages induced a marked recovery in 2010, with a four-country average growth rate of 2.9 per cent as opposed to –3.7 per cent in 2009. The year 2010 is precisely the one in which legitimation discourse temporarily shifted to the a-legitimacy (the United States), weak delegitimation (Germany, Switzerland) or intensive legitimation (the United Kingdom) scenarios, and hence to lower intensity, a less critical tone or both – confirming *ex negativo* the role of mediated economic problem pressure. Still, considering the post-crisis (2008–2011) period as a whole, the legitimation crisis was somewhat *less* pronounced than expected on the basis of the problem pressure ranking in the United Kingdom and the United States, but *more* so in Germany. Given that the financial crisis originated in the United States, while Germany weathered the storm relatively unscathed, this finding suggests that economic problem pressure does not fully translate into higher legitimation intensity and lower legitimacy levels; other political and discursive factors mitigating or exacerbating the scope of the post-2008 legitimation crisis are arguably at play.

A 'power resources' interpretation of our findings appears plausible (Esping-Andersen 1990). To the extent that the 'democratic class struggle' between labour and capital plays an important role in a national political system, it should also be reflected in legitimation discourse. Hence, the impact of the financial crisis and its economic consequences on the intensity and critical tone of legitimation discourse was presumably stronger where the labour movement is powerful and *vice versa*. In the liberal market economy of the United States (where a social democratic party has, famously, never existed and the influence of the trade union movement is waning), the discursive impact of the financial crisis was indeed mitigated. In the coordinated or 'social' market economy of Germany (where trade unions remain comparatively powerful and the Social Democrats have a 'hard' left-wing competitor), it was exacerbated. In the United Kingdom, Labour stayed in power until 2010, but it had moved to the right in economic and social policy terms, curtailed trade union influence and morphed into New Labour since Tony Blair's first election victory in 1997. During the run-up to his 2010 campaign, Blair's successor Gordon Brown closed ranks with the country's business elite and financial industry and joined them in their 'ride to the defence of capitalism' (*The Guardian*, 'Capitalism's Knight in Shining Armour', 1 October 2009), 'warn[ing] against abandoning the "gospel of free trade"' (*The Times*, 'Let's Shake Off the Shackles of Free Trade', 31 March 2009), and hence in efforts to relegitimate the beleaguered capitalist market regime.

The findings correspond less to a 'varieties of capitalism' (Hall and Soskice 2001), a 'discursive institutionalist' (Schmidt 2008, 2010) or a 'media culture' (Hallin and Mancini 2004) explanation for the varying scope of the post-2008 legitimation crisis. In line with the 'varieties of capitalism' approach, one might have expected the most pronounced differences in the discursive treatment of the legitimacy issue between liberal market economies (the United Kingdom, the United States), on the one hand, and coordinated market economies (Germany, Switzerland), on the other. The 'discursive institutionalist' perspective suggests that countries such as Germany (and presumably Switzerland) have a 'coordinative' public discourse as opposed to 'communicative' discourse in countries such as the United Kingdom (and the United States). Here, the focus is not on the mix of market and hierarchical arrangements in the liberal and coordinated versions of the capitalist market economy, and their link with ideas about the regime and its normative foundations, but on differences between *political* regimes in terms of the access ('voice'), public communication incentives and discursive opportunity structures of different types of economic, state and civil society actors (see also Tilly 1978: 98–142; Tarrow 2011: 157–82). The 'media cultures' perspective suggests varying journalistic incentives for more or less intense and critical media coverage of the economic regime and its legitimacy in liberal media systems (the United Kingdom, the United States) and corporatist ones (Germany, Switzerland). In short, all of these perspectives may be used to formulate *prima facie* plausible hypotheses on the drivers of legitimation intensity and legitimacy levels. Yet, they do not do justice to the fact that Germany and Switzerland – which belong to the same category of the three dichotomous classifications – have reacted in a starkly different way to the financial crisis, the economic pressure it created and the legitimacy challenges it entailed.

The Nature of Legitimation Discourse

While legitimation discourse on the capitalist market economy indeed became more intense and critical in the wake of the financial crisis, one might still ask what drove the varying severity of the capitalist market economy's post-2008 legitimation crisis and how relevant this development was: After all, the window of opportunity for transformative change was not used. Here, we suggest that a closer look at the nature of legitimation discourse after 2008, as captured by the speakers, objects and criteria variables of our legitimation grammar, helps to understand this outcome.

Types of Speakers

As indicated in Chapter 1, the media participate in legitimation discourse by contributing their own legitimacy assessments and by giving more or less voice to other types of (mostly) elite speakers. Different types of speakers may thus be confronted with more or less favourable opportunity structures for making their legitimacy assessments public in the quality press. Access to media discourse may also vary across national public spheres and change over time. Finally, different speaker types may be expected to have a characteristic (positive or negative) *bias* in evaluating the legitimacy of the capitalist market economy, as indicated by their respective legitimacy levels (shares of positive legitimation statements). Here, we limit ourselves to considering the voice and legitimacy levels of five broad types of speakers: journalists themselves, economic, political and civil society actors as well as speakers from the academic world, experts and public intellectuals (Table 3.3; a finer-grained coding scheme drawing on the subtypes in the right column and the actual names of individual or collective speakers participating in legitimation discourse is used in Chapter 7).[4]

Some of these speaker and actor types are closer to the 'centre' of the economic and political regimes to which they belong than others. We suggest that the window of opportunity provided by a discursive legitimation crisis is more likely to be used for transformative change if the legitimacy issue is increasingly taken up by speakers closer to the 'centre' of the capitalist market economy and to political decision-making processes – the business

Table 3.3 Speaker types, coding scheme

Speaker type	Subtype
Economic actors	Corporations Business and employers' associations Others
Political actors	National government, administration National parliament, government parties National parliament, opposition parties Central banks European Union representatives United Nations representatives Others
Civil society actors	Anticapitalists* Procapitalists* Citizens/the people Trade unions Arts/culture NGOs Protesters Religious groups Others
Academic world	
Journalists	

* This category encompasses individual or collective actors that are not explicitly identified as part of one of the other speaker groups but explicitly labelled as anti- or pro-capitalist in the examined newspaper articles.

elites and political actors who would have to support or implement this change. By contrast, the opposite scenario – legitimation discourse dominated by more 'peripheral' and less powerful speakers associated, for instance, with civil society or the academic world – is less likely to foster institutional change. The same logic applies to the *tone* of discourse contributions made by each speaker type. A legitimation crisis is unlikely to have transformative effects if business and political elites do not shift towards a more critical view on the legitimacy of the capitalist market economy, whereas even a pronounced shift towards criticism might have few consequences if it is limited to 'peripheral' speakers. Figures 3.4 and 3.5 illustrate the percentage shares of the five speaker types and their respective legitimacy levels in each of the four national public spheres, before and after the financial crisis.

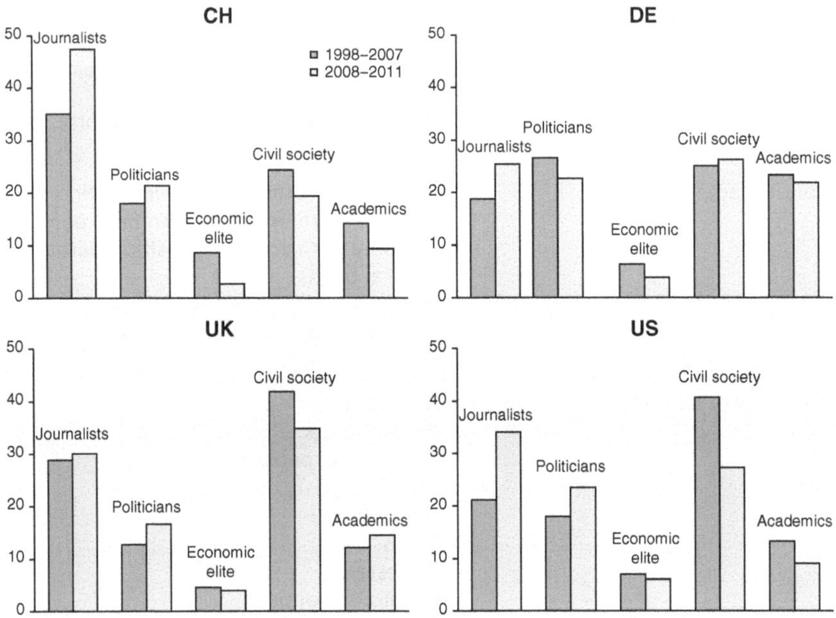

Fig. 3.4 Speaker types (%) pre-/post-financial crisis, by country

In line with the a-legitimacy claim discussed in Chapter 1, economic actors are in fact *unlikely* to acknowledge that the regime in which they operate needs to be explicitly justified; hence this speaker type should be *marginal* under normal circumstances. This is precisely what Fig. 3.4 confirms for all four countries examined: In each case, economic actors are the least prominent speaker type by far, with shares ranging from 5 per cent in the United Kingdom to 9 in Switzerland during the pre-crisis portion of our observation period (1998–2007). Yet, a legitimation crisis such as the one that occurred after 2008 challenges the taken-for-grantedness of the economic regime; it could therefore be expected to provide strong incentives for *more* – and especially more *legitimating* – discourse participation of this speaker type. However, business elites have not strongly rushed to the defence of the capitalist market economy through the media in the wake of the financial crisis. While the average yearly number of legitimation

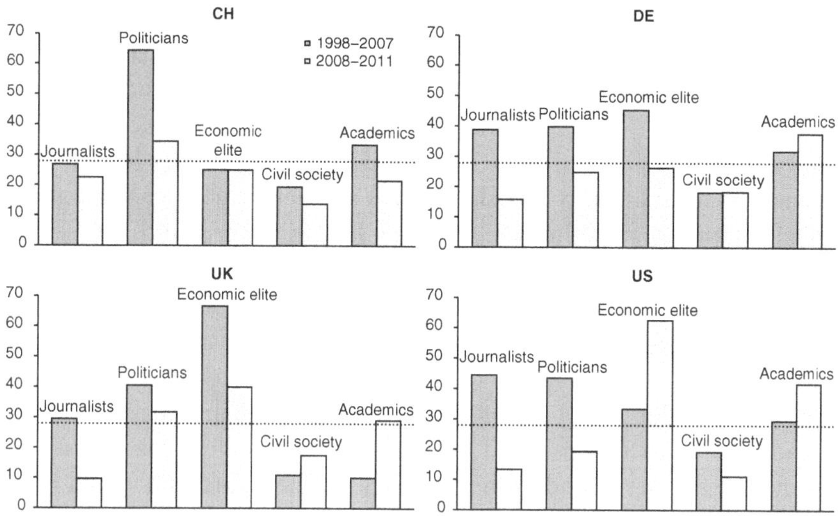

Fig. 3.5 Legitimacy levels (%) pre-/post-financial crisis, by speaker type and country

statements contributed by them indeed rises, economic actors in all four countries are crowded out by other speaker types and have an even more marginal role in legitimation discourse during the post-crisis years (2008–2011) than before, with shares from 3 per cent in Switzerland to 6 in the United States.

Before the financial crisis, economic actors are among the speakers with the highest legitimacy levels – above the 56 country-year average (27.9 per cent) indicated by the horizontal line in Fig. 3.5 – in three countries: Germany, the United Kingdom and the United States. Only in Switzerland, business elites are just as critical when they engage in legitimation discourse as journalists and civil society actors. The shares of positive legitimation statements in the other three countries range from surprisingly low 33 per cent in the United States to 67 per cent in the United Kingdom. After 2008, economic actors make conspicuous discursive concessions to the general delegitimation trend in the United Kingdom, where the legitimacy level shrinks massively, albeit to a still fairly high value (40 per cent), and in Germany, where it falls slightly below the 56 country-year average.

HSBC's world chief economist Stephen D. King's remark that 'markets are amoral [and that] there is no guarantee that the rewards will be fairly distributed' (*The Guardian*, 'After the Crunch: Boom, Bust and Then What?', 7 August 2010) is an example of such a concession. Only in the United States does the legitimacy level of the economic speaker type rise sharply (to 63 per cent) in an apparent relegitimation effort; the level remains low in Switzerland.

In addition to the self-legitimating or delegitimating voice of economic speakers, the role of political actors in legitimation discourse is crucial. They may be expected to be among the supporters of the capitalist market economy under normal circumstances but also have clear electoral incentives to take a position on economic developments such as the financial crisis and to shift blame for its negative impact to business elites. At the end of the day, they are the actors who would have to implement a transformation of the economic regime, or at least to support it with appropriate regulatory legislation. In the pre-crisis period, this speaker type – like economic actors – remains quite marginal in Swiss, UK and US legitimation discourse, with shares ranging from 13 (the United Kingdom) to 18 per cent (Switzerland and the United States), indicating relatively little preoccupation with the legitimacy of the economic regime; only in Germany, political actors are the most vocal speaker type. After 2008, the shares grow (or in the case of Germany, decrease) slightly – to values between 16 (the United Kingdom) and 23 per cent (the United States).

But what about the legitimacy levels of political actors? Are they truly among the key supporters of 'democratic capitalism' (Streeck 2011, 2014)? In the 1998–2007 period, this is indeed the case, with legitimacy levels clearly above the 56 country-year average in all four countries – ranging from 40 to 64 per cent in Germany and Switzerland, respectively. While political actors are legitimizers-in-chief – with legitimacy levels above business elites themselves – in Switzerland, they rank second in Germany, the United Kingdom and the United States. Has their support for the capitalist market economy remained unaffected by the financial crisis, though, have they come to the rescue of the capitalist market economy or have they engaged in blame shifting? Do they – like Gordon Brown – continue to 'champion the benefits of free trade and globalisation' (*The Guardian*, 'Wealth Gap', 2 February 2009) or – like Nicolas Sarkozy – turn to critical assessments of '"amoral" and uncontrolled capitalism' (*New York Times*, 'In the Lap of Luxury, Paris Squirms', 15 January 2009)? Figure 3.5 shows that political elites have indeed become considerably more sceptical. Their legitimacy levels drop to lows of 19 and 25 per cent in the United States and Germany, respectively; they also shrink massively in the United Kingdom and especially Switzerland (by whopping 30 percentage points) but remain above the long-term average in these two countries.

Yet, the more 'peripheral' speaker types – journalists, civil society actors and speakers from the academic world – continue to dominate legitimation discourse. Before 2008, a plurality of statements in Swiss discourse is contributed by journalists, followed by civil society actors. In the United Kingdom – where the latter have a share above 40 per cent – and the other two countries, the ranking of these speaker types is reversed. Only in German discourse, speakers from the academic world play a more important role than journalists. In the post-crisis period, little changes. The three speaker types dominate even more than before in Switzerland and Germany. In Switzerland, the share of journalists reaches almost 50 per cent while they move past civil society actors in the United States; in the other two countries, the latter remain (the United Kingdom) or become (Germany) the most important speaker type. Only in the United Kingdom, speakers from the academic world become more prominent.

As one might have expected, the three speaker types usually assess the economic regime more critically than economic and political actors. Before 2008, the legitimacy levels of civil society actors are already below the 56 country-year average in all four countries and range from a mere 11 to 19 per cent in Switzerland and the United States, respectively. With the exception of Switzerland, journalists are more capitalism-friendly; legitimacy levels are above the average and range from 29 per cent in the United Kingdom to 44 per cent in the United States. Apart from British discourse, speakers from the academic world also have comparatively high legitimacy levels ranging from 29 per cent in the United States to 33 per cent in Switzerland. In the post-crisis period, the legitimacy levels of journalists shrink below the 56 country-year average in all four countries, with values dwindling to a mere 10 per cent in the United Kingdom and a maximum of 23 per cent in Switzerland. In Switzerland and the United States, the values of civil society actors also sink further to 14 and 11 per cent, respectively, while they stagnate in Germany; only civil society actors in the United Kingdom buck the trend, although their legitimacy level remains well below the average line. Finally, the legitimacy levels of speakers from the academic world fall below the average in Switzerland while they rise to values between 29 (the United Kingdom) and 42 per cent (the United States) in the other three countries; in German discourse, these speakers become the most pronounced relegitimizers of the economic regime and the second most pronounced in US discourse (with an even higher legitimacy level). They state, for instance, that 'the fundamentals of our economy are strong' (Casey B. Mulligan, professor of economics at the University of Chicago, *New York Times*, 'An Economy You Can Bank On', 10 October 2008).

Legitimation Objects

All the legitimation statements in our text corpus evaluate the capitalist market economy at the regime level (see Chapter 1), but they do not necessarily evaluate the regime as a whole. Here, we draw inspiration from similar typologies in survey research (Norris 1999; Westle 2007) and our own work on the discursive legitimation of political systems (Hurrelmann et al. 2009; Schneider 2010b: 50), distinguishing four categories or levels of *legitimation objects* – each with a number of subcategories (Table 3.4). A statement may thus assess the capitalist market economy as a whole, employing unspecific terms – 'the economic system is a mess' (*Washington Post*, 'Not Capitalist, Not Socialist', 30 March 2009) – or labels such as 'capitalism' and 'the market economy' (level I); it may also focus on key principles of the regime such as free trade (level II), on varieties such as liberal or coordinated market economy (level III), and on major actor groups such as entrepreneurs or bankers (level IV). Each of these object (sub-)categories may be an 'anchor' of legitimation (and be evaluated more positively than the

Table 3.4 Legitimation objects, coding scheme

Object category	Subcategory
Economic regime (I)	Capitalism Market economy Unspecific (generic) reference to regime
Regime principles (II)	Free trade Private property Profit orientation Freedom of contract Competition
Regime variants (III)	Financial capitalism Coordinated market economy Liberal market economy
Economic actor groups (IV)	(for instance, bankers, managers)

regime as a whole) or a target of criticism (and be evaluated more negatively). Like prominent speaker types, the objects of legitimation discourse may vary across national public spheres and change over time.

Where legitimation discourse and critique increasingly focus on the upper levels of the object hierarchy – the regime as a whole (I) and its key principles (II) – the legitimation crisis is more severe in the sense that the legitimacy challenge is generalized enough to motivate calls and underpin support for transformative institutional change. More specific critique of regime varieties (III) or actor groups (IV), like John McCain's attack on 'financiers' "greed and corruption"' (*New York Times*, 'In Washington, Financial Furor Is a First-Rate Chance to Assess Blame', 18 September 2008), may be viewed as less transformative. This focused criticism implies no more than support for piecemeal regulatory reforms that do not jeopardize the core of the regime (for a similar line of reasoning, see Chapters 4 and 5). Figures 3.6 and 3.7 illustrate the percentage shares of the four object categories and their respective legitimacy levels in each of the four national public spheres, before and after the financial crisis.

Figure 3.6 indicates that even before the financial crisis, legitimation discourse was highly generalized – the bulk of legitimation statements referred to the capitalist market economy as a whole with shares ranging from 57 per cent in Switzerland to 70 in the United Kingdom and the

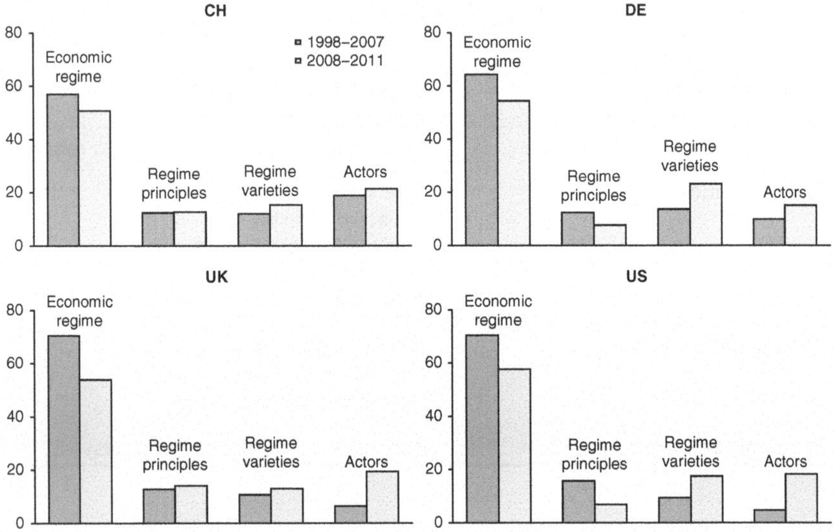

Fig. 3.6 Legitimation object categories (%) pre-/post-financial crisis, by country

United States. In the post-crisis period, generalized evaluations continue to dominate, but somewhat less than before, with shares between 51 per cent in Switzerland and 58 in the United States.

However, the legitimacy levels of this object category – and their shifts after 2008 – also matter. Before the financial crisis, the assessment that '[c]apitalism has given you everything you ever needed' (*The Guardian*, 'G2: The Ikea Anarchists', 16 December 2011) and other positive evaluations of the regime as a whole were quite widespread in the United States and Switzerland, resulting in legitimacy levels above the long-term average. By contrast, the regime as a whole already had the lowest legitimacy level of all four object categories in the United Kingdom. After 2008, the legitimacy levels of the regime fell (or in the British case, remained) below the average line across the board, with the strongest decline in US discourse.

Remarkably, there is a clear link between the labelling of the regime and the tone of evaluations. While the majority of statements using the label 'market economy' are positive both before and after the financial

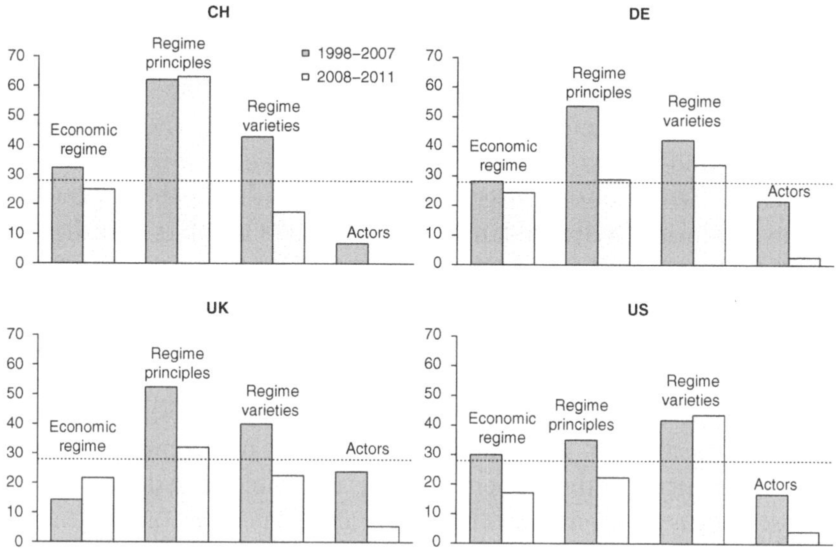

Fig. 3.7 Legitimacy levels (%) pre-/post-financial crisis, by legitimation object category and country

crisis, the label 'capitalism' is both more frequent overall and employed more often in negative statements. The legitimacy levels of these statements are below 20 per cent in the two portions of our observation period. Thus, the connotations of 'market economy' – which serves as a legitimation anchor – and 'capitalism' – a major target of delegitimation – differ greatly.

Legitimacy evaluations of specific and defining regime principles (level II) are far less frequent in all four countries than general assessments of the regime as a whole. With shares ranging from 12 to 14 per cent (in Germany and the United States), this object category ranks second in the pre-crisis period with the exception of German discourse, where it ranks third. In the post-crisis period, it becomes even more marginal, now ranking fourth or at most third (the United Kingdom); percentage shares slightly increase in Switzerland and the United Kingdom and decline in the other two countries, ranging from 7 (the United States) to 14 per cent (the United Kingdom).

Interestingly, specific regime principles are strong legitimation anchors of the capitalist market economy in the 1998–2007 period, with legitimacy levels above the 56 country-year average in all four countries – 35 per cent in the United States, more than 50 per cent in Germany and the United Kingdom, and 62 per cent in Switzerland. However, even before the financial crisis, this object category is rarely evaluated in public discourse, and its legitimacy levels shrink massively after 2008 to values only slightly above the long-term average (Germany and the United Kingdom) or even below it (the United States); only in Swiss discourse, regime principles continue to be legitimation anchors (63 per cent).

In all four countries, legitimation discourse shifts towards evaluations of specific varieties of capitalism (III) and actor groups (IV) in the wake of the financial crisis, even though the majority of statements remain level I assessments of the economic regime as a whole. The shares of level III assessments rise from values between 9 and 14 per cent (in the United States and Germany) to values between 13 and 23 per cent (in the United Kingdom and Germany). What is more, level IV assessments – which up to 2007 only rank fourth in all countries, with particularly low, single-digit values in the United Kingdom and the United States – jump to the second place in Switzerland, the United Kingdom and the United States, with values ranging from 18 to 21 per cent (and to the third place in Germany).

The legitimacy levels of the varieties of capitalism object category remain stable in US discourse but fall considerably below the 56 country-year average in Swiss and UK discourse; they shrink but remain above the average in Germany. This object category comprises a prominent post-2008 target of criticism, 'financial capitalism', whose share of statements rises to more than 9 while its legitimacy level declines below 10 per cent. The legitimacy levels of actor groups – which were already the lowest among the four object categories up to 2007 – collapse, ranging from 0 (Switzerland) to 5 per cent (the United Kingdom). Hence, much delegitimation of the economic regime after 2008 is deflected to its representatives, although this type of criticism may often be interpreted as a lukewarm, opportunistic concession to the post-crisis *zeitgeist* (Dörre et al. 2009: 15): 'The bank heads, board directors and non-executive directors who brought our financial system to the brink should stand ashamed of their failures' (*The Times*, 'Has Capitalism Failed?', 14 October 2008).

Legitimation Criteria

Finally, the positive or negative legitimacy assessments in our text corpus are usually justified on the basis of some explicit normative benchmark, a *legitimation criterion* (in addition to unspecific positive or negative evaluations such as Ayn Rand's claim that 'capitalism is splendid'; *Washington Post*, 'Global Warming? Hot Air', 23 December 2004). Frequently, public discourse links regimes and institutions with a 'logic of appropriateness' and hence with a privileged repertoire of normative ideas and legitimation criteria. Chapter 2 presented such a 'classical' repertoire for justifying or criticizing the capitalist market economy and three additional sets of justice-, democracy- and culture-centred criteria; it is this typology and its subcategories we draw on here (Table 3.5). Some of these criteria may be resources of legitimation (and be used more often in positive regime evaluations) while others are privileged by delegitimizers. As for the speaker and object variables, we may observe national peculiarities and change over time in the use of such normative ideas and standards.

We suggest that the capitalist market economy and its national varieties – such as the German social market economy, or liberal and coordinated market economy – are underpinned by specific mixes of normative ideas. In a similar vein as for speakers and legitimation objects, massive shifts in the dominant repertoires of legitimation criteria in the wake of the 2008 financial crisis – together with strong declines in the legitimacy levels of the privileged criteria – may be viewed as implying calls and mobilizing support for transformative institutional change: Where established ideas are replaced with new ones and legitimacy assessments in light of established normative standards are increasingly negative, there is presumably demand for institutional alternatives and a new 'logic of appropriateness'. Figure 3.8 illustrates the percentage shares of the four criteria groups (and unspecific statements). Figure 3.9 shows their respective legitimacy levels in each of the four national public spheres, before and after the financial crisis.

Table 3.5 Legitimation criteria, coding scheme

Groups of criteria	Individual criteria
Classical	Efficiency Public good orientation Innovation Economic stability Personal freedom Profit Self-regulation Wealth
Justice-centred	Distributive justice
Democracy-centred	Democratic stability Protection of human rights Popular sovereignty Reversibility Power/capacity to act
Culture-centred	Morality Leadership Personal virtues and vices Credibility
Unspecific	(no explicit legitimation criterion)

The repertoire of classical legitimation criteria such as efficiency discussed in Chapter 2 may be considered the gold standard for legitimacy assessments of the capitalist market economy – after all, these are the criteria traditionally used by economic theorists in justifying the regime. In the pre-crisis period, a plurality of legitimation statements indeed draws on this group of criteria. However, other groups of criteria together dominate while the classical ones are linked with only about a quarter of the statements in all four countries. Interestingly, the financial crisis has refocused discourse on these classical functional standards – their shares rise in all four countries and reach values between 33 and 41 per cent (in the United Kingdom and Switzerland) in the wake of the crisis.

Classical legitimation criteria serve as resources of legitimation in the 1998–2007 period, reaching legitimacy levels between 34 per cent in the United Kingdom and 48 per cent in Switzerland – values clearly above the 56 country-year average indicated by the horizontal line. In the wake of the financial crisis, the legitimacy levels of this group of criteria

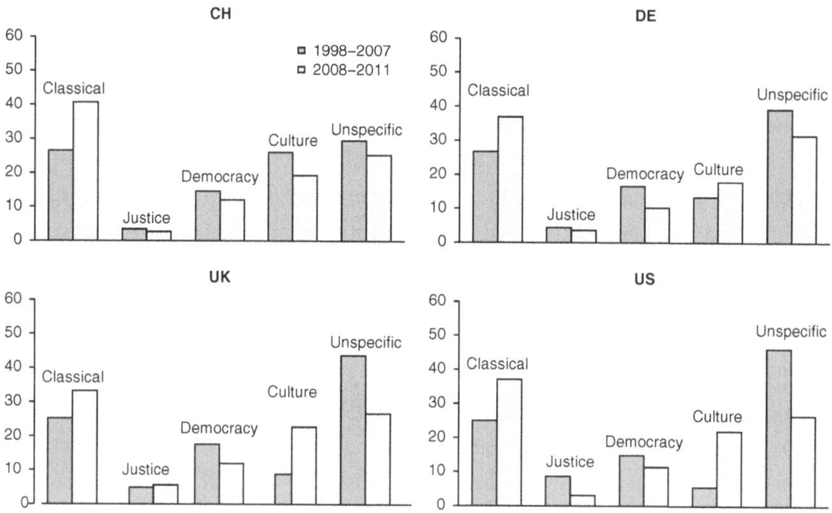

Fig. 3.8 Legitimation criteria groups (%) pre-/post-financial crisis, by country

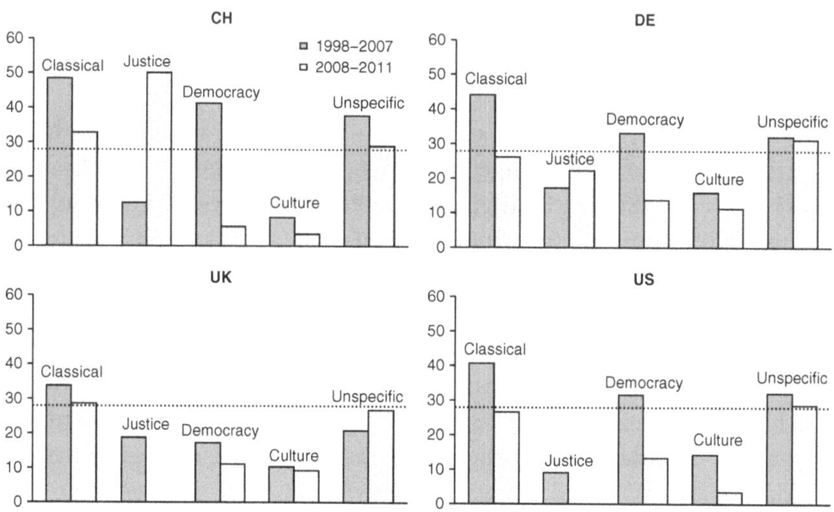

Fig. 3.9 Legitimacy levels (%) pre-/post-financial crisis, by legitimation criteria group and country

remain the highest but dwindle below the average in two countries, with values of 26 and 27 per cent (in Germany and the United States). Only in Switzerland, the legitimacy level of classical legitimation criteria still reaches 33 per cent (which is, however, lower than the 50 per cent for justice-centred criteria). Overall, classical criteria have become more important since 2008, while their thrust has become more critical. The normative foundations of the capitalist market economy have not eroded, but the regime is increasingly evaluated negatively 'on its home turf', resulting in statements such as '[t]he market is massively inefficient' (*The Guardian*, 'We've Heard the Banker's Stories', 17 September 2008) or '[c]apitalism is not self-regulating, but self-fouling' (*The Times*, 'Hooray for Red Tape', 12 December 1998).

Democracy-centred legitimation criteria are, in a sense, the farthest away from classical ones: They are 'classical' (privileged) criteria for evaluating the democratic state, not market arrangements (Schneider et al. 2010). Interestingly, however, this group of criteria is quite prominent in legitimation discourse and even second most frequent (except in Switzerland, where it ranks third) in the pre-crisis period, with shares ranging from 15 per cent (Switzerland and the United States) to 18 per cent (the United Kingdom). In the post-crisis period, democracy-centred criteria rank third, their shares falling to values between 10 per cent (Germany) and 12 per cent (Switzerland and the United Kingdom).

What is more, this group of criteria comes with remarkably high legitimacy levels which range from 32 per cent (the United States) to 41 per cent (Switzerland) in the 1998–2007 period. Only in the United Kingdom, these criteria are almost always used to attack and delegitimate the economic regime (17 per cent), as in the proposition that 'democracy is being eroded by the markets' (*The Guardian*, 'For Spain's Indignados, Last Sunday's Election Delivered a Mandate for Struggle and Resistance', 22 November 2011). In the 2008–2011 period, however, democracy-centred normative standards lose their role as resources of legitimation; legitimacy levels shrink to values between 6 and 14 per cent (in Switzerland and Germany).

The criterion of justice plays a certain role in legitimation discourse, with shares ranging from 3 to 9 per cent (in Switzerland and the United

States) up to 2007, but the weight of statements like 'poverty and injustice [are] inflicted by global capitalism' (*New York Times*, 'Czech Police and Army Get Ready for Protests at I.M.F.-World Bank Meeting', 12 August 2000) does not increase in the wake of the financial crisis. Justice-based assessments are now most important, with a 6 per cent share, in British discourse. Finally, the prominence of culture-centred criteria varies considerably across national public spheres before the financial crisis, with shares ranging from 6 (the United States) to 26 per cent (Switzerland). In the post-crisis period, this group of criteria ranks second in importance, with shares hovering around 20 per cent in all four countries.

Both groups of criteria already have low legitimacy levels even before the financial crisis. The values of justice-centred criteria range from 9 to 19 per cent (in the United States and the United Kingdom); culture-centred criteria have shares between 8 and 16 per cent (in Switzerland and Germany). However, while the post-crisis legitimacy levels of the (rarely used) justice criterion rise in two cases (slightly in Germany and to 50 per cent in Switzerland), they reach zero in the United Kingdom and the United States. The legitimacy levels of culture-centred criteria also shrink everywhere to abysmal values between 3 (Switzerland and the United States) and 11 per cent (Germany). The group of criteria becomes a key resource for delegitimizers of the capitalist market economy or its actors. The 'reckless management and casino culture on Wall Street' (*New York Times*, 'In Washington, Financial Furor Is a First-Rate Chance to Assess Blame', 18 September 2008) is, for instance, identified as a key problem and linked with the broader observation that

> [w]ith God as capital, every aspect of life gets translated into the language of economic transactions: passengers become customers, patients become clients. Where once we were souls, we are now consumers. And the problem with this is that when everything has a price, nothing has any value; especially vague notions such as human rights and dignity. In the market state, greed is good and the maximisation of profit is the only viable ethic. (*The Guardian*, 'Dogmatic Assumptions Underlie Non-religious World-views too, says Nicholas Buxton', 14 April 2007)

Conclusion

In this chapter, we used a content analysis based on our legitimation grammar to probe the scope and contours of the discursive legitimation crisis of the capitalist market economy in the wake of the Great Recession. Our indicators of intensity and tone show that the financial crisis indeed registered in media discourse. In all four countries and most years of the post-crisis period, the contours of discourse thus corresponded to the legitimation crisis scenario. We considered varying economic problem pressure and power resources to explain the few anomalies – such as the greater-than-expected scope of the discursive crisis in Germany or the temporary recovery in 2010. Overall, however, the crisis had the potential to result in a major institutional transformation of the economic regime.

In the remainder of the chapter, we considered the distribution of speaker types, legitimation object categories and groups of legitimation criteria across national public spheres and over time. Media discourse on the capitalist market economy is typically delegitimating – the 50 per cent mark is only crossed by political and economic actors in pre-crisis Swiss and UK discourse. More importantly, these speaker types keep a rather low profile in discourse even in the wake of the financial crisis. Only in the United States do business elites attempt to relegitimate the economic regime but are crowded out by other, more 'peripheral' speakers. The discursive legitimation crisis thus hardly reached the 'centre' of the regime or the political sphere; therefore, it arguably mobilized little support for transformative institutional change (see also Chapter 7).

Secondly, legitimation discourse is predominantly unspecific in the sense that the capitalist market economy as a whole rather than specific regime principles, varieties or actor groups are usually evaluated. While the legitimacy levels of all object categories – with the exception of regime principles in Switzerland and varieties in the United States – shrink in the wake of the crisis, evaluations of the regime as a whole and its principles also become somewhat less frequent. On the other end of the object hierarchy, actors such as managers and bankers shift into the focus of media discourse and become the target of particularly severe criticism. Once again, we take this finding as evidence for the limited demand or support for transformative institutional change of the capitalist market economy: If the financial crisis was caused by inappropriate behaviour of some actors rather than structural features of the regime, piecemeal regulatory reform appears sufficient.

Finally, we considered the use of four groups of normative standards – legitimation criteria – in media discourse. Overall, national differences are quite negligible in this dimension. Besides classical criteria for the evaluation of the capitalist market economy, democracy- and culture-centred criteria also play an important role while justice-based arguments are marginal. We find that the role of classical criteria grows in the wake of the financial crisis, while their legitimacy levels shrink less dramatically than the corresponding values of democracy- and culture-centred criteria. This finding suggests that the 'logic of appropriateness' tied to the capitalist market economy has survived the financial crisis relatively unscathed – whereas a Great Transformation of the regime would presumably have been accompanied and supported by a massive shift in underlying normative ideas.

Notes

1. Our cut-off point between the pre- and post-crisis time windows is 1 January 2008, as indicated in Chapter 1.
2. A z-score represents the distance between the observed value of an indicator and the population mean in standard deviation units. The score is thus negative when the observed value is below the mean and positive when above. To calculate a z-score, the population mean is subtracted from the observed value of an indicator, and this difference is divided by the standard deviation. The population mean has a z score of 0, and the standard deviation of the z scores is 1.
3. For the measurement of economic growth, unemployment and state debt, we draw on OECD data. For debt, the OECD time series for Germany, the United Kingdom and the United States were supplemented with 2011 World Bank data, and for Switzerland with information provided by the Federal Financial Administration.

4. The labour movement – trade unions and their representatives – is not subsumed under the economic but rather under the civil society speaker type: Only the representatives of capital may be plausibly expected to have a *prima facie* legitimating bias.

References

Barker, Rodney. 2007. 'Democratic Legitimation. What Is It, Who Wants It, and Why?' In *Legitimacy in an Age of Global Politics*, eds. Achim Hurrelmann, Steffen Schneider and Jens Steffek. Basingstoke: Palgrave Macmillan, 19–34.

Dörre, Klaus, Stephan Lessenich and Hartmut Rosa, eds. 2009. *Soziologie – Kapitalismus – Kritik. Eine Debatte*. Frankfurt am Main: Suhrkamp.

Esping-Andersen, Gøsta. 1990. *The Three Worlds of Welfare Capitalism*. Princeton: Princeton University Press.

Gilley, Bruce. 2006. 'The Meaning and Measure of State Legitimacy: Results for 72 Countries'. *European Journal of Political Research* 45(3): 499–525.

Hall, Peter A. and David Soskice, eds. 2001. *Varieties of Capitalism. The Institutional Foundations of Comparative Advantage*. Oxford: Oxford University Press.

Hallin, Daniel and Paolo Mancini. 2004. *Comparing Media Systems. Three Models of Media and Politics*. Cambridge: Cambridge University Press.

Hepp, Andreas and Hartmut Wessler. 2009. 'Politische Diskurskulturen: Überlegungen zur empirischen Erklärung segmentierter europäischer Öffentlichkeit'. *Medien & Kommunikationswissenschaft* 57(2): 174–97.

Hurrelmann, Achim, Zuzana Krell-Laluhová, Frank Nullmeier, Steffen Schneider and Achim Wiesner. 2009. 'Why the Democratic Nation-state is Still Legitimate: A Study of Media Discourses'. *European Journal of Political Research* 48(4): 483–515.

Norris, Pippa. 1999. 'Institutional Explanations for Political Support'. In *Critical Citizens. Global Support for Democratic Government*, ed. Pippa Norris. Oxford: Oxford University Press, 217–35.

Norris, Pippa. 2000. *A Virtuous Circle. Political Communication in Postindustrial Societies*. Cambridge: Cambridge University Press.

Norris, Pippa. 2011. *Democratic Deficit. Critical Citizens Revisited*. Cambridge: Cambridge University Press.

Schmidt, Vivien A. 2008. 'Discursive Institutionalism: The Explanatory Power of Ideas and Discourse'. *Annual Review of Political Science* 11: 303–26.
Schmidt, Vivien A. 2010. 'Taking Ideas and Discourse Seriously: Explaining Change through Discursive Institutionalism as the Fourth "New Institutionalism"'. *European Political Science Review* 2(1): 1–25.
Schneider, Steffen. forthcoming. *Precarious Legitimacy. Justifying Political Authority in the Post-National Constellation*. Book Manuscript.
Schneider, Steffen. 2010a. 'Der demokratische Nationalstaat – hohe Unterstützung'. In *Prekäre Legitimitäten. Rechtfertigung von Herrschaft in der postnationalen Konstellation*, eds. Frank Nullmeier, Dominika Biegoń, Jennifer Gronau, Martin Nonhoff, Henning Schmidtke and Steffen Schneider. Frankfurt am Main: Campus, 68–106.
Schneider, Steffen. 2010b. 'Empirische Legitimationsforschung'. In *Prekäre Legitimitäten. Rechtfertigung von Herrschaft in der postnationalen Konstellation*, eds. Frank Nullmeier, Dominika Biegoń, Jennifer Gronau, Martin Nonhoff, Henning Schmidtke and Steffen Schneider. Frankfurt am Main: Campus, 45–67.
Schneider, Steffen, Achim Hurrelmann, Frank Nullmeier, Achim Wiesner and Zuzana Krell-Laluhová. 2010. *Democracy's Deep Roots. Why the Nation State Remains Legitimate*. Basingstoke: Palgrave Macmillan.
Singer, Matthew M. 2011. 'Who Says "It's the Economy"? Cross-national and Cross-individual Variation in the Salience of Economic Performance'. *Comparative Political Studies* 44(3): 284–312.
Soroka, Stuart N. 2006. 'Good News and Bad News: Asymmetric Responses to Economic Information'. *Journal of Politics* 68(2): 372–85.
Streeck, Wolfgang. 2011. 'The Crises of Democratic Capitalism'. *New Left Review* 71: 5–29.
Streeck, Wolfgang. 2014. *Buying Time. The Delayed Crisis of Democratic Capitalism*. London: Verso.
Suchman, Mark C. 1995. 'Managing Legitimacy: Strategic and Institutional Approaches'. *Academy of Management Review* 20(3): 571–610.
Swanson, Jacinda. 2008. 'Economic Common Sense and the Depoliticization of the Economic'. *Political Research Quarterly* 61(1): 56–67.
Tarrow, Sidney. 2011. *Power in Movement. Social Movements and Contentious Politics*. Revised and Updated Edition. Cambridge: Cambridge University Press.
Tilly, Charles. 1978. *From Mobilization to Revolution*. Reading, MA: Addison-Wesley.

Westle, Bettina. 2007. 'Political Beliefs and Attitudes. Legitimacy in Public Opinion Research'. In *Legitimacy in an Age of Global Politics*, eds. Achim Hurrelmann, Steffen Schneider and Jens Steffek. Basingstoke: Palgrave Macmillan, 93–125.

Zaller, John. 1992. *The Nature and Origins of Mass Opinion*. Cambridge: Cambridge University Press.

Cited Newspaper Articles

The Guardian 14 April 2007. 'Dogmatic Assumptions Underlie Non-religious World-views too, says Nicholas Buxton'.

The Guardian 17 September 2008. 'We've Heard the Banker's Stories'.

The Guardian 2 February 2009. 'Wealth Gap'.

The Guardian 1 October 2009. 'Capitalism's Knight in Shining Armour'.

The Guardian 7 August 2010. 'After the Crunch: Boom, Bust and Then What?'.

The Guardian 22 November 2011. 'For Spain's Indignados, Last Sunday's Election Delivered a Mandate for Struggle and Resistance'.

The Guardian 16 December 2011. 'G2: The Ikea Anarchists'.

The Times 12 December 1998. 'Hooray for Red Tape'.

The Times 14 October 2008. 'Has Capitalism Failed?'

The Times 31 March 2009. 'Let's Shake off the Shackles of Free Trade'.

New York Times 12 August 2000. 'Czech Police and Army Get Ready for Protests at I.M.F.-World Bank Meeting'.

New York Times 18 September 2008. 'In Washington, Financial Furor Is a First-Rate Chance to Assess Blame'.

New York Times 10 October 2008. 'An Economy You Can Bank On'.

New York Times 15 January 2009. 'In the Lap of Luxury, Paris Squirms'.

Washington Post 23 December 2004. 'Global Warming? Hot Air'.

Washington Post 30 March 2009. 'Not Capitalist, Not Socialist'.

4

Making Sense of the Great Recession: Responsibility Attributions in Tough Times

Falk Lenke and Henning Schmidtke

The Great Recession in the wake of the 2008 financial crisis was a *critical juncture* for the capitalist market economy (Kahler and Lake 2013; Bermeo and Bartels 2014). As shown in Chapter 3, discourse on the legitimacy of the economic regime became considerably more intense and critical in Germany, Switzerland, the United Kingdom and the United States. The historical-institutionalist literature on the emergence, stability and transformation of economic institutions describes such critical junctures as 'moments in which uncertainty as to the future of an institutional arrangement allows for political agency and choice to play a decisive causal role in setting an institution on a certain path of

F. Lenke (✉)
University of Bremen, Bremen, Germany
e-mail: falk.lenke@gmail.com

H. Schmidtke
Bavarian School of Public Policy, TUM School of Governance, Technical University of Munich, Munich, Germany
e-mail: henning.schmidtke@hfp.tum.de

S. Schneider et al. (eds.), *Capitalism and Its Legitimacy in Times of Crisis*, Transformations of the State,
DOI 10.1007/978-3-319-53765-8_4

development' (Capoccia 2015: 148). Yet, wholesale institutional change of the economic regime similar in scope to the Great Transformations of the 1920s and 1970s (Polanyi 2001; Blyth 2002) failed to materialize. Instead, the capitalist market economy proved remarkably stable (Bermeo and Pontusson 2012; Mayntz 2012; Drezner 2014).

In this chapter, we show that *responsibility* for the 2008 financial crisis and its solution was discursively attributed in a way that made transformative institutional change unlikely. Theoretically, we build this argument on Mark Blyth's claim that ideas about who is responsible for a performance crisis and who should be responsible for solving it are crucial in an overall 'sequence' of institutional change (Blyth 2002: 35–7). Part of the legitimation crisis that marks a critical juncture is a debate on the nature, causes and culprits of the economic upheaval that triggered it. Moreover, any institutional response to an economic downturn requires an understanding of the actors and institutions that might be able to solve it. Analysing ideas about the causes of the 2008 financial crisis and about solutions is an important step in explaining why the Great Recession did not result in the transformation or replacement of the capitalist market economy (Rudolph 2003; Hellwig and Coffey 2011; Anderson and Hecht 2012). Our reconstruction of the discursive context of the post-2008 critical juncture thus helps to establish what choices were *historically* available, not simply *hypothetically* possible (Capoccia 2015: 159; see also Gourevitch 1986: 67; Capoccia and Kelemen 2007: 355).

We show that the legitimation crisis that resulted from the economic downturn was a lost moment for would-be reformers and challengers of the capitalist market economy for two reasons: Firstly, responsibility for the crisis was not predominantly attributed to the economic *regime* as the main culprit. Secondly, although the debate on who should be responsible for solving the crisis was highly critical of the regime itself and its main actors and institutions, the discourse coalition demanding external political regulation was weak. In short, this chapter shows that discursive attributions of responsibility for the crisis and its solution were not conducive to substantive institutional change. Rather, this dimension of legitimation discourse on the capitalist market economy supported institutional stability or, at most, marginal institutional change.

The chapter is structured as follows: The next section explains why responsibility attributions are an important element of public legitimation discourse and introduces its two main dimensions of 'causal responsibility' and 'treatment responsibility' (Iyengar 1994: 50). Taking up this distinction, we explain what the two dimensions can tell us about the likelihood of institutional transformation. Secondly, we introduce the method and data used for the empirical analysis. Thirdly, we present the empirical results. Finally, we summarize these results and discuss the implications of our findings in the light of the volume's larger question: Why did the Great Recession and the ensuing legitimation crisis of the capitalist market economy not result in wholesale institutional reform?

Legitimation Discourse and Responsibility Attribution

The financial crisis of 2008 triggered severe problems in the world economy – leaving some issues still unresolved. For two main reasons, the attribution of responsibility for these developments is important for the legitimation of the capitalist market economy and its potential transformation: Firstly, in an economic crisis, actors are confronted with high uncertainty about its nature and causes. Ideas about who is responsible for the crisis and what institutions or actors might be capable of solving it help to reduce this uncertainty. Discourse about these questions provides actors with such ideas and is thus likely to inform their responses to the crisis (Blyth 2002: 37).

Secondly, attributions of responsibility also proffer an implicit *delegitimation* of the culprits identified (van Leeuwen 2007: 92). If discourse dwells primarily on the economic regime itself as the main cause of the crisis, actors are more likely to focus their institutional responses on a genuine transformation or even the replacement of the regime. By contrast, if responsibility is mainly attributed to specific elements of the regime, for instance, financial markets or a group of actors such as bankers, institutional responses that only address these specific issues are more likely. What is more, by assigning responsibility for solving a crisis, discourse participants implicitly *legitimate* the actors or institutions trusted to handle it. If discourse participants highlight, for instance, the economic regime's ability to heal its problems without state intervention, one may conclude that the regime is still seen as legitimate and is thus not likely to be replaced any time soon. Strong demand for political intervention in the form of regulation or, even more critically, for a wholesale replacement of the regime by some alternative set of institutions suggests that it has become more vulnerable to its critics and thus more open to fundamental change.

This dichotomy of *causal* and *treatment* responsibility is well established in the literature (see, for instance, Hart 1968; Rudolph 2003; Gerhards et al. 2009). Iyengar describes both types as follows: 'Causal responsibility focuses on the origin of a problem, while treatment responsibility focuses on who or what has the power to alleviate (or forestall alleviation of) the problem' (1994: 8). In our analysis, causal responsibility is concerned with the question of who triggered the financial crisis of 2008. Treatment responsibility attributions shift the focus to the tasks that are perceived to be necessary for overcoming the crisis. To explain why the 2008 financial crisis did not result in a Great Transformation of the capitalist market economy, we analyse a set of five variables in causal and treatment responsibility attributions, which are already familiar from the legitimation grammar introduced and used in Chapters 1 and 3 of this volume (Table 4.1).

The first variable is based on the *tone* of causal responsibility attributions. A high share of causal responsibility attributions containing negative evaluations, for instance, suggesting that the crisis was caused by 'the

Table 4.1 Responsibility attributions and the potential for institutional change

Variable	High potential for change
Causal responsibility	
Evaluative tone	Mainly negative
Addressees	Mainly the economic regime
Speakers	Wide range of actor groups
Treatment responsibility	
Addressees	Mainly political actors
Speakers	Wide range of actor groups

unforced blunders by investors and banks' (*The Times*, 'Now is the Time for a Revolution in Economic Thought', 9 February 2009) indicates that discourse participants recognize the performance crisis of the capitalist market economy as a major problem. A high share of positive or neutral attributions, by contrast, indicates that the workings of the economic regime are still cast in a positive light and that reform or responses to the crisis are not considered necessary.

The second and third variables parallel the legitimation objects discussed in Chapter 3 of this volume. We distinguish three main groups of *addressees* of causal and treatment responsibility attributions, which are understood as levels of a hierarchy. At the highest level are responsibility attributions that address the capitalist market regime as a whole or its varieties. Below, we rank key economic actor groups. Finally, we also consider a set of political actors – national politicians, international politicians and civil society actors – as potential addressees (Hellwig et al. 2008).

We expect large-scale institutional change to be more likely when causal responsibility attributions are predominantly focused on the upper levels of the hierarchy of addressees, as in the following statement: '[W]hat went wrong in 2007–09 was not just a lapse in bank regulation. It was a failure of the entire market fundamentalist model of capitalism' (*The Times*, 'We Need a New Capitalism to Take on China', 4 February 2010). Causal responsibility attributions to economic or political actor groups, by contrast, are less likely to foster institutional change, because they legitimate and stabilize the economic regime and do not imply demand for strong institutional change. Statements like the following shift blame from the economic regime itself towards individual actors or even the political sphere: 'With Republicans in control of both Congress and the White House for the first six years of Mr. Bush's tenure, a climate favoring deregulation prevailed, which spawned the current crisis' (*New York Times*, 'Abroad, This Bailout Is a Shocker', 18 September 2008). They direct actors to focus less on economic institutions and more on the politics behind them. Such statements stabilize the legitimacy of the capitalist market economy and tend to undermine the legitimacy of domestic governments, intergovernmental organizations (IGOs) or civil society.

In the dimension of treatment responsibility attributions, we reverse the hierarchy of responsibility addressees to identify discursive potential for institutional change. Major institutional change is less likely when the economic regime as a whole or major economic actor groups are frequently the addressees of treatment responsibility attributions. When the capitalist market economy is considered to have the ability to correct its own flaws and solve the crisis without outside intervention from political or other societal actors, its legitimacy is stable and demand for transformative institutional change is low. An example of such statements is the following attribution of treatment responsibility: 'The financial crisis has exposed capitalism's darkest imperfections. But it is still the best hope we have of creating wealth and opportunity for the many' (*The Times*, 'Has Capitalism Failed?', 14 October 2008). By contrast, a shift of treatment responsibility attributions away from the economic regime to governments makes institutional change more likely. The legitimacy of the economic regime suffers less when it is held responsible for an economic crisis but, at the same time, considered responsible for (and trusted with) solving the crisis. It suffers more when treatment responsibility is assigned to politicians and the self-regulating powers of the capitalist market economy are questioned, as in the following statement: '[G]overnments must be much more active in taking control of the economy' (*The Times*, 'We Need a New Capitalism to Take on China', 4 February 2010).

The fourth and fifth variables turn to the speakers participating in the discourse (see also Chapter 3 and 7). In times of uncertainty about institutional reform options, *discourse coalitions* are central to mobilizing support for institutional change. We expect institutional change to be more likely if causal and treatment responsibility is attributed by speakers who represent social, economic and political elites (for a more extensive discussion of the role of discourse coalitions, see Chapter 7 in this volume). Narrower discourse coalitions which include a limited set of actors or have low political clout are rarely in a position to impose a specific interpretation of the crisis on a given public. In such a context, a dominant understanding of the crisis is less likely to emerge and many potential courses of action – including non-response and marginal re-regulation – remain on the menu.

Responsibility Analysis: Methods and Data

Our analysis of responsibility attributions is based on a subset of the text corpus presented in Chapter 1. We only analysed articles in which the financial crisis of 2008 is explicitly discussed and which include at least one responsibility attribution. The analysis is limited to newspaper articles published between 15 September 2008 (the date of the Lehman Brothers collapse) and 31 December 2010. Articles from the pre-crisis period (1998–2007) and the post-crisis year of 2011 were not considered due to our focus on immediate reactions to the crisis.

The identification and coding of responsibility attributions follows a similar logic as in Chapter 3 for legitimation statements. We describe responsibility attributions with the help of a stylized grammar (Fig. 4.1). Its structure is tailored to identify the variables discussed above. We ask: '*Who* is made responsible for *what* and by *whom*?' (Gerhards et al. 2007: 110).[1]

Firstly, to distinguish causal and treatment responsibility attributions, we examine the object of a statement. We speak of causal responsibility when discourse participants attribute responsibility to an addressee for causing the *event* of the financial crisis. The following statement is an example: 'The bank heads, board directors and non-executive directors who brought our financial system to the brink should stand ashamed of their failures' (*The Times*, 'Has Capitalism Failed?', 14 October 2008). In a treatment responsibility attribution, an addressee is given the *task* to solve the crisis.[2] This is, for instance, the case in the following statement by the British Conservative and vice-chairman of Goldman Sachs

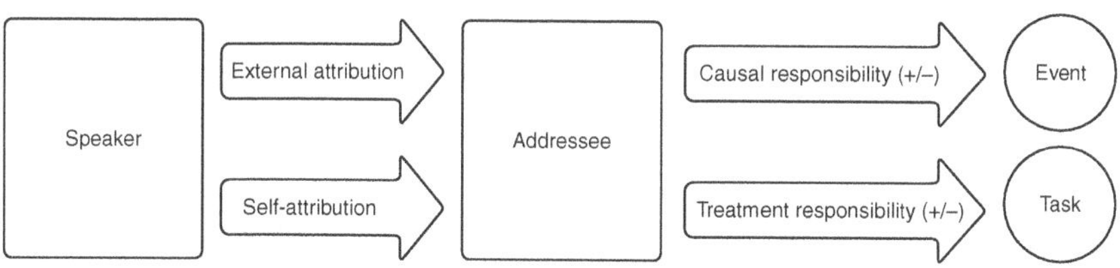

Fig. 4.1 Grammar of responsibility attributions

International, Brian Griffith, who claims that '[t]he main responsibility for change lies with the management and boards of banks. They must endeavour to create a culture of integrity, prudence and attention to detail within their institutions' (*The Times*, 'Markets Can't Be Improved by Rules', 9 April 2009).

Secondly, the tone of responsibility attributions is also dichotomous. It can be positive or negative. We do not consider the intensity of a responsibility attribution. We interpret a statement 'which blames "capitalist greed" for the economic crisis' (*Washington Post*, 'Obama's Economic Mirage', 13 April 2009) as a positive causal responsibility attribution. Statements suggesting, for instance, that 'the Americans are the only ones who can cope with the crisis' (*Frankfurter Allgemeine Zeitung*, 'Ein Gespräch mit dem Soziologen Ralf Dahrendorf', 10 October 2008),[3] that is, positive attributions of treatment responsibility, are interpreted as demanding or supporting an actor's participation in solving the crisis.

Thirdly, to identify responsibility addressees, we examine to whom discourse participants attribute responsibility. We distinguish three groups of addressees (Kim 2015). Firstly, by highlighting, for instance, that the crisis 'resulted from the nature of the system' (*Süddeutsche Zeitung*, 'Weltwirtschaftsgewitter; Karl Marx ist aktuell', 26 November 2008), causal responsibility attributions can address the economic regime as a whole and its different aspects.[4] Secondly, by attacking 'short-sellers as "bank robbers and asset strippers"' (*The Times*, 'Markets Can't Be Improved by Rules', 9 April 2009), economic actor groups are blamed for the crisis. Thirdly, by suggesting that 'the problem was too much government rather than too little' (*The Guardian*, 'After Guns and the Iraq War, Michael Moore is Now Taking on an Entire Political and Economic System in His Latest Documentary', 30 January 2010), causal responsibility is attributed to political actor groups.

Finally, we are interested in the authors of responsibility attributions. Other than (1) journalists, we distinguish three main speaker groups: (2) economic elites, (3) political elites and (4) various groups broadly related to civil society (for details on this variable, see Chapter 3).

Empirical Findings: How Responsibility Discourse Helped to Stabilize the Capitalist Market Economy

The following sections turn to the empirical results of the responsibility analysis. The analysis is based on 134 responsibility attributions in 52 articles from German, Swiss, UK and US newspapers. These numbers have to be seen in light of our constructed weeks sampling procedure (see Chapter 1). The actual number of articles and responsibility attributions is presumably 13 times as high and we may, therefore, conclude that the financial crisis has triggered public discourse about responsibility between 2008 and 2010. The causes of and solutions for the Great Recession were discussed, albeit with relatively low intensity, which we interpret as evidence for the stable legitimacy of the capitalist market economy. Despite the severe consequences of the financial crisis, public debate on what caused these events and who has responsibility for finding viable solutions was limited. Against the backdrop of the discursive legitimation crisis documented in Chapter 3, we would have expected a more intense debate about these questions.

Figure 4.2 indicates a rough balance of causal and treatment responsibility attributions in all four countries. However, it is rare to find both types of statements in a single article. The question of who is causally responsible for the crisis is not necessarily connected to the search for those who may solve it.

All four speaker groups contribute to the discourse. Almost half of the statements are made by civil society actors and journalists. Domestic political elites contribute about a third of all statements. They are the second most active group of speakers. Speakers from the economy, representing, for instance, multinational companies or banks, contribute only one-fifth of all responsibility attributions. This group is not particularly keen to attribute blame or treatment responsibility. Since these speakers are part of the economic regime in crisis, they might simply try to stay below the radar of public scrutiny and to avoid blame from other actors (Weaver 1986; Hansson 2015; Hinterleitner 2017). The

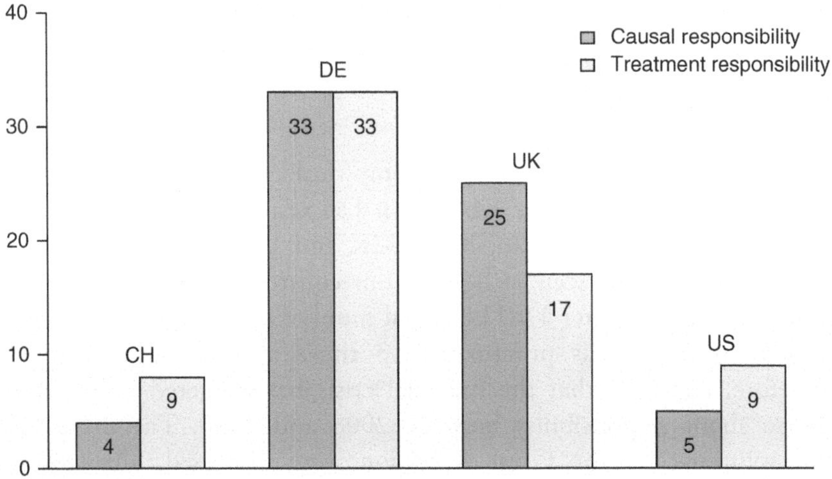

Fig. 4.2 Types of responsibility attribution, by country

following sections turn, first, to the causal responsibility attributions; secondly, we present the results for treatment responsibility attributions.

Whose Fault Is It? Causal Responsibility Attributions

With 68 statements in 41 articles, approximately half of the coded statements are causal responsibility attributions. We examine the tone of these statements – that is, the attribution of blame or praise –, the addressees of causal responsibility attributions and the discourse coalitions that present their interpretations of the crisis in the media.

As regards the *tone* of causal responsibility attributions, our data indicate a clear predominance of blame. Almost all causal attributions blame the addressee for having caused the crisis. Only a very small share of statements describes the causality between addressee and financial crisis in ambivalent or positive terms. In statements like the following the responsibility of economic and political actors is, for instance, denied but at the same time attributed to the economic regime: 'Not Alan Greenspan or Fannie Mae and Freddie Mac are primarily held responsible for the crisis, but serious malfunctions of the financial system'

(*Frankfurter Allgemeine Zeitung*, 'Greenspan war nicht schuld', 18 May 2009).[5] Overall, this finding shows that the economic performance crisis was indeed understood as a problem that had to be addressed.

Secondly, we turn to the *addressees* of these mostly negative causal responsibility attributions. Is the capitalist market economy itself blamed for the crisis, do we see a focus on economic actor groups, or is the role of political actors seen as important? Following the hierarchy of causal responsibility addressees, institutional change is more likely if the majority of statements address the economic regime or its variants.

Our data show that causal responsibility attributions to the capitalist market economy and its variants are least frequent in our sample. Attributions of blame to economic and political actor groups contribute a considerably higher share of statements. This finding suggests that the economic crisis did not translate into a Great Transformation in part because the economic regime as a whole was not seen as the root cause of the crisis. Rather, the crisis was constructed as the product of the misconduct of specific actor groups. As the behaviour of these actor groups may be easily changed without replacing the entire economic regime, the finding also suggests a comparatively low potential for institutional change. Nevertheless, a closer reading of our textual material reveals that fundamental criticism of the capitalist market economy – challenging the legitimacy of the regime – is embedded in causal responsibility attributions to the highest level of the addressee hierarchy. A prime example is the following quote from *The Times*:

> Gordon Brown believes it is time to reset capitalism's moral compass and the Pope, in his recent letter to the Prime Minister, stated that 'a key element of the crisis is a deficit of ethics in economic structures'. ('Markets Can't Be Improved by Rules', 9 April 2009)

In this quote, British Prime Minister Gordon Brown and Pope Benedict XVI call for a more ethical capitalist market economy. *Capitalism* and *economic structures* are perceived as morally wrong by two prominent public figures. This is not the only example of fundamental blame attributions that implicitly question the legitimacy of the economic regime. Yet, the number of these statements is too low to conclude that an interpretation of the crisis as being caused by the economic regime itself dominates. In addition, there are some statements, such as the following, that address the economic regime as a whole but do not suggest that the system is to blame for the crisis: 'The capitalist market economy as the strongest known form of welfare generation and distribution of wealth was not the culprit for the current crisis' (*Süddeutsche Zeitung*, 'Christliche Wege aus der Wirtschaftskrise', 22 March 2010).[6] Such statements suggest stability of the regime rather than change. There are also metaphorical causal responsibility attributions to the regime level which argue, for instance, that the crisis can be compared to the 'breakdown of a machine' (*The Times*, 'Markets Can't Be Improved by Rules', 9 April 2009). While these statements clearly question the legitimacy of the system in its current form, they do not necessarily ask for its abolition. As is discussed in more detail in Chapter 5, machine metaphors frequently imply a preference for solving the problems of the system within the existing framework instead of replacing or fundamentally reforming it. Such statements are often uttered by economic speakers. While they do not shift blame in a more direct way, for instance, by attributing causal responsibility to political actors, a strategy of blame avoidance could be behind these statements. Both the acceptance of causal responsibility in combination with the denial of viable alternatives and the use of metaphors highlighting that the system can be 'repaired' while downplaying the potential of fundamental failure can be read in this vein (Hinterleitner and Sager 2016). Although these types of statements imply responsibility of the economic regime, they do not fundamentally question its very existence and in that sense mitigate its causal responsibility for the Great Recession.

In sum, neither the share nor the quality of causal responsibility attributions to the capitalist market economy and its varieties indicate high potential for institutional change. Rather, our data indicate that the crisis was framed as the result of the behaviour of specific actor groups. These issues appear to be solvable without replacing the economic regime. To further verify this result, we now take a more detailed look at causal responsibility attributions to economic and political actor groups. Overall, statements such as the following quote from US discourse – addressing the responsibility of economic groups or specific economic actors – dominate the debate:

> That three-story, six-bedroom house, on the market for $18 million in a bank repossession sale, has emerged as a symbol of how the global financial crisis is hitting Britain, and of what many see as its cause: the raw, unchecked greed of financial barons. (*Washington Post*, 'Fall of Britain's Flamboyant Financiers Fuels a Debate about Greed', 29 September 2008)

Here, causal responsibility is shifted away from the regime level to the actor level. This suggests a high likelihood of institutional stability. Specific actors and even actor groups can be replaced or educated to avoid future economic crisis. Banks and bankers are the most prominent target of blame attributions to economic actor groups. In these statements, the role of individual banks or of banks from a specific country is barely discussed. Instead, causal responsibility is globally attributed to 'the banks'. Bankers as a group of people rather than individual banks or the banking system tend to be blamed for the financial crisis. The banks and their employees did it wrong. They took advantage of the system and are now to blame for the crisis. These statements on the causal responsibility of banks mainly refer to the legitimation criteria of morality and personal virtues and vices (for a discussion of these culture-centred legitimation criteria, see Chapter 2). It is, for instance, claimed, that 'financiers enriched themselves by selling over-priced and risky products to some of the most vulnerable citizens in America' (*The Guardian*, 'After Guns and the Iraq War, Michael Moore is Now Taking on an Entire Political and Economic System in His Latest Documentary', 30 January 2010). The focus on the wrongdoings of individuals or the business elite is, however, rarely connected to systemic causes (Sinclair 2010). Most discourse participants do not blame the system for creating incentive structures that lead actors to behave in morally improper ways. These individual vices are clearly not in need of a transformative institutional reform. By implication, the crisis could be solved and could even have been prevented if economic actors had simply behaved better.

Responsibility attributions to national politicians are second most frequent. In this category, the majority of statements addresses the failures of the US government in financial market regulation and the monetary policy of the US Federal Reserve System. In this vein, 'James Simons from [the US-American hedge fund] Renaissance [Technologies] criticized insufficient government supervision of the providers of foul US property loans and above all the rating agencies' (*Süddeutsche Zeitung*, 'Schweineohren statt seidene Handtaschen', 15 November 2008).[7] We also find statements like the following: 'In this sense the present economic crisis is actually a crisis of democracy as the market has taken from parliament the power to shape the policy of the nation' (*The Guardian*, 'Formation of a National Government Would Be an Attack on Democracy and Give Succour to Fascism', 11 December 2008). Here, it is not only a specific element of British government that is blamed for the crisis, but British democracy as a whole is considered to be a failure. Overall, these attributions of blame show that the crisis was not interpreted as a systemic failure that could only be solved through radical institutional reform. Instead, the crisis was constructed as being caused by individual wrongdoings and flawed political regulation. Both causes of the crisis can be addressed without replacing the economic regime. This suggests that room for future courses of action is substantially narrowed to institutional changes that affect the behaviour of economic and political actors.

Thirdly, we examine the *speakers* who contribute these statements, and whether an encompassing and powerful discourse coalition has emerged. Are critical responsibility attributions voiced by a limited set of politically marginal speakers? Or do the speakers in our sample form a powerful discourse coalition?

All four groups of speakers – journalists, economic actors, political elites and civil society representatives – participate in discourse. Journalists dominate. They are followed by representatives of civil society. In this group, we find scientists, public intellectuals as well as representatives of religious communities, arts and culture. They form a diverse and broad civil society group which could be considered a strong discourse coalition. As Colin Crouch (2011: 175) puts it:

> Civil society will be stronger, the more that the state and the giant firm are challenged – by churches, voluntary organizations, professions and other participants in the fragmented world of values – and required to participate in a pluralist dialogue that escapes their control.

It is this quality of civil society to express the common interest and common moral understandings without any distorting strategic considerations that could help to mobilize sufficient support for wholesale institutional reform if it focused on the economic regime as the main addressee. Yet, this is not the case. Speakers from civil society mainly blame national politics and economic actors but not the economic regime. More precisely, representatives of civil society are the only speakers that blame the banks for the crisis. This constellation of a potentially powerful discourse coalition which focuses on economic actor groups rather than the regime as a whole narrows down the menu of solutions for the crisis. Instead of putting pressure on the regime itself, the civil society coalition shifts blame to one specific group of actors, which may be substituted or educated to avoid future crashes of the economy.

National political actors appear second most frequently in causal responsibility discourse. Due to their key positions in the four countries of our sample, speakers from this group could also be considered a powerful discourse coalition. After all, political actors are at the centre of decision-making processes and would have to agree with an institutional transformation. However, our data show that this group does not tend to attribute strong blame to the economic regime as a whole either. Rather, national politicians focus on the causal responsibility of their political peers from other countries and of economic actors. About one-third of the attributions of blame made by national political actors address other political actors. This type of statements is particularly prominent in the United States and Germany. We observe a high share of blame attributions like the following to US politicians: 'The chairman of the Senate Banking Committee, Christopher J. Dodd, Democrat of Connecticut, has lambasted the White House for the crisis' (*New York Times*, 'In Washington, Financial Furor Is a First-Rate Chance to Assess Blame', 18 September 2008). Statements addressing the government of the United Kingdom are rarer. German and Swiss political actors are not at all seen to be causally responsible for the crisis.

Finally, speakers from the economy and representatives of IGOs are infrequent. Economic speakers try to avoid public appearances and blaming the economic regime or their colleagues. Representatives of IGOs put the blame for the crisis on the capitalist market economy as a whole. Yet, their marginal participation makes IGO representatives a less influential voice in discourse.

Overall, the analysis of speakers and potential discourse coalitions complements our findings for tone and responsibility addressees. The strong discourse coalition of civil society speakers mostly blaming economic actor groups and the absence of a powerful coalition focusing on the causal responsibility of the economic regime signal stable legitimacy and limited mobilization potential for major institutional reform.

Who Is Supposed to Clean Up the Mess? Treatment Responsibility Attributions

Our data on causal responsibility attributions suggest that ideas about the causes of the crisis were not conducive to the replacement of the capitalist market economy. Yet, a look at the addressees and authors of treatment responsibility might still indicate that there was demand and hence the potential for more ambitious institutional reform. In this section, we therefore turn to ideas on who should be responsible for finding solutions to the crisis. The analysis builds on 66 treatment responsibility attributions in 41 newspaper articles.

Firstly, we examine the addressees of treatment responsibility attributions. Who is supposed to solve the problems resulting from the financial crisis? Is treatment responsibility most prominently attributed to the economic regime itself (a signal of institutional stability)? Are the actors who are blamed most strongly for the crisis – that is, banks and bankers – also expected to solve it? Or is treatment responsibility frequently attributed to political actor groups (an indicator of a greater potential for change)? Most causal attributions blame economic actors for the crisis. The second most prominent addressees are national political actors. The

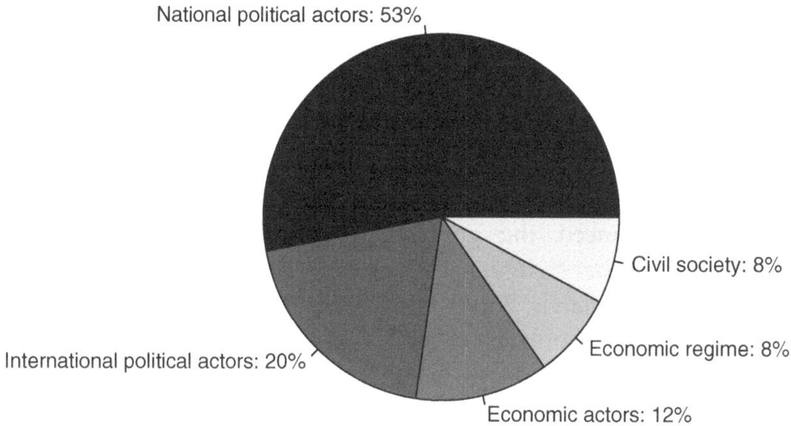

Fig. 4.3 Shares of addressees in treatment responsibility attributions

economic regime as whole is only rarely blamed for the crisis. Our data reveal a different picture for the attribution of treatment responsibility.

Figure 4.3 indicates that economic actors play a subordinate role when it comes to treatment responsibility. They are only the third most frequent addressees in our data. Hence, a direct link between causal and treatment responsibility, putting those who allegedly caused the crisis also in the driver's seat for its solution, does not seem to exist. Rather, actor groups who are at the margins of causal attributions – national and international political elites – are the actors who are mostly expected to find solutions to the crisis. Similar to the analysis of legitimation narratives in Chapter 6, our data seem to indicate the return of the state as a legitimate manager of the capitalist market economy. At first sight, this focus on political elites suggests potential for change. A shift away from the economic regime and its key actors indicates a clear demand for external intervention. This, in turn, implies potentially stronger institutional responses than those likely to be provided by insiders of the capitalist market economy, who have fewer incentives to fundamentally change the regime. As economic actors have adapted to the regime and know how to reap benefits from it, they cannot be expected to be the drivers of major transformation.

A more detailed analysis of this set of statements corroborates our diagnosis, although a relatively high share of statements addressing political elites is characterized by negative tone. These critical statements focus mainly on the performance of political elites as managers of the crisis and their specific policies. We find, for instance, that '[u]nder the slogan "we won't pay for your crisis!", demonstrators in Berlin and Frankfurt denounced the government's multi-billion-euro aid for banks' (*Frankfurter Allgemeine Zeitung*, 'Die Welt steht am Scheideweg', 28 March 2009).[8] Similarly, the late chairman of the German Liberal Democrats (FDP), Guido Westerwelle, claims that 'the biggest lesson from the financial crisis is that the state has failed as regulator and banker' (*Frankfurter Allgemeine Zeitung*, 'Die Finanzkrise hat mein Weltbild bestärkt', 7 June 2009).[9] Despite this high share of critical assessments of political elite performance, the general role of political elites as a key actor group for solving the crisis is rarely questioned. The number of these responsibility attributions is comparably low. Nevertheless, their positive tone suggests that national political elites are most welcome to intervene in the crisis: 'Financial crises are inevitable as long as the state does not intervene to regulate' (*Süddeutsche Zeitung*, 'Früher ignoriert, heute ein Star', 18 June 2009).[10]

Similarly, the less frequently addressed group of international political elites is considered to have an important role in solving the crisis. In terms of positive treatment attributions, this group is ranked first of all potential addressees. International political actors are most frequently requested to assume more treatment responsibility in the aftermath of the crisis. Angela Merkel suggests, for instance, 'establishing a new UN Economic Council, similar to the Security Council' (*Neue Zürcher Zeitung*, 'Neue Welt – neuer Kapitalismus', 9 January 2009).[11] In addition, the performance of international actors – most notably the EU – is perceived less critically than the performance of national political actors.

In sum, responsibility to solve the crisis is frequently attributed to both national and international political actors. This overall result is barely affected by the critical evaluation of their performance in this role. It suggests more potential for change than our results on causal responsibility. This conclusion needs to be qualified on the basis of a more detailed analysis of treatment responsibility attributions to economic actors and the regime as a whole. The share of these statements is comparably low. Yet, among them we find a surprisingly high number of statements attributing an important role to economic actor groups. They argue, for instance, that '[b]oards must rein in out-of-control egos. This change of ethos cannot be delegated to regulatory bodies or central banks but must become the personal responsibility of bankers themselves' (*The Times*, 'Markets Can't Be Improved by Rules', 9 April 2009). These statements express the wish that economic actors be guided by the public interest. The exclusive focus on profit is perceived to be the main reason for the crisis. Consequently, the authors of these statements consider the involvement of bankers and managers as a key element to solve the crisis and prevent future ones. Economic actors are called upon to rethink their premises and change their behaviour. In these statements, external intervention – for instance, in the form of governmental regulations – is not considered or explicitly turned down. This set of statements reinforces our results on causal responsibility. Many discourse participants attribute the crisis to the wrongdoings and moral failures of economic actors. Treatment responsibility attributions highlighting the role of economic actors continue this set of ideas as they suggest that the crisis could be solved if only those actors who caused the crisis changed their behaviour.

In treatment responsibility attributions to the economic regime as a whole, discourse is more polarized. On the one hand, a number of statements highlight that

> [t]he pursuit of profit by privately owned businesses is still the best method yet devised to create wealth and opportunity for the many. Capitalism has lifted hundreds of millions of people out of poverty and has provided unprecedented choice, material and intellectual. It has provided the backdrop for greater tolerance and understanding. (*The Times*, 'Has Capitalism Failed?', 14 October 2008)

In these rather general statements, the capacity of the capitalist market economy to correct its flaws and to create wealth is highlighted to support its treatment responsibility. Yet, on the other hand, there are also highly critical statements which argue, for instance, that 'changes in regulation are not sufficient after this financial crisis — it is time for a revolution in economic thought' (*The Times*, 'Now is the Time for a Revolution in Economic Thought', 9 February 2009). However, these strong statements are rare and do not reflect the general thrust of treatment attributions to the economic regime, which are mainly positive and frequently combined with the argument that there is no viable alternative to the capitalist market economy.

In sum, this detailed analysis of the addressees of treatment responsibility attributions suggests a qualified diagnosis. At first glance, treatment responsibility appears to have shifted away from the economic regime and its actor groups to national and international political actors. Yet, closer inspection reveals a more diverse picture. National political actors are frequently criticized for their performance in finding solutions to the crisis, a change of mind by economic actors is often seen as a necessary condition for solving the crisis and even the economic regime itself is still considered to be a legitimate part of the solution to the crisis in some statements. Strong demand for external intervention or even the replacement of the capitalist market economy is not evident. Hence, we argue that treatment responsibility attributions, similar to causal responsibility attributions, mobilize little support for transformative institutional change.

Finally, we turn to the question of whether ideas on how to solve the crisis are supported by an inclusive and dominant discourse coalition. Our data suggest a fairly balanced discourse with a wide range of speakers from all the important spheres of society. Half of the statements come from national political actors and more than a third from civil society, followed at some distance by the group of economic actors. The voices of economic actors and IGO representatives are almost absent from discourse. Although economic actors are frequently blamed for causing the crisis, they rarely try to claim treatment responsibility. Similarly, IGO representatives seldom contribute to discourse on how the crisis could be solved. The high demand for IGO intervention by other discourse participants notwithstanding, international political speakers have little voice. The strong presence of political elites and members of civil society indicates a potentially strong discourse coalition. Yet, as we have shown above, different speakers do not necessarily agree on who should solve the crisis and if they agree, they do not necessarily focus on external intervention by political elites. Instead, political elites are frequently criticized for their crisis management.

Overall, our results on treatment responsibility also suggest relatively little room for a Great Transformation. Although there is demand for external intervention, we find a large number of statements asking the capitalist market economy and its actors to correct their own mistakes. There is no strong discourse coalition pushing for external intervention and the replacement of the economic regime.

Conclusion

This chapter addressed an often neglected but relevant component of legitimation discourse: the attribution of responsibility. The detailed analysis of this specific element of legitimation discourse sheds further light on the overarching question of this volume: Why has the financial crisis of 2008 not ushered in a substantial transformation of the capitalist market economy? To probe the extent to which responsibility attributions in the wake of the economic performance crisis and the ensuing legitimation crisis have contributed to the resilience of the economic regime during this 'near-miss' critical juncture (Capoccia 2015: 165), we analysed a set of five variables. We examined the tone, addressees and speakers of causal responsibility attributions and the addressees and speakers of treatment responsibility attributions. Overall, our data show that discourse on the causes and potential solutions of the economic crisis has helped to stabilize the economic regime. Instead of highlighting the systemic failure of the capitalist market economy and asking for strong external intervention, discourse participants developed a set of ideas that directed future courses of action towards rather narrow reform and the self-correction of the economic regime.

Table 4.2 provides an overview of our empirical results. It shows that only two findings suggest potential for wholesale change while three indicate limited room for institutional reform. Clearly, discourse

Table 4.2 Summary of empirical findings

Variable	Indicator	Finding
Causal responsibility		
Evaluative tone	Mainly negative	+
Addressees	Mainly the economic regime	–
Speakers	Wide range of actor groups	–
Treatment responsibility		
Addressees	Mainly political actors	+
Speakers	Wide range of actor groups	–

Note: A plus sign in the chart indicates evidence suggesting potential for institutional change. A minus sign indicates the lack of such evidence.

participants identify the crisis as a problem for which somebody has to be blamed. In addition, we also find a strong focus on national and international political elites as potential managers of the crisis. Yet, the addressees of causal responsibility attributions and their authors do not indicate high potential for institutional change. Instead of attributing causal responsibility to the economic regime as a whole, the majority of statements blame economic actors – particularly banks and bankers – for causing the crisis. While this situation puts considerable pressure on these actor groups, it does not help to mobilize support for transformative institutional change. Actors can be substituted or re-educated without transforming or even revolutionizing the entire economic system.

Furthermore, neither causal nor treatment attributions are supported by strong discourse coalitions. In both cases, particularly critical responsibility attributions are only supported by a minority of speakers who do not have the political clout to initiate broad societal mobilization. The causal discourse is dominated by representatives of civil society and national politicians. The two groups could potentially form a powerful discourse coalition denouncing the failure of the capitalist market economy. However, empirically this is not the case, as both groups are mainly concerned with the role of domestic politics and economic actor groups. A similar picture emerges for the attribution of treatment responsibility. Although the majority of these statements allocate responsibility to solve the crisis to national and international political actors, they often criticize the role of political actors and do not highlight demand for more external intervention. Hence, we do not find a strong coalition advocating institutional change in this dimension either.

Nevertheless, the fact that domestic and international political actors are frequently called upon to solve the latest economic crisis and prevent future ones suggests an interesting transformation of legitimation discourse about the capitalist market economy. As Chapter 6 shows in more detail, governments experience a comeback as legitimate managers of the economic regime. The capitalist market economy and its actors are rarely called upon to solve the crisis. Neoliberal ideas, which made 'more people bec[o]me skeptical about the capacity of states to manage the economy [and] to look more favorably on the view that growth was likely to be restored only if the role of the state in the economy was reduced' (Hall 2015: 430) appear to be on the decline. Neoliberalism may still be alive, but 'the financial crisis did produce one solid check to the case for a diminishing role for the state, in that deregulation of the financial sector was very widely agreed to have gone too far. Even some neoliberals now concede a need for some regulation' (Crouch 2011: 170).

In short, to understand when economic crises result in legitimation crises and under what conditions such crises can trigger wholesale institutional reform or even the replacement of an economic regime, we have to systematically analyse how they are interpreted discursively and how the ideas that underpin an economic regime are transformed in legitimation discourse. Our contribution demonstrated that this kind of analysis can enrich the historical-institutionalist research agenda on critical junctures and institutional stability and change (Capoccia 2015).

Notes

1. All translations are our own.
2. In order to analyse treatment responsibility, we identified a list of tasks that were perceived as relevant and publicly discussed in the context of the crisis.
3. 'Die Einzigen, die mit der Krise fertig werden können, sind die Amerikaner'.

4. 'Diese Entwicklung liegt in der Natur des Systems'. Unlike some of the other chapters in this book, we do not differentiate between the regime and its varieties but include capitalism, the capitalist market economy and regime varieties such as financial capitalism or the social market economy in this category.
5. 'Hier werden nicht Alan Greenspan oder Fannie Mae und Freddie Mac für die Krise hauptverantwortlich gemacht, sondern in erster Linie schwere Fehlentwicklungen im Finanzsystem'.
6. 'Somit ist nach Ostheimer die freie Marktwirtschaft an sich als "beste bekannte Form der Wohlstandsproduktion und -verteilung" nicht der Grund für die gegenwärtige Krise'.
7. 'James Simons von Renaissance kritisierte mangelnde staatliche Aufsicht, die Anbieter von Paketen mit faulen US-Immobilienkrediten und vor allem die Ratingagenturen'.
8. 'Unter dem Motto "Wir zahlen nicht für Eure Krise!" prangerten die Demonstranten in Berlin und Frankfurt die Milliardenhilfen der Regierungen für die Banken an'.
9. 'Die wichtigste Lehre aus der Finanzkrise ist doch, dass der Staat als Regulierer und als Banker versagt hat'.
10. 'Finanzkrisen sind unvermeidbar, solange der Staat nicht mit starken Regeln eingreift'.
11. 'Angela Merkel blieb bodenständiger und empfahl die Bildung eines neuen Uno-Wirtschaftsrates, vergleichbar mit dem Sicherheitsrat'.

References

Anderson, Christopher J. and Jason D. Hecht. 2012. 'Voting When the Economy Goes Bad, Everyone is in Charge, and No One is to Blame: The Case of the 2009 German Election'. *Electoral Studies* 31(1): 5–19.

Bermeo, Nancy and Larry M. Bartels, eds. 2014. *Mass Politics in Tough Times. Opinions, Votes, and Protest in the Great Recession.* Oxford: Oxford University Press.

Bermeo, Nancy and Jonas Pontusson, eds. 2012. *Coping with Crisis. Government Reactions to the Great Recession.* New York: Russell Sage Foundation.

Blyth, Mark. 2002. *Great Transformations. Economic Ideas and Institutional Change in the Twentieth Century.* Cambridge: Cambridge University Press.

Capoccia, Giovanni. 2015. 'Critical Junctures and Institutional Change'. In *Advances in Comparative-Historical Analysis*, eds. James Mahoney and Kathleen Thelen. Cambridge: Cambridge University Press, 147–79.

Capoccia, Giovanni and R. Daniel Kelemen. 2007. 'The Study of Critical Junctures: Theory, Narrative, and Counterfactuals in Historical Institutionalism'. *World Politics* 59(3): 341–69.

Crouch, Colin. 2011. *The Strange Non-Death of Neo-Liberalism*. Cambridge: Polity Press.

Drezner, Daniel W. 2014. *The System Worked. How the World Stopped Another Great Depression*. Oxford: Oxford University Press.

Gerhards, Jürgen, Anke Offerhaus and Jochen Roose. 2007. 'Die öffentliche Zuschreibung von Verantwortung'. *Kölner Zeitschrift für Soziologie und Sozialpsychologie* 59(1): 105–24.

Gerhards, Jürgen, Anke Offerhaus and Jochen Roose. 2009. 'Wer ist verantwortlich? Die Europäische Union, ihre Nationalstaaten und die massenmediale Attribution von Verantwortung für Erfolge und Misserfolge'. In *Politik in der Mediendemokratie*, eds. Barbara Pfetsch and Frank Marcinkowski. Wiesbaden: VS, 529–58.

Gourevitch, Peter. 1986. *Politics in Hard Times. Comparative Responses to International Economic Crises*. Ithaca: Cornell University Press.

Hall, Peter A. 2015. 'The Changing Role of the State in Liberal Market Economies'. In *Oxford Handbook of Transformations of the State*, eds. Stephan Leibfried, Evelyne Huber, Matthew Lange, Jonah D. Levy, Frank Nullmeier and John D. Stephens. Oxford: Oxford University Press, 426–44.

Hansson, Sten. 2015. 'Discursive Strategies of Blame Avoidance in Government: A Framework for Analysis'. *Discourse & Society* 26(3): 297–322.

Hart, H.L.A. 1968. *Punishment and Responsibility. Essays in the Philosophy of Law*. Oxford: Clarendon Press.

Hellwig, Timothy and Eva Coffey. 2011. 'Public Opinion, Party Messages, and Responsibility for the Financial Crisis in Britain'. *Electoral Studies* 30(3): 417–26.

Hellwig, Timothy T., Eve M. Ringsmuth and John R. Freeman. 2008. 'The American Public and the Room to Maneuver: Responsibility Attributions and Policy Efficacy in an Era of Globalization'. *International Studies Quarterly* 52(4): 855–80.

Hinterleitner, Markus. 2017. 'Reconciling Perspectives on Blame Avoidance Behaviour'. *Political Studies Review* 15(2): 243–54.

Hinterleitner, Markus and Fritz Sager. 2016. 'Anticipatory and Reactive Forms of Blame Avoidance: Of Foxes and Lions'. *European Political Science Review* Online First DOI: 10.1017/S1755773916000126.

Iyengar, Shanto. 1994. *Is Anyone Responsible? How Television Frames Political Issues*. Chicago: University of Chicago Press.

Kahler, Miles and David A. Lake. 2013. 'Introduction: Anatomy of Crisis. The Great Recession and Political Change'. In *Politics in the New Hard Times. The Great Recession in Comparative Perspective*, eds. Miles Kahler and David A. Lake. Ithaca: Cornell University Press, 1–26.

Kim, Sei-Hill. 2015. 'Who Is Responsible for a Social Problem? News Framing and Attribution of Responsibility'. *Journalism & Mass Communication Quarterly* 92(3): 554–8.

Mayntz, Renate, ed. 2012. *Crisis and Control. Institutional Change in Financial Market Regulation*. Frankfurt am Main: Campus.

Polanyi, Karl. 2001. *The Great Transformation. The Political and Economic Origins of Our Time*. Boston: Beacon Press.

Rudolph, Thomas J. 2003. 'Who's Responsible for the Economy? The Formation and Consequences of Responsibility Attributions'. *American Journal of Political Science* 47(4): 698–713.

Sinclair, Timothy J. 2010. 'Round Up the Usual Suspects: Blame and the Subprime Crisis'. *New Political Economy* 15(1): 91–107.

van Leeuwen, Theo. 2007. 'Legitimation in Discourse and Communication'. *Discourse & Communication* 1(1): 91–112.

Weaver, R. Kent. 1986. 'The Politics of Blame Avoidance'. *Journal of Public Policy* 6(4): 371–98.

Cited Newspaper Articles

Frankfurter Allgemeine Zeitung 10 October 2008. 'Ein Gespräch mit dem Soziologen Ralf Dahrendorf'.

Frankfurter Allgemeine Zeitung 28 March 2009. 'Die Welt steht am Scheideweg'.

Frankfurter Allgemeine Zeitung 18 May 2009. 'Greenspan war nicht schuld'.

Frankfurter Allgemeine Zeitung 7 June 2009. 'Die Finanzkrise hat mein Weltbild bestärkt'.

Süddeutsche Zeitung 15 November 2008. 'Schweineohren statt seidene Handtaschen'.

Süddeutsche Zeitung 26 November 2008. 'Weltwirtschaftsgewitter; Karl Marx ist aktuell'.

Süddeutsche Zeitung 18 June 2009. 'Früher ignoriert, heute ein Star'.

Süddeutsche Zeitung 22 March 2010. 'Christliche Wege aus der Wirtschaftskrise'.

Neue Zürcher Zeitung 9 January 2009. 'Neue Welt – neuer Kapitalismus'.

The Guardian 30 January 2010. 'After Guns and the Iraq War, Michael Moore is Now Taking on an Entire Political and Economic System in His Latest Documentary'.

The Guardian 11 December 2008. 'Formation of a National Government Would Be an Attack on Democracy and Give Succour to Fascism'.

The Times 14 October 2008. 'Has Capitalism Failed?'

The Times 9 February 2009. 'Now Is the Time for a Revolution in Economic Thought'.

The Times 9 April 2009. 'Markets Can't Be Improved by Rules'.

The Times 4 February 2010. 'We Need a New Capitalism to Take on China'.

New York Times 18 September 2008. 'Abroad, This Bailout Is a Shocker'.

New York Times 18 September 2008. 'In Washington, Financial Furor Is a First-Rate Chance to Assess Blame'.

Washington Post 29 September 2008. 'Fall of Britain's Flamboyant Financiers Fuels a Debate About Greed'.

Washington Post 13 April 2009. 'Obama's Economic Mirage'.

5

Metaphorical Anticapitalism: Regulation, Not Transformation

Jennifer Gronau

The financial crisis of 2008 triggered growing contestation of capitalism's legitimacy. However, the public outcry was of only limited scope and did not usher in fundamental ideational or institutional change. To understand why the legitimation crisis of the capitalist market economy has not led to wholesale institutional change, this chapter takes a closer look at some of the rhetorical devices employed by the delegitimizers of the capitalist market economy.[1] It starts from three assumptions: Firstly, I argue that any delegitimation of the capitalist market economy with transformative consequences would have to be rooted in a radical shift of the way the regime is socially constructed. As highlighted by Mark Blyth (2002: 40), ideas about reform options or regime alternatives are underpinned by evaluations of the capitalist market economy. Negative evaluations imply both problem diagnoses and ideas about how problems

J. Gronau (✉)
Centre for Global Cooperation Research (Käte-Hamburger-Kolleg),
Duisburg, Germany
e-mail: jgronau@uni-bremen.de

S. Schneider et al. (eds.), *Capitalism and Its Legitimacy in Times of Crisis*, Transformations of the State,
DOI 10.1007/978-3-319-53765-8_5

might be solved (see Chapter 4). A consequential, transformative mobilization of anticapitalist thought can only succeed where a set of radically new ideas about the capitalist market economy arises which suggests that changing the regime is in fact possible. Secondly, like the other contributions to this volume, I assume that in order to become relevant in terms of mobilization and institutional change, this radical shift of ideas must be publicly expressed and shared. Finally, I argue that the limited discursive power of capitalism's delegitimizers after 2008 is related to – and can be gleaned from – the metaphors used in their critical statements. In line with cognitive metaphor theory, I claim that metaphors shape our worldviews, including perceptions of the capitalist market economy. They highlight some aspects of the regime while hiding others. Most importantly, metaphors entail ideas about the extent to which the regime can be reformed or replaced through political action. In that sense, metaphors strengthen or undermine anticapitalist mobilization.

In the following sections, I first sketch the theoretical rationale for an analysis of metaphors in legitimation discourse and present the research design and method of my analysis. Secondly, I identify the five metaphors used most frequently by delegitimizers of the capitalist market economy in British, German, Swiss and US legitimation discourse, and examine change in metaphorical repertoires after the 2008 financial crisis. Thirdly, I probe what margin of manoeuvring for a reform or replacement of the capitalist regime – that is, what potential for a genuine institutional *transformation* – the most prominent metaphors used in critical statements entail. Finally, I summarize the value of metaphor analysis for understanding why public criticism of the capitalist regime has failed to lay the ideational groundwork and to mobilize support for the kinds and scope of change that the anticapitalist literature calls for (see Chapter 2). While delegitimating discourse comprises a range of metaphors that, at first glance, seem to entail the possibility of such a Great Transformation, a closer look reveals that the most prominent metaphors make it difficult to envisage wholesale reform of capitalism's institutional arrangements or to think about genuine alternatives. Instead, they often imply either that a mere adjustment of the capitalist regime through *regulatory reform* is sufficient to cope with the financial crisis or that transformative institutional change is impossible.

Theoretical Rationale, Research Design and Method

Metaphors play a major role in our everyday constructions of reality. They are 'cases where one concept is metaphorically structured in terms of another' (Lakoff and Johnson 2003: 14). In a metaphor, semantic components of a 'source domain' are transferred to a 'target domain' (Kövecses 2010: 17–32), that is, familiar everyday knowledge is used to make more abstract and unknown phenomena intelligible. The capitalist market economy and its functional mechanisms are such abstract phenomena. Hence, a variety of metaphors is projected onto capitalism in public discourse to describe the regime and make sense of it, but also to criticize it and suggest alternatives to the status quo (McCloskey 1995). Metaphors produce knowledge about the capitalist market economy – and this knowledge is in turn associated with particular evaluations of the regime and ideas about the possibility of institutional change. Metaphors thus have the potential to make a course of action plausible and to mobilize support for it while making others appear inappropriate and unlikely (Wæver 2005: 35–6; Hülsse 2006: 404; Cienki and Yanow 2013).

A good example is the metaphorical representation of the capitalist market economy as a malfunctioning machine: It is possible to repair a car and to make it roadworthy again, but one cannot *educate* it. In a similar vein, discourse on the capitalist market economy and its problems often evokes ways to 'repair' the economic regime. While there is usually more than one plausible interpretation of a source domain, the scope for interpretation is definitely limited. We can switch off a machine, build a new one or re-use parts of it. But since a machine is no living organism, we can neither educate nor kill it.

The projection from a source domain to a target domain is often partial or oblique (Kuck and Scholz 2013: 251). In other words, not all of the implications entailed by a source domain are always made fully explicit in a metaphorical expression. Drawing on their personal experience (for instance, their experience with machines and possible ways to manipulate them), discourse participants are usually able to grasp the entailments of a metaphor. Yet, I suggest that metaphors are most likely to mobilize political action when they clearly entail the idea that there is a potential for institutional change and offer an 'instruction sheet' for the supporters of such a transformation. Metaphors used to criticize the capitalist market economy thus have the potential to either facilitate or limit thinking about system alternatives. As a consequence, different metaphorical accounts of the regime can foster radically different political outcomes (Blyth 2002: 33).

In particular, I suggest that a differentiation should be made between three types of entailments related to reform options and the possibility of change: Only the first group of metaphors has the potential to cognitively mobilize thought about ways to fundamentally change the economic regime by *transforming* its institutions and underlying set of ideas. The second group merely entails the possibility of a *regulatory reform*. The third group entails *institutional stability*; any potential for change induced by human actors – and thus both a genuine transformation of the capitalist market economy and regulatory reform – is denied. In line with the notion that different metaphors can be associated with varying potential for change, a legitimation crisis of the capitalist market economy is more likely to result in a genuine transformation of the regime's institutional arrangements if metaphors are used that make such a transformation appear possible.

The metaphor analysis of this chapter is based on a selection from the corpus on which the volume is based (Table 5.1). It consists of 383 legitimation statements in which the capitalist market economy – more precisely, the legitimation objects 'economic regime as a whole', 'market

Table 5.1 Number of legitimation statements (metaphors), by country and time period

	CH	DE	UK	US
1998–2007	37 (42)	118 (145)	50 (54)	20 (22)
2008–2011	22 (29)	65 (80)	50 (57)	21 (28)
Σ	59 (71)	183 (225)	100 (111)	41 (50)

economy' and 'capitalism' – is evaluated negatively. Critical evaluations of specific core principles, varieties of capitalism and groups of actors (categories II to IV of legitimation objects; see Chapter 3) were not considered with the exception of the regime variant 'financial capitalism'. Unsurprisingly, this legitimation object is frequently assessed after 2008 and has a legitimacy level (share of positive evaluations) of only 9 per cent. Hence, legitimacy evaluations of this object are 'most likely cases' of a particularly assertive critique of capitalism. The identification and coding of metaphors in these statements involved two stages.

Identification of relevant metaphors: The target domain of my analysis is the capitalist market economy. Only metaphors that underpin critical assessments of that regime were therefore considered. Each legitimation statement was examined word by word to find out whether it has the structure 'capitalist market economy (target domain) is critically connoted source domain' (Charteris-Black 2004: 35–9; Pragglejazz Group 2007; Steen et al. 2010). Hitzler's (1991) perspective of 'artificial stupidity' proved helpful to recognize metaphors. This perspective has already been successfully used for metaphor analyses in the field of political science by Hülsse (2003) and Spencer (2011). It reveals familiar or 'life-world' knowledge (Hitzler 2005: 11) typically associated with a metaphor and sensitizes the researcher for context-specific aspects related to culture and language. The purpose of this methodological approach is to downplay as much as possible the subjective knowledge of the researcher (Hitzler 2005: 10) in reconstructing the intersubjective constitution of everyday knowledge through a source domain. What interpretations are typically linked to the source domain is the key question addressed in the research process (Hitzler 2005: 10). Online dictionaries such as the Digital Dictionary of the German Language (DWDS) and the British National Corpus (BNC) proved useful in this regard, because they help to identify 'socially shared knowledge about phenomena' (Spencer 2011: 55) and thus provide a basis for the unambiguous identification of a metaphor.

Identification of the source domain: In the second step, I assigned each metaphor to a source domain. A preliminary catalogue of source domains was derived from extant metaphor analyses in the fields of economics, political science and policy studies.[2] This catalogue was pretested and inductively expanded as required. In order to keep the influence of my own interpretations as low as possible, I chose labels for source domains that remain as close as possible to the manifest linguistic content of the examined statements.

A metaphorical representation of the capitalist market economy might draw on multiple source domains (example: 'turbo capitalism must be tamed'). In such cases, all source domains were coded (here: capitalist market economy is machine *and* animal). However, where a metaphorical expression contained multiple variations of one and the same source domain, it was coded only once. If the relationship between target domain and source domain remained ambivalent even after the wider context was considered, the passage was not included. This procedure resulted in a data set of 457 metaphors with unambiguous source domains (Table 5.1). For each of the delegitimating statements using metaphorical expressions, I included the year in which it was made and the legitimation criterion used. The following sections present the quantitative and qualitative results of this analysis.

The Top Five Critical Metaphors and Regulatory Thought

What metaphors dominate critical media discourse in Germany, Switzerland, the United Kingdom and the United States? Which problem diagnoses and possibilities for change do they entail? The five most frequently mentioned source domains are, in descending order:

- person (34.0 per cent),
- animal (12.5 per cent),
- machine/mechanics (9.6 per cent),
- human body (6.4 per cent),
- gambling (3.9 per cent).

Together, they represent almost two-thirds of the metaphors identified in the context of delegitimating statements. Personifying metaphors dominate the discourse in all four countries, and there are only minor differences in the ranking of the other groups of metaphors. In US discourse, the machine metaphor ranks second. Here, one-fifth of the statements relate to the capitalist regime as a machine and the share of the machine metaphor is twice as large as in German discourse. The critique of capitalism in the German quality press is slightly more often driven by the animal metaphor than in the other countries – perhaps a discursive effect of the so-called 'Müntefering debate' in 2005. Franz Müntefering, then chairman of the German Social Democratic Party (SPD), had publicly criticized the economic regime as 'predatory capitalism' and described financial investors as 'locusts'. His statement triggered a debate in Germany about the animal nature of the economy (Münnich 2012).

All of the top five metaphors have strong 'elective affinities' with a limited set of the legitimation criteria presented in Chapter 2. Figure 5.1 illustrates these close relationships. Classical economic legitimation criteria – economic stability and the capacity of self-regulation – as well as the culture-centred criterion of personal virtues and vices take centre stage in anticapitalist discourse. The three criteria are all linked to at least two of the top five metaphors. The affinities between these criteria and prominent metaphors are readily apparent: Personifying metaphors and laments about the lack of virtue in economic affairs, animals and their inability to self-regulate by overcoming their instincts, or engines and the possibility of their breakdown provide suggestive imagery for a critique of the capitalist market economy. The imagery evoked by the top five metaphors and the potential for changing the economic regime they imply are now discussed using examples from our corpus.

Capitalism as a Human Being

In one-third of the metaphors, capitalism is depicted as an autonomously acting person. The category of personifications is dominated by metaphorical expressions relating to a lack of personal virtues. The most salient metaphor is capitalism as an *immoral person* (10.3 per cent). References to the 'misconduct of capitalism' are also manifest in its characterizations as a *thief* or *thug* (6.6 per cent) and as a *terrorist* or *murderer* (3.9 per cent). Less

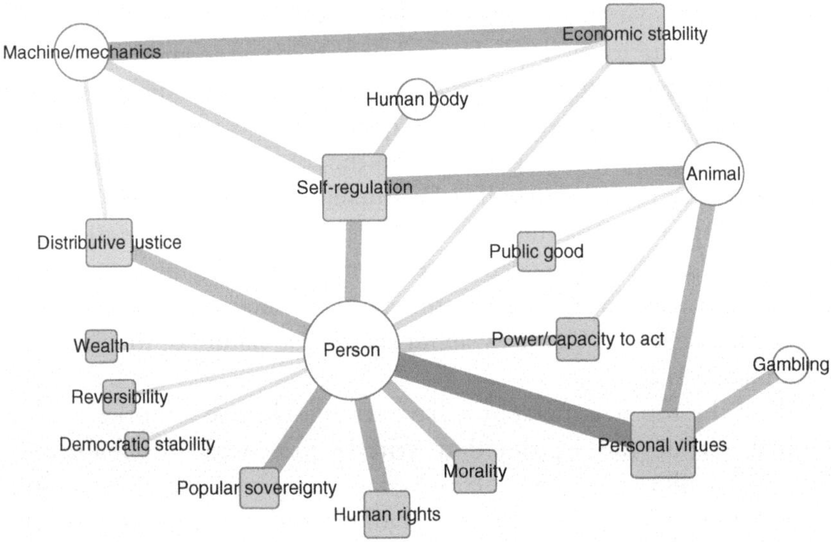

Fig. 5.1 Network of connections between metaphors and legitimation criteria, 4-slice

Note: In the network graph, metaphors are depicted by circles and legitimation criteria by squares. The size of the network nodes reflects their degree of centrality (for more details on discursive network analysis, see Chapter 7). The thickness and shading of the lines is proportional to the frequency of co-occurrences between metaphors and legitimation criteria in one and the same statement. Only connections that occurred at least four times in the data are shown (4-slice).

frequently, capitalism is depicted as a *warrior* or *soldier* (3.5 per cent) and as an *uncivilized* person (1.8 per cent).

With these variants of personification, a classical legitimation criterion of the capitalist market economy – its capacity of self-regulation – is turned into criticism and enriched by arguments from three further repertoires: In addition to the two culture-centred arguments (lack of virtue, immorality), personifications are used to criticize capitalism on democracy-centred grounds; capitalism undermines civic self-determination and fails to protect human rights. Finally, by questioning its distributive justice, critics also foster a justice-centred debate (Fig. 5.1).

'Selfish Capitalism' (*The Guardian*, 'Affluenza', 12 January 2008), then, appears far from being a benefactor of humanity. The regime is equated with a thief: While it has taken 'from parliament the power to shape the policy of the nation' (*The Guardian*, 'Gordon Brown is One of Many Using Religious Shorthand to Show Moral Purpose', 2 July 2007), society presumably has to be protected against the 'corrupt machinations of the capitalist system' (*The Guardian*, 'Paul Foot – Of Splits and Zeros', 19 February 2003), or even more pointedly: 'Inequality is inherent in the capitalist system, and meritocracy is its partner in crime' (*The Guardian*, 'Gordon Brown is One of Many Using Religious Shorthand to Show Moral Purpose', 2 July 2007). 'Whenever I hear capitalism proclaiming noble motives', American satirist Christopher Buckley suggests in a similar vein, 'something makes me check my wallet' (*New York Times*, 'Lawyer and Author Adds His Objections to Settling the Google Lawsuit', 19 August 2009). According to German political scientist Ulrike Ackermann, 'a black book about the crimes of capitalism today seems more relevant for many people than one about the crimes of communism' (*Süddeutsche Zeitung*, 'Der Terror gehörte schon mit zum Anfang', 8 June 1998).[3] Capitalism is also indicted for even more brutal and serious crimes such as running amok (*The Guardian*, 'The Hard Sell', 20 August 2011).[4] The former mayor of London, Ken Livingstone, claims that capitalism has killed 'as many people as Hitler' (*The Times*, 'Mayoral Hopefuls Put Their Case to Voters', 18 April 2000), while other observers note only somewhat more carefully that 'capitalism kills' (*Süddeutsche Zeitung*, 'Kapitalismuskritik per Graffito', 21 October 2006, reporting on a graffito slogan).[5]

What possibility of change is implied by the projection of such negative personifications onto capitalism? Capitalism is depicted as a quasi-human actor that behaves in line with its own preferences and motivations. This image entails criticism of the capitalist market economy's autonomy, as it highlights the negative consequences of leaving the regime to its own devices without restrictions or guidance. The personification of capitalism as a thief is an example for this interpretation. Thieves, as our everyday knowledge of thieves and thieving suggests, are incapable of controlling their criminal energy. Hence, they should not be tempted by their environment – and must be punished for their deeds.

This imagery suggests two courses of action: first, implementing precautionary measures that contain the immoral nature of capitalism, and second, punishing its offences (which, in turn, might have a deterrent and preventive effect). Policy measures such as the regulation of financial markets can be understood in terms of the first option. The second option, punishment, is generally not discussed. An entailment of personifying capitalism is the possibility of exonerating the 'real' actors representing the regime or at least sweeping their deeds under the carpet. As soon as discourse participants seriously consider a course of action, they do in fact tend to revert to the level of individual actors and business elites in their delegitimating statements. To the extent that the perceived problems with capitalism are grounded in structural features, it is implausible to expect behavioural change. Hence, calls for punishment are quite logically deflected to individuals and groups, the 'bangsters' and speculators (see Chapter 4). Conversely, depicting capitalism as an immoral or criminal person invites limited regulatory solutions that leave the capitalist regime principles and institutional arrangements largely untouched.

Capitalism as an Animal

The perception of capitalism as an animal underpins the frequently used metaphor of predatory capitalism. Even the late German chancellor Helmut Schmidt, hardly a radical leftist, allegedly used this expression (*Frankfurter Allgemeine Zeitung*, 'Ein Gespräch mit dem Soziologen Ralf Dahrendorf', 10 October 2008).[6] The feminist writer Sheila Rowbhotham criticizes 'unbridled capitalism': 'In the late 19th century and also in the 1930s, the impact of depression made people begin to question whether the free market and a completely unfettered form of capitalism was the best form of organising society' (*The Guardian*, 'We've Heard the Banker's Stories', 17 September 2008). In a similar vein, the journalist Jürgen Roth points out that there is no clear boundary between cleverness and crime in this unbridled capitalism (*Süddeutsche Zeitung*, 'Nur clever – oder kriminell?', 23 August 2010).[7] American writer Walter Mosley urges readers 'to look directly into the voracious maw of capitalism to see if there is a way to survive the onslaught' (*The Guardian*, 'Voice of the Excluded Debunks US Politics', 28 March 2000). The animal metaphor is often linked to other source domains such as the casino metaphor discussed below: Rules are considered necessary 'if we want to tame this casino capitalism which has the potential to ruin the whole country' (*Süddeutsche Zeitung*, 'Die Kapitalmärkte brauchen Korsettstangen', 23 September 1998).[8]

Similar to personifying metaphors, animal metaphors are closely linked with specific legitimation criteria: lack of self-regulation and lack of personal virtues and vices (Fig. 5.1). With the animal metaphor, the imagery of taming wild animals comes to the fore. This is because the animal itself is not capable of controlling its instincts. It must therefore be brought to heel, civilized and controlled by human beings before it can live a useful life. Like the casino metaphor, the animal metaphor is frequently linked with regulatory ideas. In each case, setting and effectively enforcing rules appears sufficient to solve the problems of the capitalist market economy. Wholesale institutional reform seems unnecessary.

Capitalism as a Machine

The most common metaphor of the source domain 'machine' is probably the notion of 'turbo capitalism', which is said to originate from the work of US military strategist Edward Luttwak (1995, 1999). Today, German book titles such as *Entschleunigung – Abschied vom Turbokapitalismus* ('Deceleration – Farewell to Turbo Capitalism'; Reheis 2003) echo this metaphor. In Latin, *turbo vortex* refers to a storm, a centrifugal and rotary motion. The French engineer Claude Burdin chose this phrase in 1824 to name his invention, the water wheel. Yet, which problems of capitalism are foregrounded when this originally neutral or positively connoted term is employed in critical assessments of the capitalist market economy? Like the animal metaphor, the turbo metaphor is frequently used in the context of the legitimation criteria self-regulation and economic stability. The fuel of capitalism is its workers; capitalism, unlike cars with a turbo charger, is not fuel-efficient but wasteful, runs too fast and is incapable of managing or regulating the speed of its machinery appropriately. This criticism of an inefficient system whose self-regulatory capacity is in doubt is often supported by references to the legitimation criterion distributive justice. The engine of capitalism is not only expected to produce prosperity but also to distribute it equitably – and in this it fails again: It produces injustice and 'creates islands of wealth in a sea of poverty' (*The Guardian*, 'Will the "Big Society" Bank Help Social Enterprises Do Bigger Business, in the Face of Cuts?', 23 February 2011). From the perspective of developing countries, the economy is 'rigged to the West's benefit' (*New York Times*, 'Annan Fears Backlash Over Global Crisis', 1 February 1999). A German political essayist, Jan Philipp Reemtsma, sees it as a 'generator of inequality', 'because it is a market economy, and where there is a market, there is competition, and where there is competition, there are winners and losers' (*Tagesanzeiger*, 'Wer will schon ungerecht sein?', 3 June 2003).[9] Overall, capitalism is criticized for perverting the advantages of a turbo charger, which are highly valued in the automobile industry. Consequently, some kind of regulatory intervention into the temporal malfunction of an otherwise operational machine appears necessary.

In addition, combinations of source domains occur.[10] For instance, the *Frankfurter Allgemeine Zeitung* cites German historian Hans-Ulrich Wehler with his appeal for civilizing international turbo capitalism (*Frankfurter Allgemeine Zeitung*, 'Ein Gespräch mit dem Soziologen Ralf Dahrendorf', 10 October 2008).[11] These combinations of metaphors entail the potential of both transformative and regulatory change in response to the problems of the capitalist market economy. In line with everyday knowledge, throttling or shutting down a turbo charger is the first option. It is even conceivable to use parts of the engine to construct a completely different device. Secondly, and again implying a more effective regulation instead of a transformation of the regime, domesticating it like a wild animal or civilizing it may be laborious and time-consuming, but these appear to be realistic options and feasible ways of solving its problems.

Other metaphor analyses on political regulation in the aftermath of the financial crisis (for example, Kuck and Scholz 2013: 258), however, confirm the impression that the mechanical metaphor is not stretched as widely as it could be against the background of our everyday knowledge. To switch off a turbo, to rearrange parts of an engine or to replace it is usually not suggested. Instead, as summarized by German journalist Heribert Prantl, 'financial capitalism has not become a whit more human and turbo capitalism has been kept turned on' *(Süddeutsche Zeitung*, 'Die Davids der Welt', 17 October 2011).[12] Like the person and animal metaphors, the turbo metaphor is clearly linked to regulatory ideas and serves this purpose particularly well. Unlike a living organism, a machine can be dismantled and reassembled without risking its 'death' and uncertain results. Unlike a mortal human being or living creature, the capitalist market economy can presumably be kept going and regulated at low cost.

Capitalism as a Human Body

The fourth most common metaphor explicitly conceives the capitalist market economy as a human body and thus as an entity that is more sensitive to human interference than a machine. The regime is then, for instance, depicted as 'having a tin ear for political considerations' (*Frankfurter Allgemeine Zeitung*, 'Blindflieger', 17 November 2009).[13] Frequently, the physical and mental diseases of the regime are evoked. For instance, German regional politician Janine Wissler talks about the 'madness of capitalism', as evidenced by a growing gap between the rich and the poor (*Frankfurter Allgemeine Zeitung*, 'Einigkeit im Klassenkampf', 4 October 2011).[14] Capitalism is also considered to be 'reproductively sterile' (*Frankfurter Allgemeine Zeitung*, 'Beißende Systemkritik', 15 August 2003),[15] or as 'collapsing time and again' (*Süddeutsche Zeitung*, 'Weltwirtschaftsgewitter; Karl Marx ist aktuell', 26 November 2008).[16] According to former European Commissioner Mario Monti, the crisis of 2008 struck right in the heart of the capitalist market economy, and its credibility was significantly harmed as a consequence (*New York Times*, 'In Washington, Financial Furor Is a First-Rate Chance to Assess Blame', 18 September 2008). George Soros takes a similar view when he suggests that the collapse of capitalism in the wake of the 2008 financial crisis and its lack of physical resistance are comparable to the collapse of the Soviet Union: Then as now the breakdown was not due to the inability to absorb an external shock but to design flaws of the regime that made it rot from the inside (*Süddeutsche Zeitung*, 'Auswölbungen einer Superblase', 23 February 2009).[17] In the words of British dramatist Mark Ravenhill, '[b]oom and bust are here to stay: capitalism will always be in a permanent state of crisis' (*The Guardian*,

'Theatres, Concert Halls and Opera Houses Have, Over the Years, Modelled...', 11 May 2011). The body may indeed have collapsed and be on its last legs, but it is just not dead yet: 'Yesterday, at the same time as Lehman Brothers went belly up and Merrill Lynch was bailed out, Damien Hirst made pounds 70m. This tells us that capitalism is not dead' (*The Guardian*, 'We've Heard the Banker's Stories', 17 September 2008).

These metaphors are again closely related to the classical economic legitimation criteria self-regulation and economic stability. To cope with the apparent instability of the capitalist market economy, we have to intervene and treat (regulate) the sick body, as it does obviously not have the capacity to heal itself; its immune system cannot cope. National governments are expected to act as physicians, and money is used like a drug to save the diseased body or mind of, for instance, the banks from imminent death and destruction (Kuck and Römer 2012: 87–8). However, to some observers, even surgery provides only 'a glimmer of a solution to global capitalism's ills' (*The Guardian*, 'Steve Rose on a Hallucinatory Tale of Child Abuse', 20 May 2005).

Compared to the machine metaphor, the body metaphor evokes a more limited range of options in response to the financial crisis, because the human organism works for itself, depends on itself (Hutter 1994: 290–1) and cannot be reassembled in a different way. Once we imagine capitalism as gravely sick, medical ethics obliges us to help it recover. There may be medication that can be administered as well as new therapeutic approaches such as the 'cash injection'. These measures may or may not work (Lipshaw 2010: 1558–9). In contrast to the regulation of turbo capitalism, the knock-on effect of a failed therapy is, however, momentous: We could lose that 'somebody' forever. Unlike the machine, the human body is irreplaceable. Because of its mortality, the body rejects radical transformation, and hence efforts to redesign it are limited to regulation-type options.

Capitalism as Gambling

The top five include metaphors that characterize capitalism as *gambling*. In the mid-1980s, the political economist and sociologist Susan Strange

(1986) gained public attention with her book *Casino Capitalism*. Her critique of capitalism is still attracting supporters: According to Fidel Castro, the current economic regime is unsustainable, because our planet is transformed 'into a giant casino and millions of people, sometimes even whole societies, [are] transformed into gamblers' (*Frankfurter Allgemeine Zeitung*, 'Bücher von Autoren des Reiseblatts', 15 October 2009).[18]

Since the eighteenth century, gambling has been described as 'irrational and foolish, as a defeat of civilization, and a "blind spot of the age of liberalism"' (Schnaas and Stäheli 2008: 2). The gambling metaphor and the metaphor of the immoral person are thus closely linked to each other and with the legitimation criterion personal virtues and vices (Fig. 5.1). To gamble or to encourage others to gamble has a conspicuously negative connotation – all the more so as, according to one journalist, citizens realize 'that the party is over and that the cost of expensive champagne is not necessarily borne by those who drink it' (*Neue Zürcher Zeitung*, 'Der Protest ist das Ziel', 17 October 2011).[19]

In many areas of the world, gambling is illegal or subject to strict rules. In line with this entailment of the gambling metaphor, calls for a stricter regulation of financial gambling are widespread in the public debate. Members of the German Green Party even urge a closing down of the financial manipulators' gambling operation (*Frankfurter Allgemeine Zeitung*, 'Nach dem Retten die Aufräumarbeiten', 23 September 2009).[20] Thus, the metaphor includes a variety of possible courses of action ranging from regulation to abolition. In any case, action is needed to avoid addiction or complete ruin.

Five Metaphors and One Possibility of Change

The top five metaphors do entail the possibility of human intervention in the economic regime. The entailed potential for a substantial transformation is arguably strongest in the machine and gambling metaphors, even though it is usually not made as explicit as it could be. Moreover, all five metaphors tend to evoke regulatory thought. This finding is also confirmed quantitatively, considering the number of metaphors identified for each of the legitimation criteria: Statements drawing on the legitimation criterion personal virtues and the two closely linked criteria self-regulation and contribution to economic stability use metaphors more often than the others (Fig. 5.1). In any case, the metaphors are related to legitimation criteria that make regulation seem feasible: By readjusting an existing framework, the circumstances that encourage thieves can be prevented, the predatory instincts of animals can be controlled, the error leading to the turbo charger spiralling out of control can be corrected, the human body can be healed and gambling regulated. The objects of such regulatory efforts, however, react differently to human intervention. These levels of sensitivity correspond to the possible courses of action: While a machine can be transformed into a radically different device and gambling into a game with rules (thereby substantially transforming the character of the game), the options are limited to the regulation of the status quo in the case of personifications, the animal metaphor and the body metaphor; the possibility of a transformation is not entailed in these metaphors.

Inherent in the animal and body metaphors is, at least potentially, yet another course of action: It may be impossible to transform human beings and animals, but they can be killed. Remarkably, this quite widespread social practice is not even touched upon in the metaphorical representation of the capitalist market economy. Nowhere in our text corpus is a killing of *predatory* capitalism, of capitalism as a *terrorist, murderer* or *soldier* suggested. Both the animal and the human being metaphor are used to diagnose the problems of the capitalist market economy and to provide regulatory ideas. A more radical rejection of capitalism is not entailed, and even the transformative potential of the machine and gambling metaphors is commonly not used. Instead, regulatory thought prevails.

Groups of Metaphors: Lack of Transformability

The five most common metaphors are accompanied by a range of additional ones. To shed further light on the reform options entailed in metaphorical expressions, it is helpful to categorize their source domains. I distinguish three groups of source domains in anticapitalist discourse:

- Manufactured: This category includes metaphors with source domains that underline the fact that the capitalist market economy is a manufactured human product. As discussed above, a human artefact such as a machine can be converted into a completely different one, and hence fundamentally transformed, by its creators.
- Natural: This category includes metaphors referring to natural phenomena and the animate world. The capitalist market economy appears as something naturally given. Human intervention into natural processes is usually difficult and sometimes even impossible. Regulatory options exist but are limited to exceptional cases. A sick person can undergo therapy and perhaps be healed, but it cannot be transformed into a different being because of its mortality. Unlike the machine, the body has regulatory but not transformative potential.
- Supernatural: This category comprises metaphors with source domains not covered by the laws of nature. Supernatural phenomena that cannot be explained by the human mind cannot be regulated or transformed by human beings.

This distinction implies more or less potential for changing the capitalist market economy: The transformation of a human artefact appears feasible, and minor manipulations of natural forces may also be possible, but the manipulation of supernatural forces is hardly conceivable. Table 5.2 classifies all identified source domains, ranked by frequency, into this category system. It indicates that only about a quarter of the metaphors evoke the image of an adjustable or fundamentally transformable capitalist market economy. Discourse is dominated by the idea that the capitalist market economy is something naturally given; human intervention into natural processes appears difficult or even impossible, and its outcome unclear. The key difference in entailments has already surfaced in my discussion of the machine and body metaphors: A machine can be disassembled and reassembled many times until flaws have been identified or an entirely different machine has

Table 5.2 Groups of metaphors in anticapitalist discourse

	Source domain	% metaphor group	% overall
Manufactured (transformation and regulation)	Machine/mechanics	36.1	9.6
	Gambling	14.7	3.9
	Political regime/rule	13.1	3.5
	Building	12.3	3.3
	Ruler/sovereign	8.2	2.2
	Vehicle	6.6	1.8
	Food	3.3	0.9
	Game	3.3	0.9
	Object/invention	2.5	0.7
	Manufactured, overall	100.0	26.8 (*n* = 122)
Natural (regulation in exceptional cases)	Person	52.2	34.0
	Animal	19.2	12.5
	Human body	9.4	6.4
	Plant/organism	5.7	3.7
	(Destructive) force	3.7	2.4
	Physical processes	3.7	2.4
	(Force of) nature	2.4	1.5
	Disaster, unspecific	2.0	1.3
	Pathogen/disease	1.0	0.7
	Planet	0.7	0.4
	Natural, overall	100.0	65.3 (*n* = 297)
Supernatural (no potential for human action)	Religion	70.8	3.7
	Creature/monster/vampire	16.7	0.9
	Metaphysics	12.5	0.7
	Supernatural, overall	100.0	5.3 (*n* = 24)
Other metaphors	Container	42.3	1.3
	Not classified	57.7	1.8
	Other, overall	100.0	3.1 (*n* = 14)
All metaphors			100.0 (*n* = 457)

been developed from its parts. The human body, in contrast, has potential for change but only to a certain degree – transformation is impossible. Metaphorical expressions depicting capitalism as natural and rarely adjustable are supplemented by metaphors that draw on the source domain of supernatural phenomena. Both groups of source domains entail the notion that the capitalist regime is a given order and that human beings can only partly be held responsible for its dysfunctions. As a consequence, these metaphors do not entail any realistic reform options, and people appear powerless (Peter et al. 2012: 59 reports a similar result).

Capitalism Is a Human Artefact

The machine and gambling metaphors, which dominate the category of human artefacts, have already been presented. Both metaphors strongly entail the idea that problems with capitalism can or should be dealt with through regulatory measures within the existing regime. What problem diagnoses are linked to the rest of the metaphors in this category and what potential for change do they suggest?

The late Marxist historian Eric Hobsbawm interpreted the economic turmoil in Asia towards the end of the 1990s as 'cracks in the facade of world capitalism' (*The Guardian*, 'The Marxists Return to Pronounce on the Fruit of Their Ideas – Blairism', 9 September 1998). Capitalism 'seems to be foundering on the rocks of risk, greed and general grumpiness' (*Washington Post*, 'The Power of Brand-Old Message Art', 13 January 2009). It even 'depends on disaster to clear the ground for its ceaseless rebuilding' (*The Guardian*, 'Steven Poole's Non-fiction Round-up', 27 October 2007). The building metaphor is mainly associated with classical economic legitimation criteria and used primarily to criticize the loss of economic stability (33.3 per cent of all building metaphors).

The statics of a building can be checked; its posts can be strengthened. Comparable to the total shut-down of a machine, we may tear down a building and rebuild it in parts or in its entirety, and we can assess the consequences of such human activity. The building metaphor and other metaphors in this category are indeed used for critique, but they are obviously not as effective as the top five metaphors in suggesting regulatory reform. To be sure, a new 'world economic architecture' (*Süddeutsche Zeitung*, 'Entfesselung', 27 September 2008) is sometimes called for, but tearing down the building and radically redrafting it is usually not discussed, and not even proposals for renovations and improvements within the building.[21]

The image of the economy as a *vehicle* underpins the frequent descriptions of the financial crisis as a crash of capitalism (*Süddeutsche Zeitung*, 'Und, wie schlecht geht es dir?', 28 February 2009). This metaphor, again, emphasizes inadequate self-regulation and economic instability and suggests regulatory ideas that seem appropriate for eliminating the deficits of self-regulation: Cars, ships, airplanes and other vehicles are regularly maintained to prevent technical failure and thus to minimize the risk of accidents. In line with this metaphor, at least in German-language discourse, the term brake is often used when political regulation is discussed, as in the label 'debt brake' for constitutional provisions adopted in 2009 by the German Federalism Commission to limit national debt. The possibility of recycling components of the vehicle to build something entirely new, to trade the current faulty economic regime in for a new one or to dump it in the scrap yard is rarely considered.

The same applies to metaphors describing capitalism as a human *invention* or as *food*. Sahra Wagenknecht of the German left-wing party *Die Linke* complains that Manchester capitalism is universally used as 'a blueprint for the whole globe' (*Frankfurter Allgemeine Zeitung*, 'Etwas Nettes', 3 April 2007).[22] In a similar vein, Hannah Luckcraft, a protagonist of A. L. Kennedy's novel *Paradise*, notes: 'Capitalism – whoever invented that didn't drink – no imagination' (*The Guardian*, 'The Road to Oblivion', 28 August 2004). While more and more people feel that 'the sell-by date of capitalism has expired' (*Süddeutsche Zeitung*, 'Wenn Gesetze ranzig werden', 18 August 2011),[23] others consider the capitalist market economy to be a faulty human invention. But since there are no alternatives at hand, they see no possibility to abolish it. According to the president of the US Chamber of Commerce in Germany, Fred Irwin, capitalism is 'the best system invented by people – but it also has its faults' (*Frankfurter Allgemeine Zeitung*, 'Im Gespräch: Fred Irwin, Präsident der Amerikanischen Handelskammer in Deutschland, über Krise und Kapitalismus, 10 October 2008).[24] It remains unclear how we can draw a new blueprint, grow tastier food or ensure faultless inventions. However, these metaphors entail the possibility of error correction within the framework of the existing order. And by making use of bacterial decomposition processes and genetic engineering, even a fundamental transformation of food is conceivable.

The game metaphor is often used to talk about rules that are perceived to be inappropriate. For example, the rule of the 'winner-takes-all' deal is criticized, because it destroys the incentive for the average person to play. Capitalism is depicted as a cynical game: 'Profits go to the company (and its shareholders), but the losses are borne by society at large' (*Frankfurter Allgemeine Zeitung*, 'Nach dem Retten die Aufräumarbeiten', 23 September 2009).[25] This metaphorical representation also emphasizes that capitalism is not public good-oriented. Fairer rules are therefore required. Sometimes, confidence in the game is lost. What is required, then, is again regulation: 'There can't be trust without regulation and so horse racing teaches that regulation is good rather than bad and is the thing that keeps people putting their money in' (*The Guardian*, 'Saturday Review – Profile – Jane Smiley', 2 August 2003). The game metaphor, more than any other metaphor, entails the idea of regulation by rules and more rules. However, new rules may go so far as to distort or dilute the character of the original game and to transform it into a different one altogether.

Although regimes and rulers cannot be considered to be human artefacts in the strict sense of the word, they can be thought of as products of human interaction, which is why I have assigned such metaphors to the artefact category. Everyday experience suggests that it is less easy to 'throttle' a political regime or ruler than an engine: 'Local problems can be solved or deepened by what the global economy does – often courtesy of decisions made far away from Main Street or city hall' (*Washington Post*, 'The "Glocalization" Problem', 6 June 2000). According to Tariq Ali, historian and keynote speaker at the 2002 Davos World Social Forum, the rule of capitalism and neoliberalism is a fact; it has destroyed 'basic democratic values [...], ruined the livelihood of countless people and plunged them into poverty and death' (*Neue Zürcher Zeitung*, '"Das andere Davos" im Zürcher Volkshaus', 28 January 2002).[26] The effects of this regime are often described with dramatic vocabulary, as in the following statement linking capitalism with serfdom: '[W]orkers without work or employees without rights are victims and helots of modern capitalism instead of players in a social market economy they can help shape' (*The Guardian*, 'Europe Offers Rights to Employees that are the Envy of the World', 2 July 2004). But as suggested by the daily television news, there may be large-scale transformations of regimes – and presidents, prime ministers or even kings are, at least formally, no more than 'ordinary citizens' after their abdication. Interestingly enough, this metaphor is almost always linked with democracy-centred and justice-centred legitimation criteria: Capitalism is not accountable to citizens, it violates human rights and fails to contribute to distributive justice.

However, this form of criticism is too marginal to prevail over metaphors that are more open towards regulation. The public debate is typically not driven by the question how to bring 'unaccountable capitalism' under 'democratic control' (*The Guardian*, 'Paul Foot – Of Splits and Zeros', 19 February 2003), and attacks on the 'dark empire of capitalism' (*The Guardian*, 'Pass Notes – No 1,918 – Ya Basta!', 16 July 2001) are marginalized by less fundamental criticism. Given the large shares of the other two metaphor groups (metaphors that imagine capitalism as natural or as supernatural), observers who view capitalism as a serious threat to humanity and plead for radical change are faced with considerable linguistic and cognitive hurdles.

Capitalism Is Something Natural

In the most frequent category, 'natural', I differentiate between metaphors that do not exclude the possibility of altering the capitalist market economy – although it might require a lot of patience and come at high cost – and those which deny that possibility from the outset. Both subgroups, however, entail the impossibility of a substantial transformation.

The first subgroup comprises the person, animal and body metaphors mentioned above. In the case of the animal metaphor, it seems evident that human beings need to master the animal and subject it to their will, and that unbridled capitalism and the 'debilitating nature of the capitalist system' (*The Guardian*, 'The Hard Sell', 20 August 2011) must be tamed. As in the context of the body metaphor, imagining capitalism as a harmful pathogen is accompanied by explicit treatment options: Capitalism is a 'cancer that keeps returning unless you did cut it out' (*The Times*, 'Edinburgh Theatre', 9 August 2011). But this problem-solving approach is associated with uncertainty; one can only hope that isolating the affected parts of the body will be sufficient. A plausible diagnosis in the context of the pathogen metaphor is that large parts of the body are affected and therefore the body cannot be saved.

While these metaphors still involve a certain possibility of change, the second subgroup of the category 'natural' denies human transformative power almost completely. Our experience is no real guide when we are forced to think about ways to rein in a capitalist market economy which is depicted as a destructive force, experience with early warning systems notwithstanding. In a similar vein, the notion of 'disaster capitalism', as in Naomi Klein's book *The Shock Doctrine* (published in 2007, shortly before the 2008 financial crisis), has no clear entailments related to the nature of capitalism, to the origins of its problems or to ways of solving them. The forces of nature cannot be controlled by human beings, and only Hollywood movies would have us believe that they can destroy other planets or push them out of their trajectories. Ultimately, we might only be able to mitigate damage by, for example, opening the 'rescue package'. What ensues is a feeling of helplessness: The damage cannot be undone, and what is more, it might cost lives.

In the context of gardening, certain *plants* and *organisms* are classified as 'parasites' – and even if some 'pests' can now be fought with 'weed killer' and 'pest controls', it is still a fact of life that many biological attacks and processes are beyond the control of human beings.[27] Democracy-centred legitimation criteria are most frequently associated with the plant metaphor: Capitalism as a poisonous plant harms the public good; its excesses are irreversible and – left unchecked – undermine democratic stability. Therefore, the 'rotten system of capitalist exploitation and imperialist domination must be swept away' (*New York Times*, 'Subpoena Seeks Records About Delegate Lists on Web', 30 August 2004).

Capitalism Is Supernatural

If the economic regime is conceived as a bloodsucking vampire, as the monster 'Sumsilatipak' (capitalism spelled out backwards in German, *Süddeutsche Zeitung*, 'Dietmar Dath bekämpft das Monster Sumsilatipak', 17 April 2010),[28] as an evil force or pale ghost, there is little space for even imagining that human beings might be able to introduce some kind of change. At least for those who believe, a prayer might help to appease the 'god of turbo capitalism' (*Neue Zürcher Zeitung*, 'Phantomschmerz der Leere', 10 September 2011).[29] However, gods can be neither transformed nor regulated, as explicitly stated by documentary maker Michael Moore: 'Capitalism is an evil, and you cannot regulate evil. You have to eliminate it and replace it with something that is good for all people and that something is democracy' (*The Guardian*, 'Freefall', 30 January 2010). In a similar vein, the analysis by Peter et al. (2012: 60) of figurative speech used in the wake of the 2008 financial crisis shows that metaphors from the source domain of metaphysics are rare and hardly ever linked with suggested courses of political action.

In contrast, statements of policymakers sometimes convey a sense of omnipotence when they suggest that the capitalist 'monster' can be tamed like an animal, as exemplified by Angela Merkel in a press conference following the G20 Summit in London in 2009: 'The monster, it is being tamed' (Merkel cited by Wagner and Hagelüken 2014: 12). The monster metaphor, although used only once in our data, is a particularly interesting one, because similar to religious metaphors, it does not immediately invite us to think about change brought about by human action. Yet, linked with the taming metaphor, it suggests such a potential. This belief in the human ability to tame a monster is better understood after a glance at the history of the monster narrative. Foucault (2003: 76–8, 86–8) has shown that at the beginning of the nineteenth century, criminals were dubbed as moral monsters, hybrids between humans and animals, and as acting contrary to societal rules by definition. The parallels between the monster metaphor and the immoral or criminal person metaphor are obvious.

It is worth noting that Foucault describes how the taming of the monster is accompanied by policy measures that are themselves outside the law. In a similar vein, highly unpopular policies are currently justified with the need to tame the monster of capitalism. In the context of political crisis management, exceptional situations require extraordinary measures (Kuck and Römer 2012: 81). The notion of a monster that can be tamed is gladly welcomed by some members of the political establishment; it is used to develop a narrative framework for defining and defending their actions, and to counter the image of helplessness and inactivity – for instance, in the context of criticism directed at national decision-making processes on the EU bailout packages.

Transformation Ahead?

In summary, the analysis of delegitimating metaphors reveals that capitalism is mostly regarded as something naturally given. This dominant metaphor group excludes the possibility of transforming the regime from the outset; there is only narrowly circumscribed scope for human action – and only in the sense of regulation within the given order. It is remarkable, however, that even the source domain of supernatural forces, which on the face of it entails limited reform options, gives rise to a metaphor – the monster metaphor – that suggests otherwise and is therefore actively promoted by political actors.

Overall, the impression gained in considering the five most common single metaphors is confirmed: The frequently used machine and gambling metaphors entail a transformative potential. However, this potential is generally not expressed explicitly. Even where the highest potential for change is given, entailments suggesting regulatory reform dominate.

Does the metaphorical composition of anticapitalist discourse change after the financial crisis, though, and have artefact metaphors with their transformative potential become more frequent? Figure 5.2 clearly shows that there is no such development. The notion that the economic

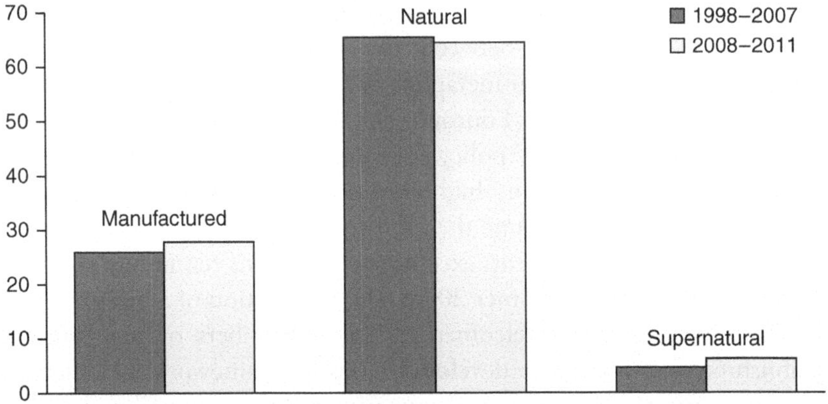

Fig. 5.2 Metaphor groups (%) pre-/post-financial crisis (*n* = 457)

regime is something naturally given is stable. Remarkably, the share of the artefact metaphors has increased only marginally after the financial crisis, mostly due to the slightly more frequent use of the gambling metaphor. The growing problem pressure in the wake of the financial crisis has not translated into a greater share of metaphors associated with uncomplicated regulatory ideas, as one might have expected. Moreover, the marginally higher share of artefact metaphors is compensated by equally strong growth in the category 'supernatural' and thus in the frequency of metaphors that portray capitalism as unsusceptible to human intervention.

Conclusion

When the international financial crisis began in the autumn of 2008, some observers immediately heard the 'death knell of capitalism' sounding (*Tagesanzeiger*, 'Nach wie vor keine Anzeichen für eine Zeitenwende', 14 October 2008).[30] Yet, with hindsight, this knell was hardly deafening; in fact, it was rather soft and has all but fallen silent today. To better understand why there were only distant rumblings of a debate instead of a more assertive and transformative critique of capitalism, I considered the metaphors used in media discourse. Central to this contribution were three questions: What metaphors are used to express anticapitalist views? Has the metaphorical repertoire changed after the financial crisis? What potential for change do the metaphors entail – and which courses of action are downplayed or hidden? To answer these questions, I focused on delegitimating metaphors from our corpus of legitimation statements.

An analysis of metaphorical anticapitalism is useful for at least three reasons: Firstly, it reveals that the metaphors employed in anticapitalist discourse entail relatively plausible regulatory ideas. This suggests that we are not completely powerless when it comes to changing the status quo of capitalism. The frequent use of machine and gambling metaphors suggests a preference for problem-solving *within* the existing framework. These regulatory ideas are also supported by the animal and body metaphors. The notions of throttling an engine, of containing a person's lack of virtue or of taming an animal instinct as well as therapies suggested for healing a diseased body are different metaphorical expressions of one and the same course of action.

Despite the frequency of such regulatory entailments, one should not forget that one-third of all metaphors interpret capitalism as a (mostly) immoral person – and that such metaphors are perhaps not the best way to open a path towards radical transformation. One can provide incentives for a more virtuous behaviour of economic actors. However, where only the punishment of actors is demanded, capitalism itself – as a structure – 'gets away scot-free'. Secondly, it is striking that metaphors that entail more transformative potential are not as widely used as they could be. It is hard to imagine how a machine which has broken down and is beyond repair could be dismantled and transformed into something radically different or how this transformative process and its outcome might look like.

This use of metaphors thus sets cognitive limits for thinking about, discussing and mobilizing support for radical change of the capitalist market economy. Only gambling, if underpinned by the right rules, might pay off. However, as shown by Emel Cetin (2012: 98, 106) for financial capitalism, no more than short-term solutions to the problems of capitalism are entailed in the gambling metaphor while demands for restructuring the financial system 'remain vague and moralizing'. If the end of capitalism fails to capture the imagination, no public debate that goes beyond the notion of short-term regulation can emerge.

Thirdly, the analysis reveals that metaphors entailing a fundamental transformative potential are rarely used and that this potential is not even fully explored. Even after the financial crisis, metaphors portraying the economy as manufactured and susceptible to human intervention entail little or no potential for change. Hence, the discursive condition that might have enabled the more effective mobilization of support for a genuine transformation of capitalism – a clearer dominance of artefact metaphors with the potential for change they entail – has not emerged. The lack of ideational blueprints for an institutional transformation explains why the window of opportunity provided by the legitimation crisis was not used more effectively by anticapitalists to challenge the status quo. Taking into account that criticism of the capitalist market economy is predominantly uttered by journalists and other representatives of the cultural sphere rather than business or political elites (see Chapters 3, 4 and 7), and that these speakers prefer metaphors without any transformative potential, more assertive anticapitalist discourse and institutional change remain quite unrealistic.

Notes

1. I would like to thank the *Käte-Hamburger-Kolleg*/Centre for Global Cooperation Research for generously supporting my research.
2. The catalogue of source domains was derived from the following studies: Charteris-Black and Musolff 2003; Beer and De Landtsheer 2004: 19–21; Charteris-Black 2004: 214–27, 2005: 200; Schneider 2008; Gronau and Schneider 2009: 15; Alejo 2010: 1140; Rojo López and Orts Llopis 2010: 3305, 3307; Wengeler and Ziem 2010: 347; Peter et al. 2012: 59.

3. 'So wie heute vielen ein Schwarzbuch über die Verbrechen des Kapitalismus wichtiger erscheint als eines über die Verbrechen des Kommunismus, kritisierte man den Kapitalismus und lobte die sozialistischen Errungenschaften der DDR'. This and all other translations of text passages in German are my own.
4. 'Sommer sagte auf dem DGB-Bundeskongress in Berlin, der "brutale Kapitalismus" der Investoren, Hedgefonds und Rating-Agenturen zu Lasten der Arbeitnehmer dürfe nicht länger hingenommen werden'.
5. '"Capitalism kills" hat jemand fein säuberlich auf den Boden vor dem Haupteingang der Sparkasse in der Unteren Stadt gesprüht'.
6. 'Von "Raubtierkapitalismus" spricht aber auch der nicht gerade als linksradikal geltende Helmut Schmidt. Und aus allen Richtungen hört man Kritik an überhöhten Managergehältern und obszönen Abfindungen'.
7. 'Im zügellosen Kapitalismus war und ist die Grenze zwischen Cleverness und Kriminalität bekanntlich fließend, und manche Schlussfolgerung Roths mag zwar naheliegend sein, ist aber nur schwer zu beweisen'.
8. 'Heute, angesichts um sich greifender Krisen, weiß man, daß gewisse Spielregeln notwendig sind, wenn man jenen "Casino-Kapitalismus" zähmen will, der ganze Länder in den Ruin treiben kann'.
9. 'Der Kapitalismus ist ein Ungleichheitsgenerator, weil er eine Marktwirtschaft ist, und wo Markt ist, gibt es Konkurrenz, und wo es Konkurrenz gibt, gibt es Gewinner und Verlierer. Es werden Chancen ungleich verteilt'.
10. 'Dem Raubtier auf die Zähne gefühlt: Turbokapitalismus versus Soziale Marktwirtschaft'.
11. 'Der internationale Turbokapitalismus muss zivilisiert werden! Der Schlussgedanke von Hans-Ulrich Wehlers "Deutscher Gesellschaftsgeschichte" klingt prophetisch. Kehrt die Klassenfrage zurück?'
12. 'Der Finanzkapitalismus wurde keinen Deut menschlicher, der Turbo des Kapitalismus blieb angeschaltet'.
13. 'Nein, Imageprobleme eines, der fürs Allerwichtigste zuständig ist, das Schicksal nämlich, von dem zugleich doch alle wissen, dass die Wirtschaft auf dem politischen Ohr ganz taub ist. Siehe Boni, siehe General Motors'.
14. 'Die Fraktionsvorsitzende im Landtag, Janine Wissler, sprach vom "Wahnsinn des Kapitalismus"; dieser führe dazu, dass die Kluft zwischen Reich und Arm immer größer werden müsse – und deshalb in Frage zu stellen sei'.

15. ‘In Washingtons Grundphilosophie (“Washington Consensus”) vom ungehinderten Marktzugang und einer möglichst geringen Rolle des Staates in der Wirtschaft sieht der Verfasser so etwas wie die ideologische Kampagne eines “Raubtierkapitalismus” (Helmut Schmidt) zu Lasten der Mehrzahl der Menschheit im allgemeinen und einer ausgewogenen Sozialpolitik im besonderen. Eine Weltregion nach der anderen, so Kurz, erweise sich als kapitalistisch “reproduktionsunfähig”’.
16. ‘Seit Beginn der siebziger Jahre des 20. Jahrhunderts haben die Regierungen die Marktwirtschaft entfesselt – erst in den Industrieländern, später in den Schwellenländern. Sie haben Zoll- und Handelsschranken beseitigt, Staatskonzerne privatisiert und die Finanzmärkte dereguliert. Doch der Kapitalismus stürzt immer wieder in die Krise’.
17. ‘Für Soros ist das Fiasko an den Finanzmärkten höchstens mit dem Zusammenbruch der Sowjetunion vergleichbar. Damals wie heute kollabierte ein soziales System – nicht weil es unfähig war, einen äußeren Schock zu absorbieren, sondern weil es Konstruktionsfehler aufwies, die es von innen marode machten’.
18. ‘Er ist sogar ein Prophet, denn in seiner Rede zum vierzigsten Jahrestag der kubanischen Revolution hat er die aktuelle Weltfinanzkrise vorausgesehen: “Dass die gegenwärtige Wirtschaftsordnung unhaltbar ist, zeigt die Schwäche und Verletzlichkeit des Systems, das unseren Planeten in ein gigantisches Kasino, Millionen Menschen und gelegentlich sogar ganze Gesellschaften in Glücksspieler verwandelt hat. Eine derartige Deformation führt die Weltwirtschaft zum unvermeidbaren Desaster”’.
19. ‘Die Bürger realisieren, dass die Party ein Ende hat – und die Kosten des teuren Sekts nicht zwingend von jenen getragen werden, die am meisten getrunken haben’.
20. ‘Die Grünen wollen ebenfalls. Denn sie wollen “die Spielhölle der Finanzjongleure” schließen, “Exzessen bei Managergehältern einen Riegel vorschieben”’.
21. ‘Jenseits des unmittelbaren Krisenmanagements ist eine neue Weltwirtschaftsarchitektur gefragt, die dem Treiben der Märkte auf allen Ebenen enge Grenzen setzt’.
22. ‘Es ist schon ziemlich ärgerlich, dass in Gesprächsrunden wie dieser immer erst jemand von Linksaußen (hier also Sahra Wagenknecht) darauf hinweisen muss, dass wir in einer Zeit leben, die den Manchester-Kapitalismus als Blaupause für den ganzen Globus kennt’.

23. 'Das Brot verschimmelt, das Fleisch vergammelt, die Sache stinkt. In der Finanzwelt stinkt auch ziemlich viel; daher haben immer mehr Leute das Gefühl, dass das Haltbarkeitsdatum des Kapitalismus abgelaufen ist'.
24. 'Und Kapitalismus ist das beste System, das die Menschen erfunden haben – aber es hat auch Fehler'.
25. 'Der Casino-Kapitalismus habe abgewirtschaftet. Er sei ein zynisches Spiel nach dem Muster gewesen: "Die Gewinne dem Unternehmen (und seinen Anteilseignern), die Verluste trägt die Gesellschaft"'.
26. 'Die Herrschaft von Kapitalismus und Neoliberalismus sei nun einmal eine Tatsache. Sie hätten grundlegende demokratische Werte zerstört, die Existenz zahlloser Menschen ruiniert und sie in Armut und Tod getrieben'.
27. The German Nazi regime of the 1940s propagated the parasite metaphor to carry out the dehumanization and mass destruction of millions of people (Urban 2014).
28. 'Hier verschanzt sich das leibhaftige Geld, ein bleiches Gespenst mit "ungesunden gelben Augen", bewacht von Sumsilatipak (Kapitalismus rückwärts gelesen), einem Monster, das die Welt im Würgegriff hat, und hier kommt es zum Endkampf zwischen Gut und Böse in Dietmar Daths neuem Buch "Deutschland macht dicht"'.
29. 'Doch wer wollte behaupten, der Gott des Turbokapitalismus sei in seinen Trümmern begraben worden?'
30. 'Wir erleben eine Finanzkrise von historischem Ausmaß. Einige hören bereits das Totenglöckchen auf den Kapitalismus läuten'.

References

Alejo, Rafael. 2010. 'Where Does the Money Go? An Analysis of the Container Metaphor in Economics: The Market and the Economy'. *Journal of Pragmatics* 42(4): 1137–50.

Beer, Francis A. and Christ'l De Landtsheer. 2004. 'Metaphors, Politics, and World Politics. Introduction'. In *Metaphorical World Politics*, eds. Francis A. Beer and Christ'l De Landtsheer. Michigan: Michigan State University Press, 5–52.

Blyth, Mark. 2002. *Great Transformations. Economic Ideas and Institutional Change in the Twentieth Century*. Cambridge: Cambridge University Press.

Cetin, Emel. 2012. '"Denn sie wissen nicht, was sie tun." Eine Diskursanalyse über die Finanzkrise in deutschen Zeitungen'. In *Krise, Cash &*

Kommunikation. Die Finanzkrise in den Medien, eds. Anja Peltzer, Kathrin Lämmle and Andreas Wagenknecht. Konstanz: UVK, 95–110.

Charteris-Black, Jonathan. 2004. *Corpus Approaches to Critical Metaphor Analysis*. Basingstoke: Palgrave Macmillan.

Charteris-Black, Jonathan. 2005. 'Myth, Metaphor and Leadership'. In *Politicians and Rhetoric. The Persuasive Power of Metaphor*. Basingstoke: Palgrave Macmillan, 197–212.

Charteris-Black, Jonathan and Andreas Musolff. 2003. '"Battered Hero" or "Innocent Victim"? A Comparative Study of Metaphors for Euro Trading in British and German Financial Reporting'. *English for Specific Purposes* 22(2): 153–76.

Cienki, Alan and Dvora Yanow. 2013. 'Why Metaphor and Other Tropes? Linguistic Approaches to Analysing Policies and the Political'. *Journal of International Relations and Development* 16(2): 167–76.

Foucault, Michel. 2003. *Die Anormalen. Vorlesungen am Collège de France (1974-1975)*. Frankfurt am Main: Suhrkamp.

Gronau, Jennifer and Steffen Schneider. 2009. *Metaphorical Concepts in the Construction of International Legitimacy*. IPSA Working Paper Series of the Committee on Concepts and Methods 37 (November), http://www.concepts-methods.org/Files/WorkingPaper/PC_37_Schneider_Gronau.pdf (last accessed September 15, 2016).

Hitzler, Ronald. 1991. 'Dummheit als Methode: Eine dramatologische Textinterpretation'. In *Qualitativ-empirische Sozialforschung. Konzepte, Methoden, Analysen*, eds. Detlef Garz and Klaus Kraimer. Opladen: Westdeutscher Verlag, 295–318.

Hitzler, Ronald. 2005. 'The Reconstruction of Meaning. Notes on German Interpretive Sociology'. *Forum Qualitative Social Research* 6(3), www.qualitative-research.net.

Hülsse, Rainer. 2003. 'Sprache ist mehr als Argumentation. Zur wirklichkeitskonstituierenden Rolle von Metaphern'. *Zeitschrift für Internationale Beziehungen* 10(2): 211–46.

Hülsse, Rainer. 2006. 'Imagine the EU: The Metaphorical Construction of a Supra-nationalist Identity'. *Journal of International Relations and Development* 9(4): 396–421.

Hutter, Michael. 1994. 'Organism as a Metaphor in German Economic Thought'. In *Natural Images in Economic Thought*, ed. Philip Mirowski. Cambridge: Cambridge University Press, 289–321.

Klein, Naomi. 2007. *The Shock Doctrine. The Rise of Disaster Capitalism*. New York: Metropolitan Books.

Kövecses, Zoltan. 2010. *Metaphor: A Practical Introduction*. Second Edition. Oxford: Oxford University Press.

Kuck, Kristin and David Römer. 2012. 'Metaphern und Argumentationsmuster im Mediendiskurs zur "Finanzkrise"'. In *Krise, Cash & Kommunikation. Die Finanzkrise* in *den Medien*, eds. Anja Peltzer, Kathrin Lämmle and Andreas Wagenknecht. Konstanz: UVK, 71–93.

Kuck, Kristin and Ronny Scholz. 2013. 'Quantitative und qualitative Methoden der Diskursanalyse als Ansatz einer rekonstruktiven Weltpolitikforschung. Zur Analyse eines internationalen Krisendiskurses in der deutschen Presse'. In *Rekonstruktive Methoden der Weltpolitikforschung. Anwendungsbeispiele und Entwicklungstendenzen*, eds. Ulrich Franke and Ulrich Roos. Baden-Baden: Nomos, 219–69.

Lakoff, George and Mark Johnson. 2003. *Metaphors We Live By*. New Edition. Chicago: University of Chicago Press.

Lipshaw, Jeffrey M. 2010. 'The Financial Crisis of 2008-2009: Capitalism Didn't Fail, but the Metaphors Got a "C"'. *Minnesota Law Review* 95(5): 1532–67.

Luttwak, Edward. 1995. 'Turbo-charged Capitalism and Its Consequences'. *London Review of Books* (2 November), 6–7.

Luttwak, Edward. 1999. *Turbo-Capitalism. Winners and Losers in the Global Economy*. New York: Harper Collins.

McCloskey, Donald. 1995. 'Metaphors Economists Live By'. *Social Research* 62(2): 215–37.

Münnich, Sascha. 2012. 'Von Heuschrecken und Bienen: Profit als Legitimationsproblem'. In *Der Aufstieg der Legitimitätspolitik. Rechtfertigung und Kritik politisch-ökonomischer Ordnungen*, eds. Anna Geis, Frank Nullmeier and Christopher Daase. Baden-Baden: Nomos, 283–301.

Peter, Nina, Christine Knoop, Catarina von Wedemeyer and Oliver Lubrich. 2012. 'Sprachbilder der Krise. Metaphern im medialen und politischen Diskurs'. In *Krise, Cash & Kommunikation. Die Finanzkrise in den Medien*, eds. Anja Peltzer, Kathrin Lämmle and Andreas Wagenknecht. Konstanz: UVK, 49–70.

Pragglejazz Group. 2007. 'MIP. A Method for Identifying Metaphorically Used Words in Discourse'. *Metaphor and Symbol* 22(1): 1–39.

Reheis, Fritz. 2003. *Entschleunigung. Abschied vom Turbokapitalismus*. Munich: Riemann.

Rojo López, Ana María and María Ángeles Orts Llopis. 2010. 'Metaphorical Pattern Analysis in Financial Texts: Framing the Crisis in Positive or Negative Metaphorical Terms'. *Journal of Pragmatics* 42(12): 3300–13.

Schnaas, Dieter and Urs Stäheli. 2008. 'Die kalkulierte Unvernunft. Interview des Wirtschaftswoche-Chefreporters Dieter Schnaas mit Urs Stäheli'. *Wirtschaftswoche (online)*, http://www.wiwo.de/finanzen/boersenpsychologie-die-kalkulierte-unvernunft/5123156.html (last accessed September 15, 2016).

Schneider, Steffen. 2008. 'Exploring the Metaphorical (De-)Construction of Legitimacy: A Comparison of Legitimation Discourses in American and British Newspapers'. In *Political Language and Metaphor*, eds. Terrell Carver and Jernej Pikalo. London: Routledge, 83–102.

Spencer, Alexander. 2011. 'Bild Dir Deine Meinung: Die metaphorische Konstruktion des Terrorismus in den Medien'. *Zeitschrift für Internationale Beziehungen* 18(1): 47–76.

Steen, Gerard, Aletta Dorst, Berenike Herrmann, Anna Kaal, Tina Krennmayr and Trintje Pasma. 2010. *A Method for Linguistic Metaphor Identification from MIP to MIPVU*. Amsterdam: John Benjamins.

Strange, Susan. 1986. *Casino Capitalism*. Oxford: Blackwell.

Urban, Monika. 2014. *Von Ratten, Schmeißfliegen und Heuschrecken. Judenfeindliche Tiersymbolisierungen und die postfaschistischen Grenzen des Sagbaren*. Konstanz: UVK.

Wæver, Ole. 2005. 'European Integration and Security: Analysing French and German Discourses on State, Nation, and Europe'. In *Discourse Theory in European Politics. Identity, Policy and Governance*, eds. David Howarth and Jacob Torfing. Basingstoke: Palgrave Macmillan, 33–67.

Wagner, Lorenz and Alexander Hagelüken. 2014. 'Freut euch nicht zu früh'. *Süddeutsche Zeitung Magazin* (21 May), 8–19.

Wengeler, Martin and Alexander Ziem. 2010. '"Wirtschaftskrisen" im Wandel der Zeit: Eine diskurslinguistische Pilotstudie zum Wandel von Argumentationsmustern und Metapherngebrauch'. In *Diskursiver Wandel*, ed. Achim Landwehr. Wiesbaden: VS, 335–54.

Cited Newspaper Articles

Frankfurter Allgemeine Zeitung 15 August 2003. 'Beißende Systemkritik'.

Frankfurter Allgemeine Zeitung 3 April 2007. 'Etwas Nettes'.

Frankfurter Allgemeine Zeitung 10 October 2008. 'Ein Gespräch mit dem Soziologen Ralf Dahrendorf'.

Frankfurter Allgemeine Zeitung 10 October 2008. 'Im Gespräch: Fred Irwin, Präsident der Amerikanischen Handelskammer in Deutschland, über Krise und Kapitalismus'.
Frankfurter Allgemeine Zeitung 23 September 2009. 'Nach dem Retten die Aufräumarbeiten'.
Frankfurter Allgemeine Zeitung 15 October 2009. 'Bücher von Autoren des Reiseblatts'.
Frankfurter Allgemeine Zeitung 17 November 2009. 'Blindflieger'.
Frankfurter Allgemeine Zeitung 4 October 2011. 'Einigkeit im Klassenkampf'.
Süddeutsche Zeitung 8 June 1998. 'Der Terror gehörte schon mit zum Anfang'.
Süddeutsche Zeitung 23 September 1998. 'Die Kapitalmärkte brauchen Korsettstangen'.
Süddeutsche Zeitung 21 October 2006. 'Kapitalismuskritik per Graffito'.
Süddeutsche Zeitung 27 September 2008. 'Entfesselung'.
Süddeutsche Zeitung 26 November 2008. 'Weltwirtschaftsgewitter; Karl Marx ist aktuell'.
Süddeutsche Zeitung 23 February 2009. 'Auswölbungen einer Superblase'.
Süddeutsche Zeitung 28 February 2009. 'Und, wie schlecht geht es dir?'.
Süddeutsche Zeitung 17 April 2010. 'Dietmar Dath bekämpft das Monster Sumsilatipak'.
Süddeutsche Zeitung 23 August 2010. 'Nur clever – oder kriminell?'
Süddeutsche Zeitung 18 August 2011. 'Wenn Gesetze ranzig werden'.
Süddeutsche Zeitung 17 October 2011. 'Die Davids der Welt'.
Neue Zürcher Zeitung 28 January 2002. '"Das andere Davos" im Zürcher Volkshaus'.
Neue Zürcher Zeitung 10 September 2011. 'Phantomschmerz der Leere'.
Neue Zürcher Zeitung 17 October 2011. 'Der Protest ist das Ziel'.
Tagesanzeiger 3 June 2003. 'Wer will schon ungerecht sein?'
Tagesanzeiger 14 October 2008. 'Nach wie vor keine Anzeichen für eine Zeitenwende'.
The Guardian 9 September 1998. 'The Marxists Return to Pronounce on the Fruit of Their Ideas'.
The Guardian 28 March 2000. 'Voice of the Excluded Debunks US Politics'.
The Guardian 16 July 2001. 'Pass Notes – No 1,918 – Ya Basta!'
The Guardian 19 February 2003. 'Paul Foot – Of Splits and Zeros'.
The Guardian 2 August 2003. 'Saturday Review – Profile – Jane Smiley'.
The Guardian 2 July 2004. 'Europe Offers Rights to Employees that are the Envy of the World'.

The Guardian 28 August 2004. 'The Road to Oblivion'.
The Guardian 20 May 2005. 'Steve Rose on a Hallucinatory Tale of Child Abuse'.
The Guardian 2 July 2007. 'Gordon Brown is One of Many Using Religious Shorthand to Show Moral Purpose'.
The Guardian 27 October 2007. 'Steven Poole's Non-fiction Round-up'.
The Guardian 12 January 2008. 'Affluenza'.
The Guardian 17 September 2008. 'We've Heard the Banker's Stories'.
The Guardian 30 January 2010. 'Freefall'.
The Guardian 23 February 2011. 'Will the "Big Society" Bank Help Social Enterprises Do Bigger Business, in the Face of Cuts?'
The Guardian 11 May 2011. 'Theatres, Concert Halls and Opera Houses Have, Over the Years, Modelled . . . '.
The Guardian 20 August 2011. 'The Hard Sell'.
The Times 18 April 2000. 'Mayoral Hopefuls Put Their Case to Voters'.
The Times 9 August 2011. 'Edinburgh Theatre'.
New York Times 1 February 1999. 'Annan Fears Backlash Over Global Crisis'.
New York Times 30 August 2004. 'Subpoena Seeks Records About Delegate Lists on Web'.
New York Times 18 September 2008. 'In Washington, Financial Furor Is a First-Rate Chance to Assess Blame'.
New York Times 19 August 2009. 'Lawyer and Author Adds His Objections to Settling the Google Book Lawsuit'.
Washington Post 6 June 2000. 'The "Glocalization" Problem'.
Washington Post 13 January 2009. 'The Power Of Brand-Old Message Art'.

6

Narrative Legitimation: The Capitalist Market Economy as a Success Story

Dominika Biegoń

The previous chapter examined the *critical* side of media debates on the legitimacy of capitalism by scrutinizing the use of metaphors in delegitimating statements. It could be shown that delegitimizers lacked the discursive power to mobilize support for a process of institutional change in the wake of the 2008 financial crisis. The present chapter focuses on the *other* side of media debates – pro-market discourse – to further explore the conditions that fostered the stability of the economic regime. In line with the theoretical framework developed in Chapter 1, I argue that the existence of a stable and coherent pro-market discourse that reduced uncertainty by providing a conclusive story on the merits of the capitalist market economy contributed to warding off any transformative change of the regime.

A qualitative approach to the data – narrative analysis – has been selected to scrutinize the content and structure of market-friendly

D. Biegoń (✉)
Friedrich-Ebert-Stiftung, Berlin, Germany
e-mail: dominika.biegon@fes.de

S. Schneider et al. (eds.), *Capitalism and Its Legitimacy in Times of Crisis*, Transformations of the State,
DOI 10.1007/978-3-319-53765-8_6

discourse. The method concentrates on narratives as configurations of ideas about the functioning and legitimacy of the capitalist market economy and thus focuses on how certain discourse elements relate to each other even if taken up by different speakers in different texts. More than a mere combination of discourse elements, a narrative is a cohesive and stable form of discourse combining a range of elements that are mutually dependent. A cohesive configuration of such elements can have a decisive impact on the political significance of discourse. Defenders of capitalism are likely to be more successful in stabilizing the capitalist market economy if they can rely on a coherent narrative that justifies the benefits of capitalism.

The chapter is therefore concerned with the following questions: Is it possible to reconstruct market-friendly narratives in our text corpus? Has there been a change of narratives over time? In a first step, the method of narrative discourse analysis is described. The next two parts of the chapter present the empirical results in greater detail. I argue that there are two market-friendly narratives structuring public debates on the acceptability of the capitalist economic regime – a wealth narrative and a freedom narrative. The chapter ends with a comparative analysis of these two narratives and classifies them according to the typology of legitimation criteria proposed in Chapter 2.

Method: Narrative Discourse Analysis

Narrative has recently become a widely used concept in the social sciences. The origins of narrative analysis as a text-analytical method go back to two strands of literature. While a range of works draw on literary studies, categorizing texts with the help of Northrop Frye's (1965) famous typology of four archetypal plots, the theoretical roots of other social scientific narrative analyses lie in structural linguistics, particularly in the field of narrative semiotics.

The analysis of texts on the basis of the four archetypal plots has been increasingly taken up by the social sciences in the wake of Hayden White's (1987) seminal narrative analysis of theories of history. White argues that the description and interpretation of historical events typically takes the form of one of four archetypical plot structures (tragedy, satire, romance or comedy). By establishing a connection between history and literary studies, White pursues a methodological approach that negates the radical distinction between historical and fictional narratives. Social science applications use White's distinction of the four archetypical plot structures in a similar vein (King and Langston 2008; Kuusisto 2009; Rovisco 2010; Schneider et al. 2010).

Narrative semiotics is another important starting point for narrative analysis. The works of Vladimir Propp and Algirdas Julien Greimas are particularly pertinent. Initially, the objective of these two authors was to reconstruct the deep narrative structure of Russian fairy tales and other types of texts (Propp 1968; Greimas 1971, 1987). Their method of text analysis was subsequently adapted for the social sciences (Barthes 1994; for an overview, see also Titscher et al. 1998: 161–9).

The following narrative analysis is based on this second research tradition and employs the actant model developed by Algirdas Julien Greimas (1971, 1987) to reconstruct the fundamental meanings and structures shaping pro-market discourse in the British, German, Swiss and US quality press. I draw on a selection of articles from the joint text corpus. As my focus is on the pro-market side of legitimation discourse, only articles that contain at least one positive evaluation of the following legitimation objects (see Chapter 3) were considered: 'capitalist market economy as a whole'; 'market economy'; '(financial) capitalism'; different variants of the capitalist market economy (in particular, 'free market economy' v. 'social market economy'). Moreover, only articles in which authors provided a reason for their positive evaluation of the capitalist market economy – that is, an explicit legitimation criterion – were considered. This procedure yielded 159 articles (Table 6.1).

Table 6.1 Pro-market discourse, articles by country and time period

	CH	DE	UK	US
1998–2007	14	39	17	10
2008–2011	11	38	22	8
Σ	25	77	39	18

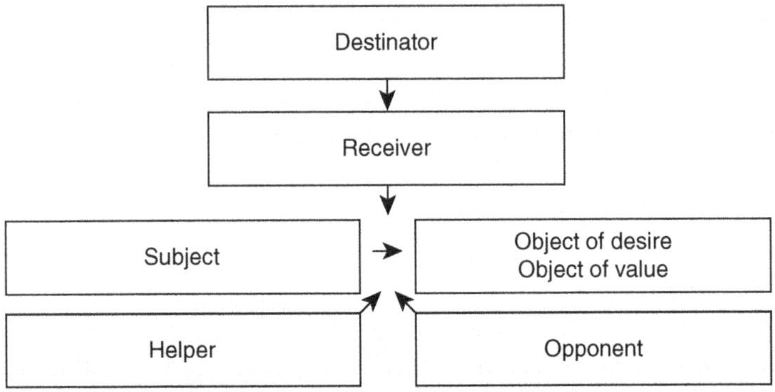

Fig. 6.1 Greimas's actant model

The narrative analysis of this subcorpus was guided by Greimas's actant model. According to Greimas, each actant assumes a particular function in the narrative.[1] As such, actants are not to be confounded with the characters of a narrative (Bal 1999: 114–32). The concept encompasses human beings and other active and inactive forces if they assume a particular role in the story (Greimas and Courtés 1982: 294).[2] More specifically, Greimas distinguishes six actants (Fig. 6.1):

- *Destinator*: The function of the destinator is to provide a horizon of norms and values for the other actants. Therefore, some authors define the destinator as the 'source of values in a narration' (Viehöver 2006: 196; Fiol 1990: 381). The subject of the narrative (see below) feels obliged to act according to this system of norms and values.
- *Receiver:* The receiver is the addressee of the norms and values promoted by the destinator of a narrative.
- *Subject*: The subject is the hero of the narrative and as such the central figure in the story. It is the destiny of the subject that is traced in the narrative. The core of every narrative is the subject seeking to acquire the object, thereby bringing about the norms and values of the destinator.
- *Object*: The object is the desire of the subject and is thus the goal towards which the subject directs its actions and reflections. In the

following analysis, I employ the distinction made by Kim (2002), who differentiates between a narrative's *object of desire* and *object of value* – a distinction already hinted at by Greimas (1987: 84–105). This distinction is based on the idea that the value system of a subject does not necessarily correspond to the value system constructed as generally accepted by the destinator. Thus, the subject can desire a certain object (object of desire), yet the generally accepted object in a given story (object of value) can be something entirely different, something that the subject does not necessarily intend to acquire.

- *Opponent* and *helper:* Typically, the opponent and the helper are forces in the discourse that prevent the subject from acquiring the object or support it in doing so (see, for instance, Bal 1999: 201–3). Here, I employ a slightly broader definition of the two actants (see also Viehöver 2006: 198). All highly positively connoted forces in a narrative are coded as helpers and all highly negative constructions as opponents. Thus, a range of positive and negative representations varying in intensity are subsumed under the categories of the helper and the opponent; very strong or very weak types of helpers and opponents may therefore underpin the narrative.

This adapted version of Greimas's actant model provides a suitable framework of analysis for an in-depth examination of discourse structure, because the framework takes into account whole configurations of structures. A narrative analysis based on Greimas takes his abstract model as its starting point and examines whether such configurations – that is, narratives – can be reconstructed in the text material.[3]

The identification of narratives proceeded as follows: All articles were read and coded several times. I started with a preliminary classification of discourse elements as actants. All six actants together rarely occur in one and the same text. To identify narratives, I therefore began by looking for frequent actant couples and triplets. Based on this procedure, typical actant patterns could be reconstructed. After a first reading of all texts, it became clear that only two fundamentally different principles, namely wealth and freedom, were constructed as objects of value. Two types of narratives were therefore clearly defined at a very early stage in the analysis, and variants as well as deviations from these two types were specified in the course of the analysis. A leading article entitled 'Has Capitalism Failed?', published by *The Times* on 14 October, 2008, may be used to illustrate the procedure:

> The financial crisis has exposed capitalism's [*destinator*] darkest imperfections. But it is still the best hope we have of creating wealth and opportunity for the many [*object of value*]. [. . .].
>
> Spain, Germany and France yesterday followed Britain in bailing out their banks. Russia halted stock trading. Iceland seemed to soften its opposition to EU membership. When government is the only port in the storm [*helper*], what does this say about free markets? The short, and not terribly comforting, answer is that boom-and-bust is an inherent feature of free-market capitalism [*destinator*]. The current financial crisis is only the latest in a series stretching over a century.
>
> The bank heads, board directors and non-executive directors who brought our financial system to the brink should stand ashamed of their failures [*opponent*]. They need to do more to explain themselves, both their mistakes and the mistaken criticisms of them. [. . .]. But their mistakes do not mean that capitalism [*destinator*] is the wrong way to organise our economy. The pursuit of profit [*object of desire*] by privately owned businesses [*subject*] is still the best method yet devised to create wealth and opportunity for the many [*object of value*]. Capitalism has lifted hundreds of millions of people out of poverty and has provided unprecedented choice, material and intellectual [*object of value*]. It has provided the backdrop for greater tolerance and understanding [*object of value*].
>
> Greater transparency and global supervision are needed [*helper*]. The financial markets were regulated; but their complexity left regulators staring at corners of the jigsaw when they should have been piecing together the picture on the box [*opponent*].
>
> Can the State [*helper*] save capitalism from itself? The Government's approach is instructive [*helper*]. Yesterday's intervention gave the Treasury a controlling stake in RBS. In return, ministers have demanded an end to bonuses and dividends for this year. [. . .].

> Policymakers who thought that they had abolished boom-and-bust have had a brutal shock. But the greed of one group [*opponent*] has not fatally compromised the entire economic system. It is the many well-run businesses remaining [*subject*] that will return us to prosperity [*object of value*]. Capitalism [*destinator*] has faltered. But it could emerge the stronger, if prudence [*helper*] goes from being a political slogan to a watchword in the private sector.

As in all examined articles, the capitalist market economy is here represented as the destinator of the narrative. It sets the framework of norms and values within which the other actants can manoeuvre. Capitalism is mentioned at the beginning of the text segment and its nature is further specified later. 'Boom-and-bust' is presented as 'an inherent feature of capitalism' – an aspect which is again taken up at the end of the text segment. 'Privately owned businesses' are constructed as the subject in the text segment. They are the positively connoted heroes. Businesses are usually 'well-run' and play a central role in market processes. An inherent characteristic associated with businesspeople is the fact that they seek profit. The 'pursuit of profit' thus emerges as the object of desire. 'Wealth and opportunity for the many' are constructed as the generally accepted and desirable consequence of a businessperson's actions. Hence, wealth and opportunity are the objects of value in the narrative. Wealth is constructed as the direct but unintended consequence of a businessperson's pursuit of profit. The objects of value are further specified in later passages of the text segment. Poverty reduction, 'unprecedented choice', 'prosperity' and even 'greater tolerance and understanding' are depicted as the consequences of the private businessperson's profit orientation. Finally, the text segment is populated with different helper and opponent constructions. In the second and fourth paragraph, 'government' is presented as an important helper. According to these two paragraphs, state intervention plays a decisive role in ensuring the functionality of the economic regime. Furthermore, transparency, supervision and more prudence in the private sector are constructed as vitally important helpers in the text example. By contrast, financial market actors are constructed as the chief opponents. 'Bank heads, board directors, and non-executive directors', who 'brought our financial system to the brink', 'should be ashamed of their failures'.

Their 'greed' is utterly condemned. Overall, the failures leading to the financial crisis are clearly attributed to a specific group of financial market actors.

With the help of narrative analysis, two fundamentally different narratives were reconstructed. In one narrative, the generation of wealth takes centre stage, as is the case in the analysed text segment. In the other narrative, the capitalist market economy is primarily justified on the basis of freedom, which is represented as a superior value. I now go on to describe both narratives in greater detail. I identify the actants constituting the two narratives and substantiate my findings by giving concrete examples.

The Wealth Narrative

The two narratives are categorized according to the object of the narrative. In the wealth narrative, the object is divided into the object of desire (that is, the object that the subject wishes to acquire) and the object of value (the object that is constructed as being generally accepted and desirable in a given narrative). Furthermore, subject, destinator and receiver are central 'figures' in the narrative. These four actants are the basic framework of the wealth narrative. Considering helpers and opponents, two variants of the wealth narrative can be distinguished: the state-as-helper narrative and the state-as-opponent narrative.

While the destinator of the wealth narrative is, by definition, the capitalist market economy, the regime appears in a range of representations, indicating the malleability and adaptability of the capitalist market economy. An illustrative example can be found in *The Guardian* (Brian Cordley, 'The State Shirked Its Role while City Stupidity and Greed Slid into Thieving', 17 September, 2008):

> Is this the end of capitalism? Absolutely not. The key feature of capitalism is that it's malleable. It has been through antiquity, feudalism, the industrial era, it has worn the guise of fascism and now it's wedding itself to the ecology cause. After this latest event, it will take on a new form. It is indestructible and works like the Hydra of Lerne, cut off one head and another grows in its place.

This quotation is typical for the wealth narrative: The system of norms and values provided by capitalism is depicted as being indestructible, applicable in different contexts and thus universally valid. Society is the *receiver* of the norms and values provided by the free market economy. Yet, in the analysed text material there are hardly any concrete representations of what such a capitalist society looks like. The examples in the text corpus depict capitalist society, where 'all are responsible for their own happiness', as individualistic and as obsessed with money and credit (*Süddeutsche Zeitung*, 'Abschied von der Gier', 27 September, 2008).[4]

By contrast, the *subject* of the narrative is clearly delineated. In the wealth narrative, it is largely the self-interested businessperson that is constructed as the subject. A specific understanding of the businessperson is prevalent: The subject of the wealth narrative is virtuous, middle class, responsible, innovative and prepared to take risks. Moreover, ideal businesspeople are liable with their own capital. In other text passages, authors complain that 'the traditional society of property owners has transformed itself into a society of managers' (*Tagesanzeiger*, 'Der Kapitalismus hat seine Seele verloren', 23 January, 2006). The virtuous businessperson is thus distinguished from the manager. There are only a few cases in which the manager is constructed as the subject of the wealth narrative.[5]

The defining characteristic of businesspeople is the fact that they seek to maximize their profit. The pursuit of profit is thus the *object of desire* in the wealth narrative.[6] It is represented as desirable because it generates wealth as a side effect. The latter emerges as the central *object of value* in the narrative. In pro-market discourse, there is a range of statements that either implicitly or explicitly refer to Adam Smith's metaphor of the 'invisible hand'. The text segment analysed above is a prime example in which the author emphasizes that 'the pursuit of profit of privately owned businesses is still the best method yet devised to create wealth and opportunity for the many' (*The Times*, 'Has Capitalism Failed?', 14 October, 2008). A similar example can be found in the *Süddeutsche Zeitung* ('Christliche Wege aus der Wirtschaftskrise', 22 March, 2010):

> A baker sells bread not because he wants to do something good for his fellow human beings but to earn money. Other bakers do the same, and

> competitive pressure leads to falling prices and increasing quality. Ultimately, the customer profits.[7]

Occasionally, the wealth narrative also refers to the principle of 'private vices, public benefits' (*Süddeutsche Zeitung*, 'Das Hohe Lied vom Eigennutz', 5 October, 2001) or to the 'Mephisto principle', as in the following text passage from the same article:

> Pursuit of profit, cold calculation, craving for pleasure and laziness are no shame [. . .] but create the very things that the do-gooders of this world constantly call for: social and ecological progress. Or to paraphrase Goethe's Mephisto in *Faust*: 'Those who think primarily about their own benefit are part of the power that would always wish Evil, and always work the Good' – very much like Adam Smith's 'invisible hand'.[8]

The good that is created by self-interest is material wealth in both variants of the wealth narrative. This type of story advances the idea that the capitalist market economy promotes economic growth, increases individual earnings, improves people's living standards and heightens the gross domestic product. These are the basic meanings attributed to wealth in the market-friendly wealth narrative. Occasionally, a broader understanding of wealth, for instance including happiness, is evoked as the object of value. Reduced poverty, the promotion of the common good and economic or ecological progress are also sporadically constructed as side effects of the capitalist market economy and as the object of value.

The State-as-Helper Narrative

A variety of fundamentally different discourse elements are constructed as helpers and opponents in texts that represent wealth as the central object of value, which makes it sensible to distinguish between two different variants of the wealth narrative. The state is constructed as the *helper* of the hero in the state-as-helper narrative (Fig. 6.2). Ordoliberals such as Germany's late minister of external affairs, Guido Westerwelle, assign a central role to the 'strong state' in market processes (*Frankfurter Allgemeine Zeitung*, 'Die

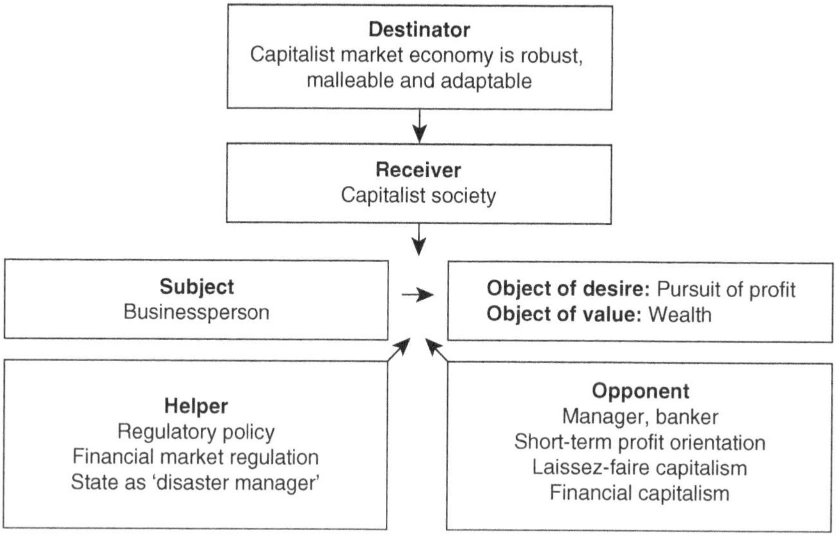

Fig. 6.2 Actant structure of the state-as-helper narrative

Finanzkrise hat mein Weltbild bestärkt', 7 June, 2009). In the state-as-helper narrative, the role of the state is to enforce rules, to provide and monitor a regulatory framework in order to 'maximize the positive effects of the market mechanism' (Helmut Maucher, then chairman of the board of directors of Nestlé, in *Neue Zürcher Zeitung*, 'Daran haben die Väter der Marktwirtschaft nicht gedacht', 28 November, 1998).

Regulatory measures such as those pertaining to liability law and the protection of property rights play a key role. More generally, guaranteeing the smooth functioning of a competition regime emerges as a core task of the state in this context. Consider, for instance, the following statement in which the position of the Archbishop of Munich and Freising, Reinhard Marx, is depicted (*Frankfurter Allgemeine Zeitung*, 'Im Gespräch: Reinhard Marx, Erzbischof des Erzbistums München und Freising', 23 December, 2008):

> [He argued that] he was a supporter of the market economy. Yet, competition [for him] was a 'cultivated plant' that needed to be tended. A market economy could not exist without risk. However, [he concluded that] a form of capitalism without a regulatory framework damaged the common good.[9]

In the wake of the 2008 financial crisis, the state has increasingly been portrayed as a helper of crucial importance. The state is not only mentioned more often, but a change of state representations can also be discerned. A more encompassing regulatory role is assigned to the state, particularly with regard to reorganizing the financial market: More regulation and tighter control of market processes are demanded. Sometimes even additional state intervention is called for in the context of the state-as-helper narrative. The idea of the state as a 'disaster manager' (Bieling 2010: 38) gains significance. The state is constructed as an entity that extensively intervenes to nationalize banks and to launch economic stimulus programmes to cushion the effects of the crisis. Yet, the temporary nature of these interventions is underlined. The tasks of the state in the state-as-helper narrative are limited to enforcing free market principles. The state is to refrain from further interventions. The demand for a stronger state does not, therefore, imply a defence of far-reaching state interventions in economic processes. Thus, a paradigm shift back to a state that is expected to intervene massively in the economic sphere does not take place (Bieling 2010; see also Kutter 2013). The narrative remains fundamentally market-liberal – the state is supposed to 'govern in accordance with market laws and not against them' (Demirović 2010: 25). There is no revision of the pro-market discourse; what we observe instead is a modest shift within the wealth narrative from the state-as-opponent to the state-as-helper narrative.

The most frequently mentioned *opponents* in the state-as-helper narrative are bankers and managers. This actor group is represented as greedy and only interested in short-term profits; it is often equated with criminals: This 'new class of managers and asset administrators threatens to destroy the foundations of capitalism' (*Tagesanzeiger,* 'Der Kapitalismus hat seine Seele verloren', 23 January, 2006). These actors are the 'sorcerer's apprentices of the financial market', the 'technocrats of profit' (*Neue Zürcher Zeitung,* 'Konstanten jenseits der Krise', 31 December, 2008) and 'fat cat financiers' (*The Guardian*, 'The State Shirked Its Role while City Stupidity and Greed Slid into Thieving', 17 September, 2008) – the opposite of virtuous businesspeople.

What is more, a marked distinction between the capitalist market economy and an economic regime without any regulatory framework is characteristic for the state-as-helper narrative. *Laissez-faire* capitalism functions as an important negative foil. In British and American newspapers, narratives refer to the 'dark forces of Thatcherism and Reaganomics' (*The Times*, 'We're All Blairites Now', 22 April, 1999) to denounce a *laissez-faire* form of capitalism. Further pejorative labels for this kind of capitalism include 'cowboy capitalism' (*The Times*, 'Has Capitalism Failed?', 14 October, 2008), 'primitive capitalism' (*Frankfurter Allgemeine Zeitung*, 'Im Gespräch: Reinhard Marx, Erzbischof des Erzbistums München und Freising', 23 December, 2008), 'capitalism without responsibility' (*Süddeutsche Zeitung*, 'Die Balance zwischen Markt und Demokratie ging verloren', 27 September, 2008) and 'predatory capitalism' (*Frankfurter Allgemeine Zeitung*, 'Wirtschaftsbücher', 19 January, 2004). Similarly, a specific sector of the capitalist system, financial capitalism – called the 'Frankenstein of deregulated global financial markets' by the *New York Times* ('Amid a Global Financial Crisis, Calls for Regulation Spread', 14 November, 1998) – is harshly criticized and thus assumes the role of an opponent in the narrative. By demarcating capitalism both from financial capitalism and from *laissez-faire* capitalism, proponents of the state-as-helper narrative try to establish an idea of capitalism that is loaded with positive associations.[10]

A further specificity of the state-as-helper narrative is that representatives of particular interests and powerful multinational companies also play the role of opponents. The state-as-helper narrative condemns interest groups and multinational corporations engaging in lobbying activities; it claims that by lobbying the government these actors exert pressure and obtain a competitive advantage. The following quotation by Viktor Vanberg, the director of the Walter Eucken Institute, exemplifies this antipluralist stance (Biebricher 2012: 47; see also Ptak 2008) of proponents of the capitalist market economy:

> The political process opens the opportunity for single groups to fight for the privilege of warding themselves off competition pressure. The more these groups are successful in gaining this privilege, the weaker the productive power of the market economy. Therefore, democratic societies are in danger of destroying the institutional basis of an economic system that has brought them wealth. Yet, many people do not recognize the reasons for these erosion processes.[11] (*Frankfurter Allgemeine Zeitung*, 'Global robust, lokal verwendbar', 20 July, 2009)

The State-as-Opponent Narrative

The state-as-opponent narrative is characterized by the fact that the state is represented as an extremely negative force. It is the central *opponent* in the story (Fig. 6.3). A quotation illustrating this hostility towards the state that is often taken up in the UK and US quality press is a remark originally made by Ronald Reagan: 'The nine most terrifying words in the English language are: I'm from the government and I am here to help' (for example, *The Guardian*, 'Genius, Risk and the Secret of Capitalism', 7 August, 2010). This narrative criticizes any form of state intervention. Rescue packages for banks, state aid for companies, subsidies for buying properties in the United States, a tighter regulation of banks, trade barriers and the German agreement on fixed book prices are wholly condemned. Redistributive tax measures and the welfare state as a whole are attacked (*Frankfurter Allgemeine Zeitung*, 'Edmund Phelps über geldpolitische Experimente, die verkrustete Wirtschaftsordnung und Rachsucht gegenüber Unternehmern', 8 December, 2006):

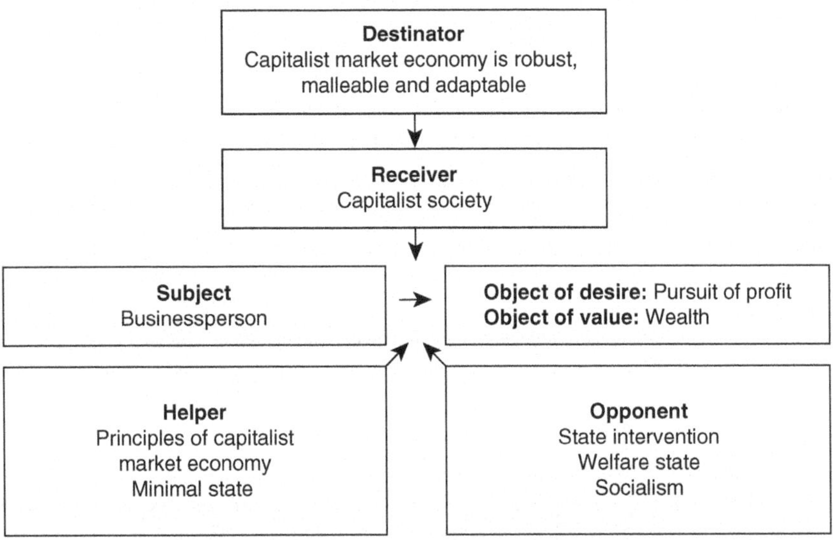

Fig. 6.3 Actant structure of the state-as-opponent narrative

> Even though economies are complex dynamic systems with many unclear causal chains, we can nevertheless theoretically deduce harmful factors. And hence, we know that there are many further harmful influences, in particular tax policy and the welfare state. The welfare state, as it is organized in Europe, establishes entitlements without a real basis. It makes people independent from their performance and from their employers. It emancipates them. This is even the welfare state's foundational idea – and, at the same time, its problem. The welfare state thus emancipates people from a benevolent force, the dynamic entrepreneur, who constantly tries to find new ways to earn money.[12]

Moreover, the state-as-opponent narrative is based on the opposition between the capitalist market economy, on the one hand, and Marxism, socialism or the planned economy, on the other. Alliances of opponents are constructed such as the following 'socialist coalition' consisting of Keynesians, social democrats, Stalin and Marx (*Frankfurter Allgemeine Zeitung*, 'Edmund Phelps über geldpolitische Experimente, die verkrustete Wirtschaftsordnung und Rachsucht gegenüber Unternehmern', 8 December, 2006):

> All of a sudden everyone is talking about Keynes, and Mussolini's corporatist state is popular again; sooner or later we will witness the resurrection of Karl Marx. However, not only the inveterate Keynesians and Stalin's orphans draw the wrong conclusions from the crisis but also allegedly sensible social democrats who sing capitalism's song of death.[13]

The core principles of the capitalist market economy are constructed as forces that help businesspeople in their pursuit of profit and are, at the same time, the central preconditions of wealth generation. The market principle, competition, the freedom of contract, free trade, free prices and the principle of risk and liability are the central *helpers* of the state-as-opponent narrative.[14]

However, even the state-as-opponent narrative cannot exist completely without the state. The state is depicted as being responsible for guaranteeing a favourable economic framework for the profit-seeking businesspeople to work in. There are, therefore, always minimal references to and representations of the state in the narrative to assume the function of helper. This narrative propagates a 'lean state' which concentrates on core tasks and favours the idea of 'self-restrained policy' (*Frankfurter Allgemeine Zeitung*, 'Globalisierung bietet neue Chancen', 14 January, 2000). Such a minimal conception of the state, the narrative argues, strengthens the personal responsibility of the citizen and ultimately creates more wealth.

The Freedom Narrative

The main difference between the wealth and the freedom narrative lies in the *object* of the narrative. In the freedom narrative, the principle of unlimited, individual freedom is central for the justification of the capitalist market economy (Fig. 6.4). The narrative defends the regime on the grounds that unlike any other economic regime, it respects individual freedoms. Germany's former minister of economic affairs, Otto Graf Lambsdorff, for instance, appears as a major representative of the freedom narrative, because he views the capitalist market economy as the 'key pillar of [. . .] a society founded on freedom as the highest value' (*Frankfurter Allgemeine Zeitung*, 'Standpunkte: Otto Graf Lambsdorff'), 10 October, 2000).[15]

The capitalist market economy as the *destinator* in the freedom narrative is constructed in two particularly pertinent ways: Firstly, there is a line of reasoning that can be described as a democratic justification of the regime. The freedom narrative perceives the capitalist market economy as an 'emancipatory idea' (*Frankfurter Allgemeine Zeitung*, 'Angela Merkel', 24 September, 2003) or as a 'revolutionary power' (*Süddeutsche Zeitung*, 'Seid umschlungen', 21 August, 2010). These descriptions imply that the capitalist market economy has a positive effect on political systems, because it creates the material basis for opposition against particular rulers. The regime thus has the power to revolutionize political processes. By providing several historical arguments, Nikolaus Piper in the *Süddeutsche Zeitung* (21 August, 2010, 'Seid umschlungen') pursues this line of reasoning. In his view, the wealth of the bourgeoisie played a central role in overcoming

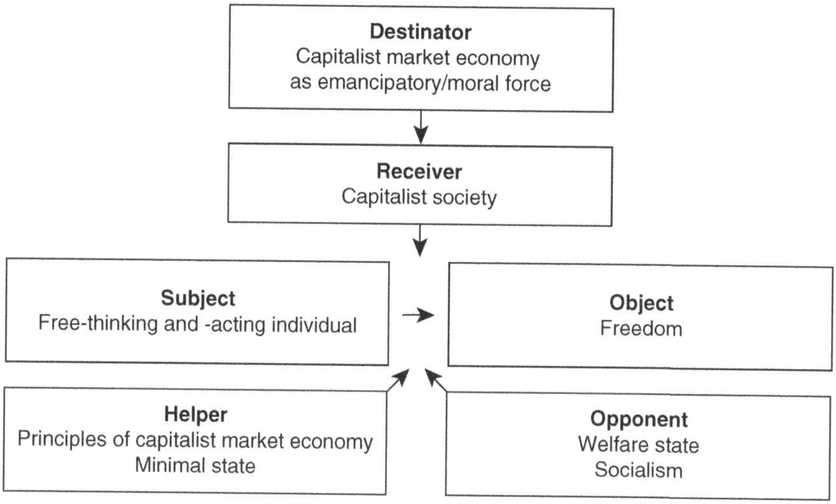

Fig. 6.4 Actant structure of the freedom narrative

feudalism in Europe and later also in democratizing the United States. Hence, 'capitalist competition' is portrayed as an 'instrument of disempowering' aristocrats and the undeservedly privileged. In a similar vein, the journalist Konrad Lischka writes: 'Capitalism [frees] people from political and economic oppression' (*Süddeutsche Zeitung*, 2 May, 2001, 'Brüder im Wettbewerb').

Furthermore, justifying the capitalist market economy on the basis of freedom rights is often linked with an emphasis on the cultural and moral power of capitalism. More specifically, it is underlined that the 'market exerts an educational influence' on market participants (*Frankfurter Allgemeine Zeitung*, 'Standpunkte: Otto Graf Lambsdorff', 10 October, 2000), facilitating the development of social norms such as tolerance.

Those affected by the values and norms of such a politically and morally valuable type of capitalism are the *receivers* of the narrative. In the analysed discourse, capitalist society assumes this role. However, a more specific characterization of the nature of capitalist society is missing to a large degree. The journalist Alexander Kissler touches on this aspect in a discussion of Ayn Rand's theory. Rand conceptualizes the capitalist society as individualistic, antipolitical and egoistic – and egoism itself as 'the basis of every peaceful society' (*Süddeutsche Zeitung*, 'Kapitalismus für Kluge', 17 March, 2009).

Similarly, the *subject* of the freedom narrative is only vaguely sketched. Different from the wealth narrative, the freedom narrative does not cast the self-interested businessperson in a leading role. Instead, the free-thinking and free-acting individual is paramount. This image of the subject is, again, most clearly illustrated in Kissler's discussion of Ayn Rand's theory: 'For Galt human beings are those creatures who "act at their own discretion" and who only accept the imperative "you shall think" as their single moral commandment.'[16]

As mentioned above, guaranteeing freedom is the primary objective in this narrative and the object of the story. Freedom is the goal that the subject seeks to achieve and is at the same time represented as the highest and most fundamental principle by the freedom narrative – the object of desire and the object of value thus merge. Central to this narrative is the close connection between political and economic freedom. Following this narrative, the value of economic freedom lies in the fact that it facilitates political freedom. This argument, which has been famously made by Milton Friedman (1962: 7–22), assumes that economic freedom guaranteed by the capitalist market economy is a necessary precondition for political freedom. Thus, the freedom narrative consists of a unique mixture of freedom-centred and democracy-centred justifications in which a liberal understanding of democracy is prevalent. Without specifying the mechanisms by which economic freedom can nourish political freedom (in the form of democracy), several instances in the text corpus can be found which implicitly rely on this automatism:

> For [Ludwig von] Mises, the value of freedom is superior to all others. He is convinced that freedom of ownership is the most fundamental form of freedom as it safeguards all other basic freedoms. The system that is irrevocably connected to individual freedom is capitalism.[17] (*Frankfurter Allgemeine Zeitung*, 'Wirtschaftsbücher', 19 January, 2009)

> To the extent that American business or government even attempt to square the circle, the argument they most frequently adduce is that modernity – that is, the integration of a nation into the global

> economy – will transform that nation into a more pluralistic democracy. (*Washington Post*, 'Wanna Buy a Port?', 22 February, 2006)

Finally, the freedom narrative comprises an array of opponents and helpers. The most important *helpers* are the central principles of the capitalist market economy. These helpers also play a role in the state-as-opponent variant of the wealth narrative. In the freedom narrative, the principles of the regime help individuals in their pursuit of freedom while in the wealth narrative these principles are constructed as being beneficial for economic growth. In the following quotation, the market principle and the principle of competition are presented as helpers. Further principles that are typically referred to in this context are private ownership and freedom of contract:

> For Federal Councillor Pascal Couchepin, the faith in the market is indestructible – even as far as human rights are concerned. This conviction was not even shattered on his trip to China. If market forces develop freely, if there is competition, then human rights will be safeguarded, then democracy will prevail over the despotism of the party apparatus, then rulers will start to respect individuals in society.[18] (*Tagesanzeiger*, 'Abseits stehen bringt nichts', 25 November, 2003)

However, the capitalist market economy and its principles alone cannot guarantee freedom. The freedom narrative often concedes that a modicum of state presence is necessary to establish a regime in which capitalist principles can fully unfold. Besides such conceptions of a minimal role for the state, certain requisite attributes of market participants are presented as helpers in the state-as-opponent narrative. In this context, 'self-responsibility' and 'temperance' (*Neue Zürcher Zeitung*, 'Wenn die Gleichheit mehr zählt als die Freiheit', 25 June, 2011) are, for instance, put forward as useful in the individual's pursuit of freedom.

Lastly, the freedom narrative constructs radical opponents. The most prominent opponent of this story is the welfare state, or more specifically, state redistribution measures. Moralism and paternalism, two further opponents typically attacked by libertarianism, are practically non-existent in this type of discourse. A particularly aggressive image of an opponent is again evoked by Otto Graf Lambsdorff (*Frankfurter Allgemeine Zeitung*, 'Standpunkte: Otto Graf Lambsdorff', 10 October, 2000). He holds the welfare state responsible for excesses of violence and nationalist movements:

> The welfare state's material entitlements are always exclusive and are assigned to clearly defined target groups according to unclear and non-universal criteria. Consequently, contestation about who is excluded and who is not is always a question of political power. This should not and does not necessarily lead to excessive violence, yet it strengthens a culture in which welfare is more important than performance, and equality of higher value than freedom. Generally, this nourishes the attitude that there are individual entitlements that are threatened by out-groups. Such an attitude can unveil the potential for violence. Political processes in Eastern Europe confirm this proposition, as previous communist political elites quickly turned to nationalist authoritarianism after the collapse of Soviet Communism. [...]. In the long run, no state relying on comprehensive redistributive measures can do without aggressive nationalism.[19]

Socialism is often revived as an enemy in this context; authors refer to the concept of 'collectivism' as propagated by Hayek and Röpke, and employed to express the antisocialist stance of neoliberal thinkers. The term stands for a range of rather disparate social and political phenomena, linked only through the negation of individualism (Ptak 2008: 24), which is similar to the way it is employed in the text corpus:

> The collectivist seducers and enemies of the open society promise a land of milk and honey through nationalization and redistribution; in doing so, they curtail freedom and self-determination. That is why we are ready to oppose the enemies of freedom and to put up a fight against those who want to lead us back to the past with quaint doctrines of salvation.[20] (*Frankfurter Allgemeine Zeitung*, 14 July, 2007,'Fremde Federn: Volker Kauder')

The Wealth and Freedom Narratives Compared

Table 6.2 summarizes differences and similarities between the wealth and freedom narratives. The wealth narrative differs fundamentally from the freedom narrative with respect to its object. In the first narrative, the generation of wealth is constructed as a leading principle while in the second this role is assumed by the principle of freedom. Similarly, the subject is represented entirely differently in each narrative. The clear-cut conception of the self-interested businessperson is constitutive of the wealth narrative. The freedom narrative, in contrast, has no equivalent actant. The subject is only vaguely conceptualized as a free-thinking and free-acting individual. At the same time, however, there are similarities: Both advocate *laissez-faire* capitalism; the state, on the other hand, assumes the role of the main opponent. The state-as-opponent narrative and the freedom narrative are generally hostile to more than minimal state intervention into economic processes.

What is more, it is evident that both narratives are embedded in different theoretical traditions. While the freedom narrative has its theoretical roots in libertarian philosophy, the wealth narrative is fundamentally market-liberal. Narratives structuring market-friendly media discourse are constituted by a mixture of market-liberal and libertarian premises, yet a deeper engagement with philosophical theories and concepts – such as the concept of 'self-ownership' in libertarian political philosophy – does not take place. The lack of left-libertarian lines of reasoning in our text material is also striking.

Overall, the empirical analysis shows that there are two relatively stable discursive configurations structuring market-friendly discourse, which remain relevant throughout the examined time period. Both narratives consist of configurations of actants standing in different relations and mutually stabilizing each other. The market-friendly discourse gains cohesion as a result of this discursive structure. Questioning one discourse element is not possible without doubting others. Criticizing, for instance, the subject of the wealth narrative, that is, the self-interested businessperson, automatically entails questioning the aim of wealth generation. The two are intrinsically linked. Because of this tightly knit

Table 6.2 Wealth narrative and freedom narrative compared

	Wealth narrative		Freedom narrative
Variants	State-as-helper narrative	State-as-opponent narrative	
Destinator	Capitalist market economy	Capitalist market economy	Capitalist market economy
Receiver	Society	Society	Society
Subject	Businessperson	Businessperson	Free-thinking and free-acting individual
Object of desire	Pursuit of profit	Pursuit of profit	Freedom
Object of value	Wealth	Wealth	Freedom
Opponent	Manager, banker, short-term profit orientation, *laissez-faire* capitalism, financial capitalism	State intervention, welfare state, socialism	Welfare state, socialism
Helper	Regulatory policy, financial market regulation, state as disaster manager	Principles of the capitalist market economy, minimal state	Principles of the capitalist market economy, minimal state
Theoretical background	Classical, market-liberal	Classical, market-liberal	Libertarianism

relationship between discourse elements, criticizing the capitalist market economy in a differentiated manner becomes more difficult. By radically excluding anticapitalist voices even in the form of the opponent, the discourse gains additional strength.

Moreover, the empirical analysis has shown that four actants – subject, object, opponent and helper – play a decisive role for the coherence and stability of discourse. Concentrating on these four actants as basic units of a narration, it becomes evident that the wealth narrative is characterized by a clear-cut construction of actants. In contrast, the freedom narrative is more ambivalent. The subject of this story is not sufficiently specified. The exact characteristics of the freedom-seeking individual remain unclear. Similarly, the narrative largely lacks constructions of a capitalist society, supporting individuals in their pursuit of freedom. This constitutes a moment of instability in the discourse. At the same time, the freedom narrative gains coherence through radical helper and opponent constructions.

The narratives also display a range of inconsistencies and contradictions. So far I have only illustrated typical representations of actants for each of the narratives. Deviant constructions can be found in the text material as well. There is, for instance, occasionally an alternative construction of the subject in the wealth narrative, depicting the latter not as a self-interested businessperson but as a person that wishes to put into practice a particular idea that she is convinced of. Parts of the wealth narrative are also composed of Schumpeterian representations of the capitalist market economy in which it is depicted as a 'creative power', that is, as an economic regime that facilitates progress and innovation. Here, the dynamic version of a classical line of justification (Chapter 2) is highlighted at the expense of the static version underlining self-regulation and balance. Finally, the capitalist market economy is also represented as a moral power that has an educative impact on market participants. These representations occur sporadically and are not connected with further actants, which would integrate them into a narrative. Yet, these ideas suggest possible variants of market-friendly narratives and constitute a moment of instability in the discursive space since a significant deviation away from the regular characteristics of actants leads to a transformation of the narrative.

With regard to the typology of justifications presented in Chapter 2, the narratives reconstructed in the text material are constituted by configurations of classical justifications of the market economy. Non-classical – that is, justice-, culture- and democracy-centred – arguments defending the capitalist market economy do play a role. Yet, these justifications do not link up with other ideas and, therefore, do not constitute independent narratives.

Conclusion

The analysis of pro-market discourse revealed that market-friendly ideas tend to be linked with each other and to have the form of narratives. Classical market-liberal and freedom-centred justifications are key in constructing coherent narratives. Both narratives are constituted by configurations of actants that are mutually dependent; this mutual interdependence of discourse elements strengthens and stabilizes the two market-friendly narratives.

The financial crisis did not fundamentally change the structure of these narratives. The two variants of the wealth narrative appear to have moved towards the state-as-helper narrative since 2008. The narrative now assigns a more significant role to the state in economic processes, and the 'ordering hand' of the state is highlighted; the state is temporarily given a new and important regulatory task, namely, the fundamental reorganization of the financial market. Nevertheless, the narrative remains market-liberal.

Overall, pro-market discourse is characterized by structures that remain remarkably stable after the crisis. Ruptures or inconsistencies in pro-market discourse cannot be discerned. The increasing criticism of the capitalist market economy (Chapter 3) has virtually no effect on the nature of market-friendly discourse. It remains stable and continues to be based on classical, market-liberal and freedom-centred justifications of the market economy. Therefore, defenders of the capitalist market economy continue to have a coherent story to tell, which contributes to the stability of the economic regime.

Notes

1. Greimas's definition is wider than the actant definition proposed by Bruno Latour, who writes (1996: 337): 'An "actor" in ANT [actor-network theory] is a semiotic definition – an actant – that is something that acts or to which activity is granted by others. It does not imply any special motivation of human individual actors, nor of humans in general. An actant can be literally anything provided it is granted to be the source of an action'. Thus, while action and capability to act play a central role in Latour's definition, actants do not have to act according to Greimas nor are they considered to be the source of an action. Actants are primarily defined by the fact that they take over a functional role in the narrative. For instance, the object of a narrative is typically an actant that does not act.

2. Greimas's own conceptualization has been frequently modified. Helpful clarifications and applications of the model in the field of literary studies can be found in Bal (1999) and Kim (2002). A social scientific application of the model is provided by Arnold (2012), Fiol (1990), Titscher et al. (1998) and Viehöver (2006). The following definition of actants draws on these works that have further developed and specified Greimas's original actant model.
3. Narrative analyses drawing on structural semiotics are characterized by a structural bias that 'invites' the researcher to arrange ideas into coherent wholes. By applying narrative discourse analysis, I aim to reconstruct typical configurations of ideas. However, empirical analysis should be open enough to take into account rare and deviant constructions of particular actants. When summarizing the empirical results, I will therefore also hint at atypical actant constructions and incoherencies in the discourse.
4. All translations of text passages in German are my own.
5. An example can be found in the *Süddeutsche Zeitung*: 'Bonus payments for managers are "really a good idea". Managers' self-interest helps businesses to succeed, creating a collective benefit' ('Bonuszahlungen an Manager seien laut Ostheimer "eigentlich eine sinnvolle Idee". Durch ihr Eigennutzdenken könnten sie den Unternehmen zum Erfolg verhelfen und so einen kollektiven Vorteil erzeugen'; *Süddeutsche Zeitung*, 22 March, 2010, 'Christliche Wege aus der Wirtschaftskrise').
6. Besides self-interest and profit maximization, there are other rather marginalized constructions of the object of desire in the text corpus. According to this alternative construction, the driving force of the businessperson is the desire to pursue an idea and to invent something new (*Frankfurter Allgemeine Zeitung*, 26 February, 2002, 'Ein Narrenhaus, bedingte Nutzung weiter möglich'). Compare the following quotation from *The Guardian*: 'What gets Branson, Murdoch, Gates and Jobs up in the morning is not the prospect of making more millions, but the passion to invent, the thrill of risk, the hunger to compete' (7 August, 2010, 'Genius, Risk and the Secret of Capitalism').
7. 'Ein Bäcker verkauft Brot, nicht weil er seinen Mitmenschen etwas Gutes tun möchte, sondern um Geld zu verdienen. Andere Bäcker tun es ihm gleich, unter dem Konkurrenzdruck sinkt der Preis und die Qualität steigt, was wiederum den Kunden zu Gute kommt'.
8. 'Gewinnstreben, kalte Berechnung, Vergnügungssucht und Faulheit, so schreiben die Autoren, sind keine Schande, sondern bringen genau das

hervor, was die Gutmenschen dieser Welt immer wieder anmahnen: sozialen und ökologischen Fortschritt. Oder frei nach Goethes Mephisto im Faust: "Wer vor allem an den eigenen Vorteil denkt, ist ein Teil von jener Kraft, die stets das Böse will und stets das Gute schafft" – ganz im Sinne der "unsichtbaren Hand" des Adam Smith'. The translation of the verse from Faust (by A.S. Kline) is available at http://www.poetryintranslation.com/PITBR/German/Fausthome.htm.

9. 'Zuvor hatte sich in der F.A.Z auch der Erzbischof von München und Freising, Reinhard Marx, zu Wort gemeldet. Er sei ein Anhänger der Marktwirtschaft. Aber der Wettbewerb sei "eine Kulturpflanze", die gestaltet werden müsse. Eine Marktwirtschaft könne ohne Risiko nicht funktionieren. Aber ein Kapitalismus ohne Rahmenordnung schädige das Gemeinwohl'.
10. A similar point is made in Chapters 3 and 4, where financial capitalism is identified as a central target of criticism.
11. 'Um Wählerstimmen werbende Politiker sind immer in Versuchung, solche Illusionen zu nähren. Der politische Prozess eröffnet einzelnen Gruppen die Möglichkeit, für sich das Privileg der Verschonung von Wettbewerbsdruck oder seinen Folgen zu erstreiten. Je mehr Gruppen bei solcher Privilegiensuche erfolgreich sind, desto mehr wird die produktive Kraft der Marktwirtschaft geschwächt. Auch demokratische Gesellschaften sind aus diesem Grunde in Gefahr, die institutionellen Grundlagen einer Wirtschaftsordnung zu zerstören, der sie ihren Wohlstand verdanken, ohne dass den Menschen unbedingt klar würde, wo die Ursachen für diesen Erosionsprozess liegen'.
12. 'Auch wenn die Volkswirtschaft ein komplexes dynamisches System mit vielen unklar verknüpften Wirkungsketten ist, so können wir doch theoretisch herleiten, was ihr schadet. Und so wissen wir, daß es eben auch noch viele andere schädliche Einflüsse gibt, insbesondere durch die Steuerpolitik und den Sozialstaat. Der Sozialstaat, so, wie er in Europa organisiert ist, begründet Ansprüche ohne reale Grundlage. Er macht die Leute unabhängig von ihrer Leistung und von ihren Arbeitgebern. Er emanzipiert sie. Das ist sogar der Grundgedanke dabei – aber zugleich das Problem. Denn er emanzipiert sie von einer wohlwollenden Kraft, nämlich von dem dynamischen Unternehmer, der versucht, neue Wege zu finden, um Geld zu verdienen'.
13. 'Mit einem Mal ist Keynes in aller Munde und Mussolinis korporatistischer Staat wieder populär; früher oder später werden wir wohl die Auferstehung

von Karl Marx erleben. Doch nicht nur die unverbesserlichen Keynesianer und die Waisen Stalins ziehen die falschen Schlüsse aus der Krise, sondern auch angeblich vernünftige Sozialdemokraten haben sich in den Chor derer eingereiht, die den Tod des Kapitalismus ausrufen'.

14. Thus, the narrative integrates a range of legitimation objects that have been identified as 'legitimation anchors' in Chapter 3, that is, as institutions of the capitalist market economy that tend to be evaluated more positively than the regime as a whole.
15. In our text corpus, other prominent representatives of the freedom narrative are Ayn Rand, Robert Nozick, Ludwig von Mises, Milton Friedman and the lesser-known libertarian economist Hans-Hermann Hoppe (2003), who propagates a purely private property society. The position of these authors is either presented directly through guest commentaries or indirectly in articles, discussing the work of libertarian thinkers.
16. 'Für Galt ist der Mensch jenes Wesen, das 'nach eigenem freien Ermessen handelt' und das als einziges moralisches Gebot den Imperativ "Du sollst denken" akzeptiert'. John Galt is the protagonist of Ayn Rand's novel *Atlas Shrugged*, which introduces Rand's philosophy.
17. 'Über alle anderen Werte stellt Mises die Freiheit, wobei er davon überzeugt ist, dass nur durch die Freiheit des Eigentums auch andere Grundfreiheiten gewährt werden können. Das System, das unwiderruflich mit der individuellen Freiheit verknüpft ist, ist der Kapitalismus'.
18. 'Der Glaube an den Markt ist bei Bundesrat Pascal Couchepin unerschütterlich – selbst wenn es um die Menschenrechte geht. Diese Überzeugung liess sich Couchepin auch auf seiner Reise nach China nicht nehmen. Wenn sich die Marktkräfte frei entfalten könnten, wenn der Wettbewerb spiele, dann werde es auch mit den Menschenrechten besser, dann gewinne die Demokratie die Oberhand über die Willkür des Parteiapparates, dann setze sich der Respekt der Staatsführung gegenüber dem Individuum in der Gesellschaft durch'.
19. 'Die materiellen Anspruchsrechte des Wohlfahrtsstaats sind immer exklusiv und müssen in ihrer Gültigkeit auf klar definierte Zielgruppen nach eher unklaren und nichtuniversellen Kriterien angewendet werden. Die Auseinandersetzung darum, wer ausgegrenzt wird und wer nicht, ist daher immer eine Frage politischer Macht. Dies sollte und muß in einer Demokratie nicht unbedingt zu Gewaltexzessen führen, stärkt aber eine Mentalität, die Fürsorge vor Leistung, Gleichheit vor Freiheit stellt. Dies fördert tendenziell die Einstellung, daß man selbst Rechte habe, die von

Außenstehenden bedroht sind. Damit können zugleich Gewaltpotentiale freigelegt werden. Bestätigt wird dies durch die Leichtigkeit, mit der sich in Osteuropa die ehemaligen kommunistischen Führungseliten [. . .] nach dem Zusammenbruch des Sowjetkommunismus einem nationalistischen Autoritarismus zuwandten. [. . .]. Langfristig kann kein umfassender Umverteilungsstaat gänzlich ohne aggressiven Nationalismus auskommen'.

20. 'Die kollektivistischen Verführer und Feinde der offenen Gesellschaft versprechen stattdessen ein Schlaraffenland durch Verstaatlichung und Umverteilung; sie legen damit die Axt an Freiheit und Selbstbestimmung. Deshalb sind wir bereit, uns den Feinden der Freiheit entgegenzustellen und denen die Stirn zu bieten, die uns mit den Heilslehren von gestern in die Vergangenheit führen wollen'.

References

Arnold, Markus. 2012. 'Erzählen. Die ethisch-politische Funktion narrativer Diskurse'. In *Erzählungen im Öffentlichen. Über die Wirkung narrativer Diskurse*, eds. Markus Arnold, Gert Dressel and Willy Viehöver. Heidelberg: VS, 17–64.

Bal, Mieke. 1999. *Narratology. Introduction to the Theory of Narrative*. Toronto: University of Toronto Press.

Barthes, Roland. 1994. *The Semiotic Challenge*. Berkeley: University of California Press.

Biebricher, Thomas. 2012. *Neoliberalismus zur Einführung*. Hamburg: Junius.

Bieling, Hans-Jürgen. 2010. 'Metamorphosen des "integralen Staates": Konkurrierende Leitbilder in der Krisendiskussion'. In *Die Rückkehr des Staates? Nach der Finanzkrise*, eds. Elmar Altvater, Hans-Jürgen Bieling, Alex Demirović, Heiner Flassbeck, Werner Goldschmidt, Mehrdad Payandeh and Stefanie Wöhl. Hamburg: VSA, 37–60.

Demirović, Alex. 2010. '"Politik und Wirtschaft kann man nicht trennen": Zur Aktualität eines Gemeinplatzes'. In *Die Rückkehr des Staates? Nach der Finanzkrise*, eds. Elmar Altvater, Hans-Jürgen Bieling, Alex Demirović, Heiner Flassbeck, Werner Goldschmidt, Mehrdad Payandeh and Stefanie Wöhl. Hamburg: VSA, 19–35.

Fiol, C. Marlene. 1990. 'Narrative Semiotics: Theory, Procedure and Illustration'. In *Mapping Strategic Thought*, ed. Anne Sigismund Huff. New York: Wiley, 377–402.

Friedman, Milton. 1962. *Capitalism and Freedom*. Chicago: University of Chicago Press.

Frye, Northrop. 1965. *Anatomy of Criticism. Four Essays*. Princeton: Princeton University Press.

Greimas, Algirdas J. 1971. *Strukturale Semantik. Methodologische Untersuchungen*. Braunschweig: Vieweg.

Greimas, Algirdas J. 1987. *On Meaning. Selected Writings in Semiotic Theory*. Minneapolis: University of Minnesota Press.

Greimas, Algirdas J. and Joseph Courtés. 1982. *Semiotics and Language. An Analytical Dictionary*. Bloomington: Indiana University Press.

Hoppe, Hans-Hermann. 2003. *Demokratie. Der Gott, der keiner ist*. Leipzig: Manuskriptum.

Kim, Taehwan. 2002. *Vom Aktantenmodell zur Semiotik der Leidenschaften. Eine Studie zur narrativen Semiotik von Algirdas J. Greimas*. Tübingen: Narr.

King, Ronald F. and Thomas S. Langston. 2008. 'Narratives of American Politics'. *Perspectives on Politics* 6(2): 235–52.

Kutter, Amelie. 2013. 'Totgesagte leben länger. Die Fortschreibung ökonomischer Ordnung in Krisenlektionen der deutschen Finanzpresse'. In *Ökonomie, Diskurs, Regierung. Interdisziplinäre Perspektiven*, ed. Jens Maeße. Wiesbaden: Springer VS, 95–120.

Kuusisto, Riikka. 2009. 'Comic Plots as Conflict Resolution Strategy'. *European Journal of International Relations* 15(4): 601–26.

Latour, Bruno. 1996. 'On Actor-Network Theory: A Few Clarifications'. *Soziale Welt* 47(4): 369–82.

Propp, Vladimir. 1968. *Morphology of the Folktale*. Second Edition. Austin: University of Texas Press.

Ptak, Ralf. 2008. 'Grundlagen des Neoliberalismus'. In *Kritik des Neoliberalismus*, eds. Christoph Butterwegge, Bettina Lösch and Ralf Ptak. Wiesbaden: VS, 13–85.

Rovisco, Maria. 2010. 'One Europe or Several Europes? The Cultural Logic of Narratives of Europe – Views from France and Britain'. *Social Science Information* 49(2): 241–66.

Schneider, Steffen, Dominika Biegoń, Jennifer Gronau, Martin Nonhoff, Frank Nullmeier and Henning Schmidtke. 2010. 'The Legitimacy of the

European Union: Four Academic Narratives, Four National Perspectives'. In *Europe on Trial. Shortcomings of the EU with Regard to Democracy, Public Sphere, and Identity*, eds. David Tréfás and Jens Lucht. Innsbruck: Studienverlag, 140–68.
Titscher, Stefan, Ruth Wodak, Michael Meyer and Eva Vetter. 1998. *Methoden der Textanalyse. Leitfaden und Überblick*. Wiesbaden: Westdeutscher Verlag.
Viehöver, Willy. 2006. 'Diskurse als Narrationen'. In *Handbuch Sozialwissenschaftliche Diskursanalyse*, Volume 1: *Theorien und Methoden*, eds. Reiner Keller, Andreas Hierseland, Werner Schneider and Willy Viehöver. Wiesbaden: VS, 179–208.
White, Hayden V. 1987. *The Content of the Form*. Baltimore: Johns Hopkins University Press.

Cited Newspaper Articles

Frankfurter Allgemeine Zeitung 14 January 2000. 'Globalisierung bietet neue Chancen'.
Frankfurter Allgemeine Zeitung 10 October 2000. 'Standpunkte: Otto Graf Lambsdorff'.
Frankfurter Allgemeine Zeitung 26 February 2002. 'Ein Narrenhaus, bedingte Nutzung weiter möglich'.
Frankfurter Allgemeine Zeitung 24 September 2003. 'Angela Merkel'.
Frankfurter Allgemeine Zeitung 19 January 2004. 'Wirtschaftsbücher'.
Frankfurter Allgemeine Zeitung 8 December 2006. 'Edmund Phelps über geldpolitische Experimente, die verkrustete Wirtschaftsordnung und Rachsucht gegenüber Unternehmern'.
Frankfurter Allgemeine Zeitung 14 July 2007. 'Fremde Federn: Volker Kauder'.
Frankfurter Allgemeine Zeitung 23 December 2008. 'Im Gespräch: Reinhard Marx, Erzbischof des Erzbistums München und Freising'.
Frankfurter Allgemeine Zeitung 19 January 2009. 'Wirtschaftsbücher'.
Frankfurter Allgemeine Zeitung 7 June 2009. 'Die Finanzkrise hat mein Weltbild bestärkt'.
Frankfurter Allgemeine Zeitung 20 July 2009. 'Global robust, lokal verwundbar'.
Süddeutsche Zeitung 2 May 2001. 'Brüder im Wettbewerb'.
Süddeutsche Zeitung 5 October 2001. 'Das Hohe Lied vom Eigennutz'.
Süddeutsche Zeitung 27 September 2008. 'Abschied von der Gier'.

Süddeutsche Zeitung 27 September 2008. 'Die Balance zwischen Markt und Demokratie ging verloren'.

Süddeutsche Zeitung 17 March 2009. 'Kapitalismus für Kluge'.

Süddeutsche Zeitung 22 March 2010. 'Christliche Wege aus der Wirtschaftskrise'.

Süddeutsche Zeitung 21 August 2010. 'Seid umschlungen'.

Neue Zürcher Zeitung 28 November 1998. 'Daran haben die Väter der Marktwirtschaft nicht gedacht'.

Neue Zürcher Zeitung 31 December 2008. 'Konstanten jenseits der Krise'.

Neue Zürcher Zeitung 25 June 2011. 'Wenn die Gleichheit mehr zählt als die Freiheit'.

Tagesanzeiger 25 November 2003. 'Abseits stehen bringt nichts'.

Tagesanzeiger 23 January 2006. 'Der Kapitalismus hat seine Seele verloren'.

The Guardian 17 September 2008. 'The State Shirked Its Role while City Stupidity and Greed Slid into Thieving'.

The Guardian 7 August 2010. 'Genius, Risk and the Secret of Capitalism'.

The Times 22 April 1999. 'We're All Blairites Now'.

The Times 14 October 2008. 'Has Capitalism Failed?'

New York Times 14 November 1998. 'Amid a Global Financial Crisis, Calls for Regulation Spread'.

Washington Post 22 February 2006. 'Wanna Buy a Port?'

7

(De-)Legitimating Discourse Networks: Smoke without Fire?

Sebastian Haunss

The previous chapters have shown that the 2008 financial crisis has indeed left its imprint on the public spheres of Germany, Switzerland, the United Kingdom and the United States. Chapter 3 indicates that the debate on the legitimacy of the capitalist market economy has become more intense and the overall evaluation of the economic regime more negative in all four countries. But why has the declining legitimation of the regime not been the beginning of a process of institutional change leading to another Great Transformation (Blyth 2002)? Why has the more negative evaluation of the capitalist market economy in the wake of the crisis remained an ephemeral phenomenon that has left the institutions of the regime largely unchanged? Chapter 4 on responsibility attributions, Chapter 5 on the metaphors of delegitimating discourse and Chapter 6 on legitimating narratives

S. Haunss (✉)
Research Centre on Inequality and Social Policy (SOCIUM),
University of Bremen, Bremen, Germany
e-mail: sebastian.haunss@uni-bremen.de

S. Schneider et al. (eds.), *Capitalism and Its Legitimacy in Times of Crisis*, Transformations of the State,
DOI 10.1007/978-3-319-53765-8_7

before and after the financial crisis have already offered some explanations. Responsibility for the crisis is attributed mainly to individual economic actors (especially bankers) and national political actors, not to the economic regime as a whole. The legitimation narratives of the capitalist market economy have remained largely intact and have only been slightly adapted to allow for a stronger role of the state. And the metaphors employed in delegitimating discourse show no signs of emerging new ideas and interpretations that challenge the dominant ideational foundations of the economic regime.

Based on an analysis of discursive interactions in the public sphere, this chapter provides further explanation for the surprising fact that critics of capitalism were not able to seize the opportunity the crisis offered – especially considering the magnitude of the economic downturn, which was comparable to the Great Recession of the 1930s (Drezner 2014) and from which many European countries, among them the United Kingdom (Banks et al. 2014), are still struggling to recover. Why were radical and moderate critics of capitalism not able to use the post-2008 legitimation crisis to mobilize support for a more comprehensive institutional transformation of the capitalist regime? Why did they, to paraphrase Philip Mirowski (2013), let this crisis go to waste?

In order to answer these questions, I will systematically analyse the changing topography of legitimating and delegitimating discourse over time, looking at the *discursive connections* between individual speakers and the *relations* between actors and statements. This relational perspective considers individual actors to be always embedded in a web of relationships and interactions with other actors and is interested in the networks of interaction – here: *discursive* networks – among them (Jansen 2006; Hennig et al. 2012).

The network perspective builds on the same data as the statistical analysis in Chapter 3 and draws on the speaker and legitimation criteria variables to examine why a delegitimating actor coalition using a developed anticapitalist master frame has not emerged in the wake of the financial crisis. It examines first whether a coherent repertoire of arguments questioning the legitimacy of the economic regime has developed and then looks at the evolution of discourse coalitions after the crisis.

Discourse Networks

The following analysis of discursive interaction in the public sphere draws on the growing literature on policy and discourse networks (Sabatier and Weible 2007; Rhodes 2008; Schneider et al. 2009; McClurg and Young 2011; Leifeld 2013), especially on Maarten Hajer's (1993, 1995, 2002) concept of discourse coalitions. Hajer argues that political problems do not simply exist but are constructed as problems in a discursive process. The act of defining a problem takes place in a structured political space in which different actors fight for discursive hegemony. They do not act in isolation but form discourse coalitions, characterized by their joint use of frames, argumentative figures and practices (Hajer 1993: 46). Their shared ideas function as coalition-building resources (Blyth 2002: 39).

Discourse coalitions can, in principle, be examined in every public sphere. However, quality newspapers are an especially prominent arena of public discourse in which claims and opinions are usually substantiated with arguments. In this arena, various actors position themselves discursively (or are positioned by journalists) and interact with or respond to other actors' discursive interventions. This discursive interaction generates complex connections between actors who rely on the same pool of criteria to criticize or to legitimate the economic regime. Analysing the complexity of this discursive web requires a method that is able to deal with the relational nature of the discursive interaction. If there is only a small number of statements and actors, this can be done with a classical qualitative text-analytical approach. But for a large number of statements contributed by many actors over a long period of time, discourse network analysis offers a better tool to capture the changing patterns of discursive interaction.

I therefore conceptualize discourse on the legitimacy of the capitalist market economy in the four national publics as discourse *networks* (Leifeld and Haunss 2012; Leifeld 2013). The nodes of discourse networks are the actors involved and the arguments (legitimation criteria) they use. The resulting network contains two separate classes of nodes: actors and legitimation criteria (Fig. 7.1). Discourse networks thus

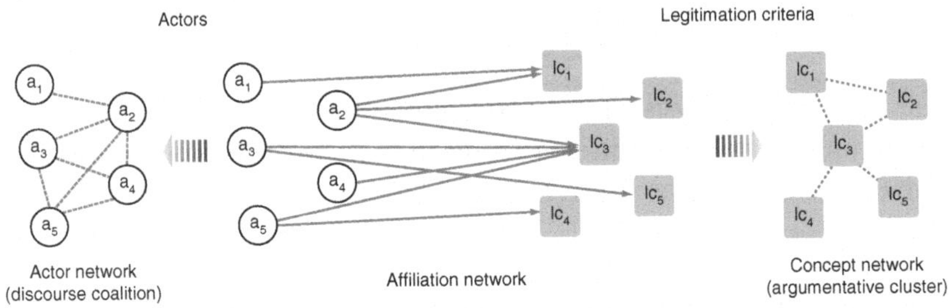

Fig. 7.1 Model of a discourse network

belong to the class of affiliation or bipartite networks (Borgatti and Everett 1997) where links (edges) can only exist between nodes of different classes. In discourse networks, an edge between two nodes in the network is formed when an actor uses a specific legitimation criterion in her evaluative statement.

Conceptualizing legitimation discourse as affiliation networks makes it possible to identify the discursive relationships between actors that emerge when different actors base their arguments on the same legitimation criteria. These indirect connections between actors should be interpreted as discourse coalitions, as conceptualized by Hajer. They are, in the conceptual frame of network analysis, tightly connected clusters of actors, linked to each other by several edges.

From a network analytical perspective, discourse coalitions are one of two possible co-occurrence networks, resulting from a projection of the original affiliation network onto one of the sides.[1] Projecting the affiliation network onto the side of actors produces links between actors whenever they share one or more legitimation criteria. An edge in the actor network thus refers to an overlap of arguments employed by the two actors it connects. If actors share more than one legitimation criterion, this is reflected in the weight of the edge, which is visualized in the network graphs as the thickness of an edge. Projecting the affiliation network onto the side of legitimation criteria creates concept networks in which edges are created between criteria whenever they are used by the same actor. In this case, a higher edge weight reflects the simultaneous use of two (or more) legitimation criteria by several actors.

Concept networks should thus be interpreted as repertoires or clusters of arguments used by one or more actors.

Conceptualizing the debates in the public sphere as affiliation networks, and thus considering only relationships between actors and legitimation criteria, is a methodological decision resulting from the present volume's overall focus on public discourse. While there are presumably other direct relationships between some of the actors involved in media discourse (e.g. two actors may be members of the same organization, be friends, relatives or have formal relations), these other relations cannot be systematically reconstructed based on the evaluation of newspaper articles, since the source material provides only sporadic information about possible direct relationships between the actors. Only relationships between actors and legitimation criteria can be reliably mapped based on our corpus of newspaper data.

Among all the possible discourse networks, some ideal-typical network topographies can be identified, corresponding to ideal-typical discursive constellations. Figure 7.2 shows three such network topographies. In the graphs, white circles denote actors and blue squares legitimation criteria. Green arrows represent the legitimating use of a legitimation criterion and orange arrows indicate delegitimating use. The network topography on the left-hand side is a classic case of an unconnected, scattered discourse, characterized by the actors' use of

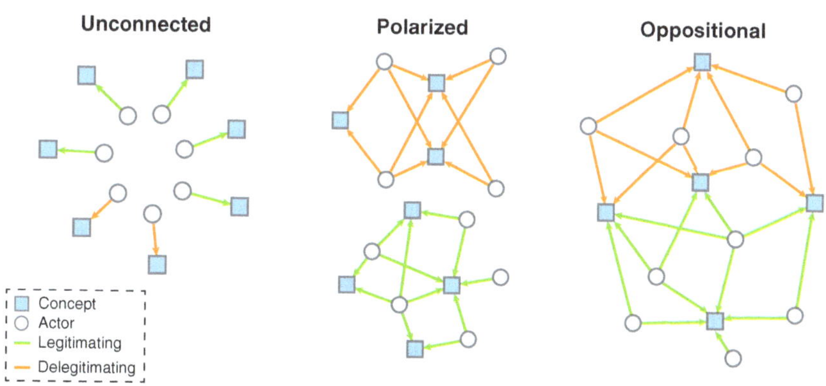

Fig. 7.2 Ideal-typical network topographies

separate legitimation criteria (concepts). As a result, there is no discursive connection between the actors; instead of a coherent discourse, only individual and scattered utterances exist which remain unconnected and do not reverberate in the public. Since the actors speak only for themselves, without referring to each other, I call this structure an *autistic* discourse constellation. If this constellation goes along with a network consisting of only a small number of actors and statements, it indicates an a-legitimacy scenario of the capitalist market economy, in which occasional and unconnected statements represent nothing more than the background noise of political discourse.

The network topography in the middle represents a polarized discourse, characterized by two clearly differentiated and separate discourse coalitions. In this constellation, connections exist only within each discourse coalition. Participating actors thus substantiate their legitimacy evaluations according to coalition-specific criteria, and as a result the two sides are effectively speaking about something different. An example of such a constellation is a delegitimating discourse coalition criticizing the capitalist economic regime as undemocratic and unjust, with a legitimating coalition praising it as efficient and promoting innovation. Whether such a *disjunction* of coalitions legitimating and delegitimating the capitalist market economy leads to a profound delegitimation of the economic regime and thus potentially to its institutional transformation depends primarily on the size and density of the two coalitions. A clear hegemony of densely connected anticapitalist positions accompanied by an unwillingness or inability of proponents of the market economy to respond to the arguments of critics should clearly be interpreted as a constellation with transformative potential – at least when the anticapitalist coalition is 'large enough' in absolute terms.[2] If, on the other hand, both coalitions are approximately the same size, such a constellation should be interpreted as evidence for the weakness of the anticapitalists and their arguments, indicating relatively stable legitimacy of the capitalist market economy.

The network topography on the right-hand side depicts a discourse characterized by two opposing discourse coalitions with largely overlapping legitimation criteria. This constellation represents a political dispute that corresponds most closely to Habermas's ideal of a deliberative democracy, one in which actors engage with the arguments of the opposite side. Such a constellation should be interpreted as an *integrated* political discourse about the economic regime. If there is a strong numerical imbalance between the two discourse coalitions, the network shown on the right in Fig. 7.2 may develop into a hegemonic constellation, with one side dominating the discourse and the other side playing only a marginal role. Such a constellation may destabilize the discursive legitimacy foundations of the capitalist market economy if critical evaluations dominate the discourse or even become hegemonic, and if the anti-capitalist coalition surpasses a certain threshold in terms of size and density.

Empirically observed discourse networks are usually combinations of these ideal types with additional factors affecting the substantive interpretation of the network topographies and thus also the interpretation of the transformative potential of the constellation. Network analysis enables the researcher not only to identify network topographies but also to determine the importance of an individual actor or an individual legitimation criterion within the overall discourse network. The importance of individual nodes can be measured by their centrality. In this study, Kleinberg's (1999) measure of hub centrality is used, because it focuses not only on individual nodes but also considers their respective neighbourhoods.[3] An actor has a particularly high hub centrality if the legitimation criteria used by this actor are also employed by other actors, whose criteria are again used by many other actors. Similarly, the hub centrality of a legitimation criterion depends on whether it is used by many actors who also draw on other criteria, which are in turn employed by many other actors. An actor with a high hub centrality value thus acts as a hub within the network and has relatively strong discursive authority. Legitimation criteria with high hub centrality values are core elements of a complex and coherent argumentation consisting of a range of densely connected concepts.

Discourse Networks over Time

Whereas descriptive statistical analysis of legitimacy communication provides a bird's eye view of developments over time and of differences between countries, discourse network analysis permits a closer and more detailed look at those general dynamics. In the years 1998–2011, public communication about the legitimacy of the economic regime follows a broadly similar pattern in all four countries. Before the financial crisis, statements about the legitimacy of the economic regime tend to be only weakly connected. In some years, discourse even comes very close to the ideal type of an autistic constellation. In their evaluations of the economic regime, actors present in the media only seldom draw on the same legitimation criteria. The small size and disconnectedness of the networks thus suggest – at least in some of the years before the financial crisis – an a-legitimacy constellation of the economic regime. This is especially true for the United States and Switzerland, where public communication about the legitimacy of the capitalist market economy is very sparse over the whole period; in the United States, it disappears almost completely between 2001 and 2005.

In the wake of the financial crisis, the interconnectedness of legitimating or delegitimating statements has grown in all four countries. Nevertheless, in Switzerland and the United States in particular, public discourse on the legitimacy of the economic regime remains rather weak. In Switzerland, the public debate is clearly dominated by a small number of journalists – notably two journalists from the *Neue Zürcher Zeitung*, Gerhard Schwarz and Markus Spillmann. Between 2008 and 2011, only two politicians participate in the debate, both with an overall ambiguous evaluation of one delegitimating and one legitimating statement.

The general pattern of growing intensity and interconnectedness of legitimation discourse is most evident in the network graph showing the discourse networks in the United Kingdom (Fig. 7.3). For each year, the graph depicts all statements in which an actor evaluates the economic regime negatively or positively. White circles represent actors, blue squares legitimation criteria. Orange lines indicate delegitimating, green lines legitimating use of the particular legitimation criterion. The graphs show at a glance that the networks have grown in size and cohesion since 2007. In the United Kingdom, prior to 2007, the largest connected component and thus the largest group of discursively connected actors never comprises more than seven actors, and the connection usually consists of

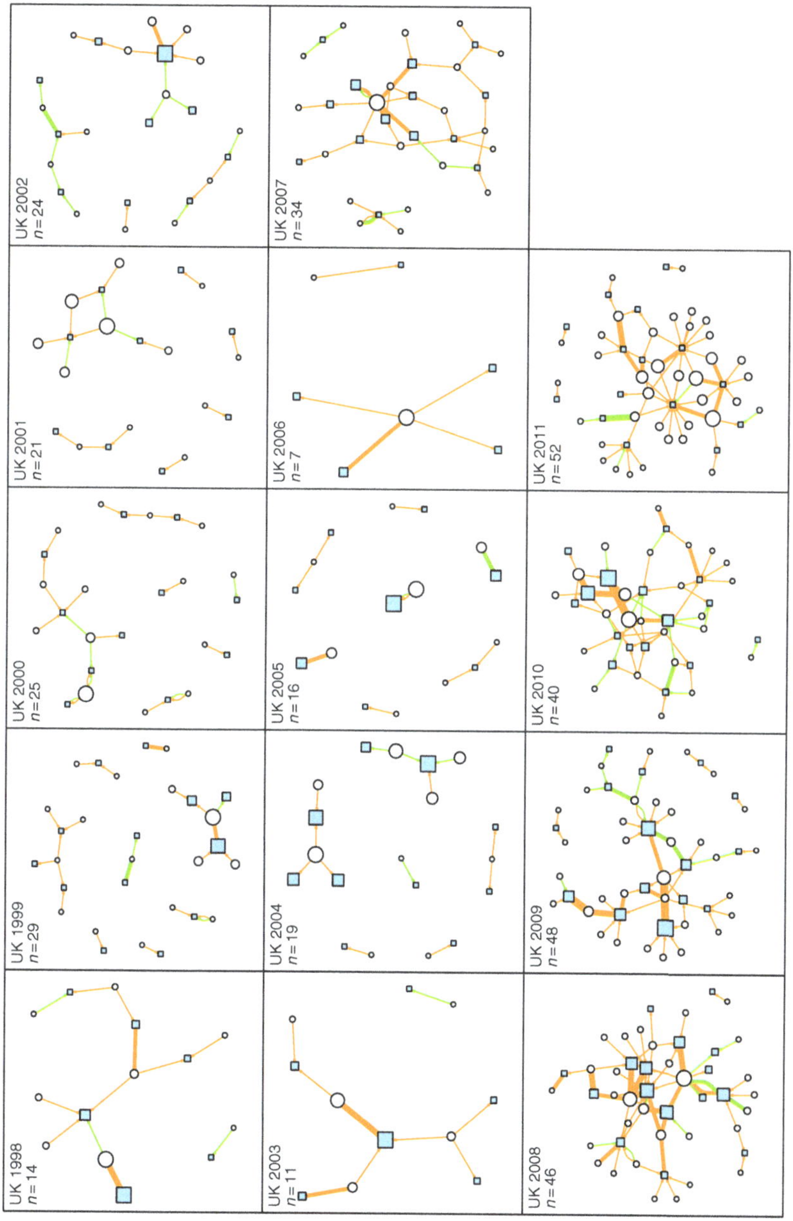

Fig. 7.3 Discourse networks in the United Kingdom, 1998–2011

exactly one shared legitimation criterion. These graphs illustrate that vivid legitimation discourse depends not only on the number of speakers but also on the number of statements each of them makes. Equally important, however, is the overall connectedness among speakers through shared arguments. For example, the size of the discourse networks for the years 1999 and 2007 increases only moderately from 29 to 34 nodes, but during the same time period the density of the network (measured as average degree centrality) increases from 1.5 to 2.2 – indicating a substantial increase of discursive links between actors.

Since 2008, the discourse networks in the United Kingdom have consisted of one contiguous main component and several isolated sub-networks, the latter consisting each of one single actor and the legitimation criteria they use. The discourse network analysis thus shows that the statistically observed increase in terms of discourse intensity during the financial crisis is accompanied by increasingly tight connections between the actors involved in the debate about the legitimacy of the economic regime and their arguments. Together, the growing intensity of the debate and the more densely connected discourse networks suggest a critical development with regard to the legitimacy of the capitalist market economy.

The discourse networks for the same period in Germany (Fig. 7.4) provide a similar picture. However, in contrast to the other countries, relatively large connected sub-networks can be detected even before 2008. This finding reflects intensive debates about the legitimacy of the economic regime triggered by and grouped around prominent politicians and their discursive interventions. In the years 1998 and 2000, these debates developed around contributions by Otto Graf Lambsdorff, a prominent member of the German Liberal Party (FDP), defending the capitalist market economy against anti-neoliberal critique (*Frankfurter Allgemeine Zeitung*, 'Der Bürger entscheidet selbst', 4 April, 1998) and praising it as a system that promotes tolerance (*Frankfurter Allgemeine Zeitung*, 'Standpunkte: Otto Graf Lambsdorff', 10 October, 2000). In 2005, Franz Müntefering (SPD) set off the 'Heuschreckendebatte', a political controversy in which he used the biblical metaphor of the

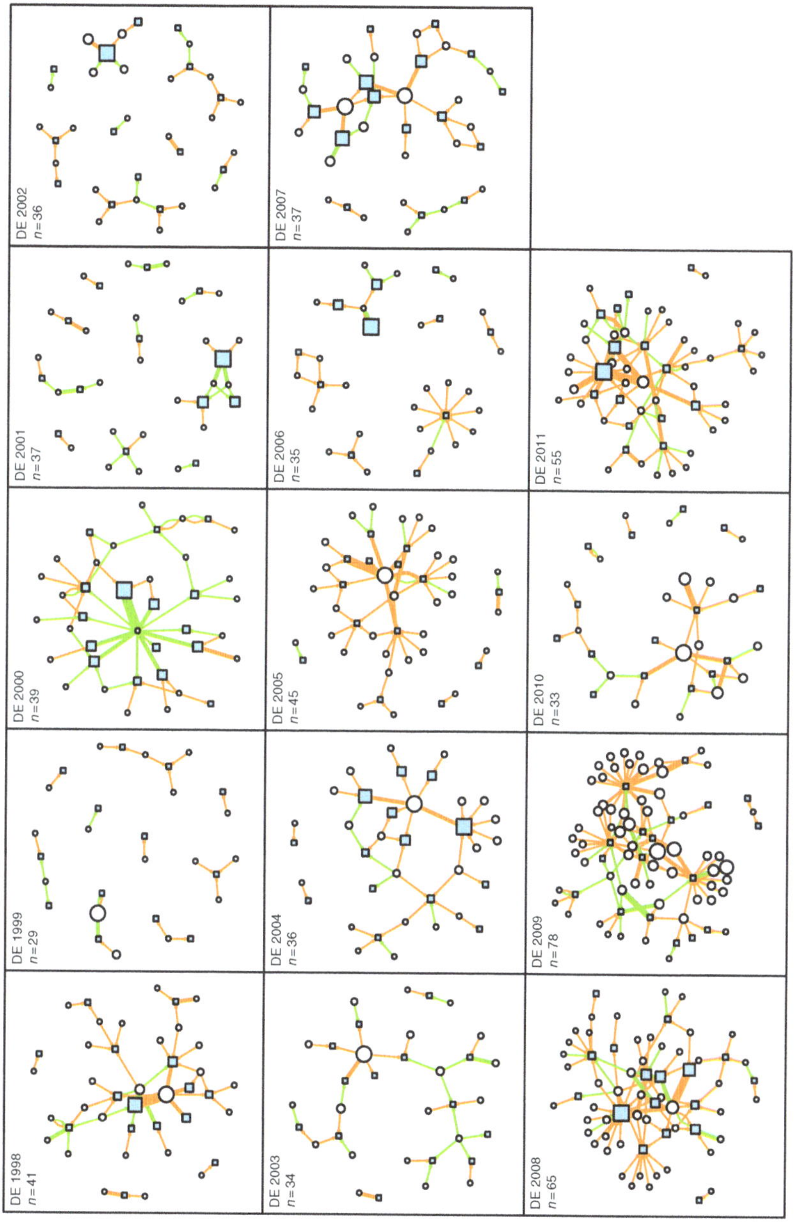

Fig. 7.4 Discourse networks in Germany, 1998–2011

'plague of locusts' to denounce the irresponsible profit maximization strategies of international investors (*Süddeutsche Zeitung*, 'Balsam für die linke Seele', 14 April, 2005). While these were lively debates, German discourse nevertheless changed significantly with the onset of the financial crisis. Between 1998 and 2007, the analysis reveals some years with largely unconnected discourse networks, consisting of many individual components, and some years with densely connected networks, mainly composed of one principal element and some individual unconnected sub-networks. Since the financial crisis, however, the discourse networks have always consisted of one large main component that includes all stakeholders, with the exception of a small number (one to four) of unconnected actors. Within the main component, many actors are connected through more than one shared legitimation criterion, leading to a densely connected discourse.

Overall, in two of the four countries, Germany and the United Kingdom, the financial crisis did not only lead to a higher intensity of legitimation communication but also to an intensification of the conflict as expressed in stronger discursive links between actors. In the United States and Switzerland, the salience of the issue has remained so low that discourse network analysis is not able to identify clear trends.

How should the more intense and more tightly connected discourse in Germany and the United Kingdom be interpreted? In general, both countries move from an a-legitimacy or weak-delegitimation scenario to a more integrated political discourse on the legitimacy of the capitalist market economy, in which critical evaluations outweigh support even more strongly than before 2008. Thus, at least for Germany and the United Kingdom, the first results from the discourse network analysis support the findings of the statistical analysis in Chapter 3 and suggest a scenario in which the legitimation crisis *might* have developed into an institutional transformation of the capitalist market economy. However, looking only at the topographies of the discourse networks is not enough. To understand why this transformative potential was not mobilized despite the growing density of delegitimating discourse, a closer look at the structure of arguments and at the actors is necessary.

What Is Being Said? The Structure of Arguments

Which repertoires of arguments are used in the public debate? Do we see the emergence of new repertoires that represent a shifting interpretation of the legitimacy of the economic regime, a new set of ideas with the potential to initiate institutional change? In order to answer this question, the analysis now turns to the concept networks that represent the repertoires of arguments used by actors involved in legitimacy communication.

A discursive constellation in which the legitimacy of the economic regime is fundamentally challenged would be characterized by the emergence and stabilization of an argumentative core of anticapitalist criticism built around several tightly connected legitimation criteria. In such an argumentative core, shared legitimation criteria link groups of actors. These legitimation criteria function as frame bridges between varying interpretive frames held by different actor groups (Snow et al. 1986; Benford and Snow 2000). Ideally, a repertoire of arguments used by a strong discourse coalition comprises only a limited number of closely linked legitimation criteria, with the criteria that are most important for the shared argumentation at the centre of the concept network. In addition, one would also expect the shared and thus connected criteria to be coherent at a substantive level, since otherwise a coherent and consistent argumentation would be hard to develop. In other words, in a transformative scenario, an anticapitalist coalition effectively produces a delegitimating master frame that is able to bridge actors' more specific frames and to fundamentally question the legitimacy of the economic regime.

The following analysis of the changing structures of argumentation is based on the 3-slices of the concept networks, that is, the networks of legitimation criteria that are shared by at least three actors in the same way. The analysis focuses here on network cores (3-slices) because they represent the relatively stable underlying structures of the networks. Focusing on the network cores also reduces the effect of missing observations resulting from our sampling strategy.[4] In the graph, the size of the nodes corresponds to their hub centrality in the original affiliation network. Nodes are colour-coded according to the following pattern: Blue nodes represent legitimation criteria that address the functional core of the capitalist market economy and thus focus primarily on its economic performance. These criteria belong to the clusters of classical justification or criticism introduced in Chapter 2. Green nodes represent legitimation criteria that focus on aspects outside the core of classical justifications of the economic regime and address, for example, issues of (distributive) justice or moral values.

In Germany, both before and after the financial crisis, the networks show a set of connected legitimation criteria and thus a coherent repertoire of arguments (Fig. 7.5). However, the legitimation criteria are not very strongly connected, particularly in the period leading up to the financial crisis. The maximum normalized edge weight, that is, the edge weight divided by the number of years for each observation period, is 0.5 in Germany before the financial crisis. This means that the two most strongly connected concepts are on average shared by 0.5 actors per year, or more intuitively: Once every four years, two actors agree on more than one legitimation criterion. After the crisis, this value rises to 2.75, indicating that on average less than three actors have used two or more legitimation

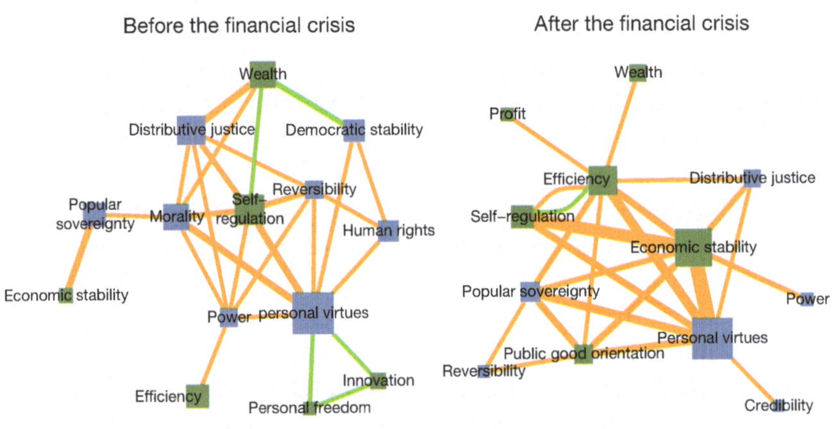

Fig. 7.5 Germany, concept networks pre-/post-financial crisis, 3-slice

criteria concurrently in one and the same year between 2008 and 2011. While we see more coherent criticism of the capitalist market economy in Germany after the financial crisis, the absolute level of discursive cohesion remains very low.

In the United Kingdom, the cluster of densely connected legitimation criteria before the financial crisis is much smaller than in Germany (Fig. 7.6). Between 1998 and 2007, only five criteria are connected by three or more actors sharing at least two of them, with the criticism of insufficient provision of public goods having the highest hub centrality value (1.0). As in Germany, with a value of 0.6 the maximum normalized edge weight is very low. On average, we have to aggregate data over more than three years before two actors agree on at least two legitimation criteria. After the financial crisis, the bundle of strongly connected legitimation criteria grows significantly in the United Kingdom, and the maximum normalized edge weight increases to 2.0. Again, this is a very low value as it means that on average in any given year no more than two actors agree on more than one legitimation criterion. This hardly indicates a strongly connected emerging repertoire of arguments on which powerful criticism of the capitalist market economy might be based.

Substantially, the legitimation criteria used have changed less in Germany than in the United Kingdom. In Germany, both before and after the financial crisis, the most central legitimation criterion is the lack

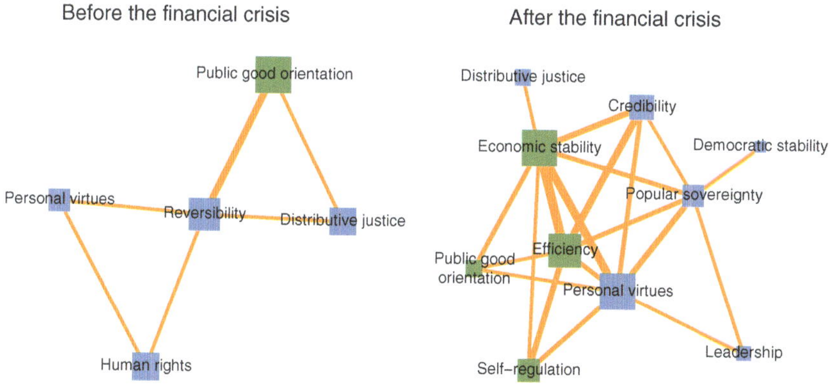

Fig. 7.6 United Kingdom, concept networks pre-/post-financial crisis, 3-slice

of personal virtues of economic agents (hub centrality 1.0 in both periods).[5] Before the crisis, other central concepts are criticism of the deficient provision of wealth (0.61), distributive justice (0.55), democratic stability (0.41) and human rights (0.38). The most central arguments before the crisis thus draw mainly on non-classical legitimation criteria, relying on culture-, justice- and democracy-centred criticism of the market economy. After the crisis, classical criteria addressing the functional core of the capitalist market economy move to the centre of the repertoire of arguments. The economic regime is now criticized for its failure to ensure economic stability (hub centrality 0.88) and the provision of common goods (0.32), and for its deficits in terms of effectiveness and efficiency (0.63).

In the United Kingdom, the negative impact of the market on the personal virtues of economic actors only takes centre stage after the crisis (hub centrality before the crisis 0.33, after the crisis 1.0), followed by lack of economic stability (0.99), effectiveness/efficiency (0.89), credibility (0.60), self-regulation (0.53) and popular control (0.51). At a substantial level, the anticapitalist line of argument in Britain since 2008 has thus become remarkably similar to discourse in Germany at the same time.

Figure 7.7 shows this comparison of hub centrality values in the original affiliation networks containing the complete set of legitimation criteria and not just those present in the concept network cores discussed above. In this graph, we clearly see that discourse in Germany has indeed changed only moderately in the wake of the financial crisis. Many legitimation criteria more or less keep their position in relation to the other criteria. Only legitimation criteria that address a lack of stability and efficiency see a steep increase in their centrality and thus their importance within the discourse. Before the financial crisis, arguments focus on culture-centred arguments about personal virtues and morality combined with justice- and democracy-centred criticism of distributive injustice, lacking democratic control of economic processes and the negative impact of the economy on democracy in general. After the financial crisis, personal virtues and culture-centred criticism of the economic regime have retained their central role for the argumentation, but they are now joined by legitimation criteria that focus on the

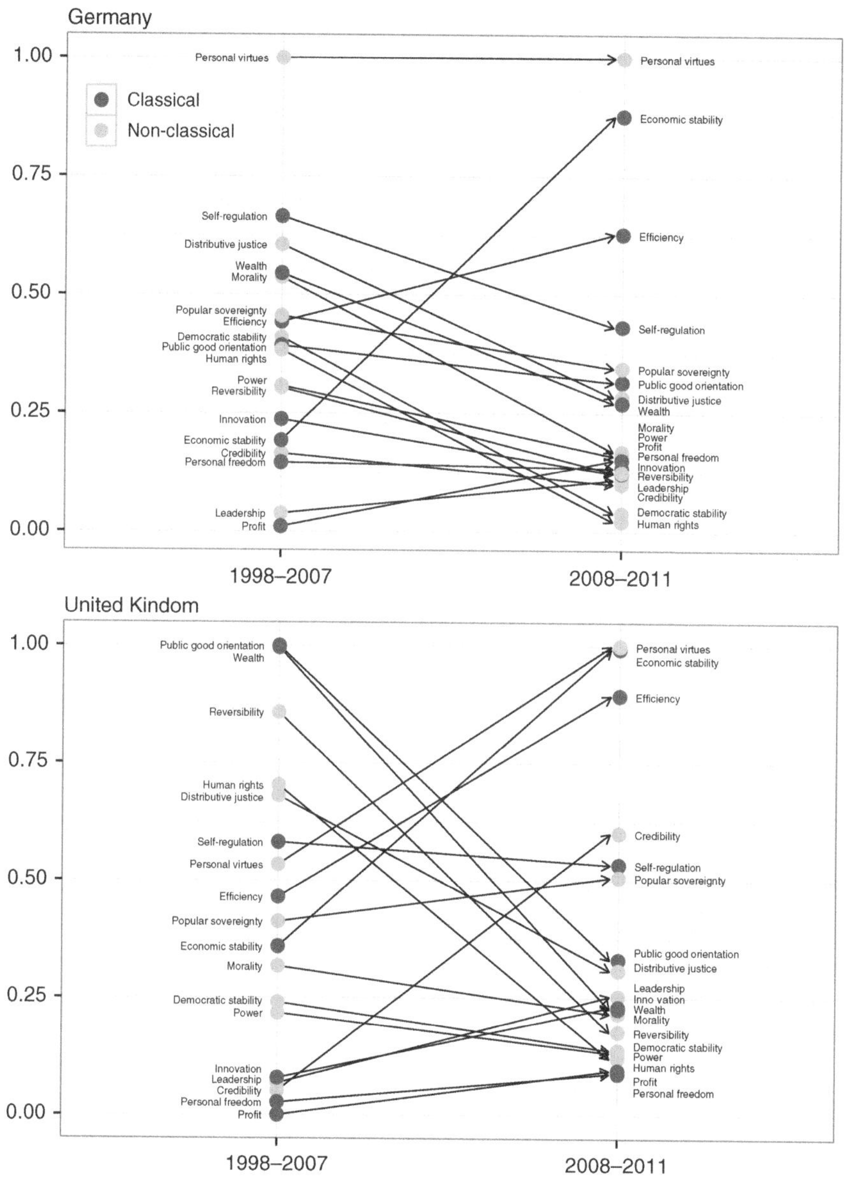

Fig. 7.7 Hub centrality values pre-/post-financial crisis

economic stability of the capitalist market economy, thus indicating a loss of confidence in its proper functioning.

In the United Kingdom, where discourse changed more dramatically than in Germany, personal virtues and culture-centred aspects did not play such a prominent role before the financial crisis. Instead, before 2008, criticism of the consequences of capitalism was based in its core on democracy- and justice-centred arguments. After the crisis, the rank order of legitimation criteria based on their hub centrality values changed much more than in Germany, resulting in structurally similar delegitimating discourse in both countries. Since 2008, criticism of the capitalist market economy's lacking personal virtues, diminishing economic stability and efficiency has moved to the centre stage of discourse in the United Kingdom. As in Germany, aspects of democratic control and distributive justice have lost their central role in the debate.

This is remarkable especially for the aspect of (distributive) justice, which has traditionally formed the centre of anticapitalist critique voiced by the labour movement and its organizations and parties. The current framing in Germany and the United Kingdom thus breaks with a tradition that Boltanski and Chiapello have called 'social critique' and which denounces the 'egoism of private interests [. . .] and the growing poverty of the popular classes in a society of unprecedented wealth' (2007: 38). As this line of argument has become less integrated into delegitimating discourse after the financial crisis, an important bridging frame between political and cultural actors is now missing. As I will show in the next section, this paradoxically goes along with a very pronounced shift towards actors from the cultural sphere in the centre of the discourse coalitions criticizing the capitalist market economy.

Who Speaks? Networks of Actors and Discourse Coalitions

The final step of the analysis provides the strongest clues on why the financial crisis only provoked an ephemeral legitimation crisis that did not lead to institutional change of the capitalist market economy. Going back to the diagnosis of a discursive legitimation crisis (see Chapter 3), we need to answer the following question: Under what circumstances should more intense debate with a more negative tone, and hence with stronger and more integrated delegitimating discourse coalitions, have been able to push the critical juncture of the financial crisis towards institutional change of the capitalist market economy?

In principle, higher density of discourse networks can be driven by two mechanisms: It can be the result of a differentiation of arguments, where a small number of central actors use a large number of legitimation criteria concurrently. Or it can be the result of a large number of actors agreeing on multiple points. In both cases, it is only appropriate to classify this as a development with transformative potential if the judgements are clearly negative and if the discourse coalition also becomes politically relevant. To be politically relevant, members of the delegitimating discourse coalition should either control important power resources, for instance, as representatives of the state or large business organizations, or represent major societal stakeholders such as unions or churches (Korpi 1985). A discourse coalition may also be regarded as politically relevant if it represents a broad social base and includes members from the societal elite, thus creating an opportunity for broad and contentious mobilization (Kriesi 2004).

In order to check whether such a development can actually be observed, I now analyse the discourse coalitions in more detail and examine the actor networks consisting of actors connected through their shared use of the same legitimation criteria. As already mentioned, only in Germany and the United Kingdom can discourse coalitions of a sufficient size be identified in our evaluation of quality newspapers, and therefore a closer inspection of the actor networks is limited to comparing these two countries. This first result already indicates that anti-capitalist positions have not significantly gained traction in the wake of the financial crisis in the United States and Switzerland. Even though the intensity and negative tone of the legitimacy evaluations of the economic regime have also grown in these countries, the emergence of only weak discursive connections between actors and a discourse heavily dominated by very few core speakers without relevant power resources may explain why the legitimation crisis never developed into a serious danger for the economic regime and remained without lasting consequences.

Figure 7.8 shows the cores (2-slice) of the two actor networks in Germany for the periods before and after the financial crisis. Aggregation over several years and the fact that there was already a comparatively lively debate before 2008 resulted in relatively dense discourse coalitions

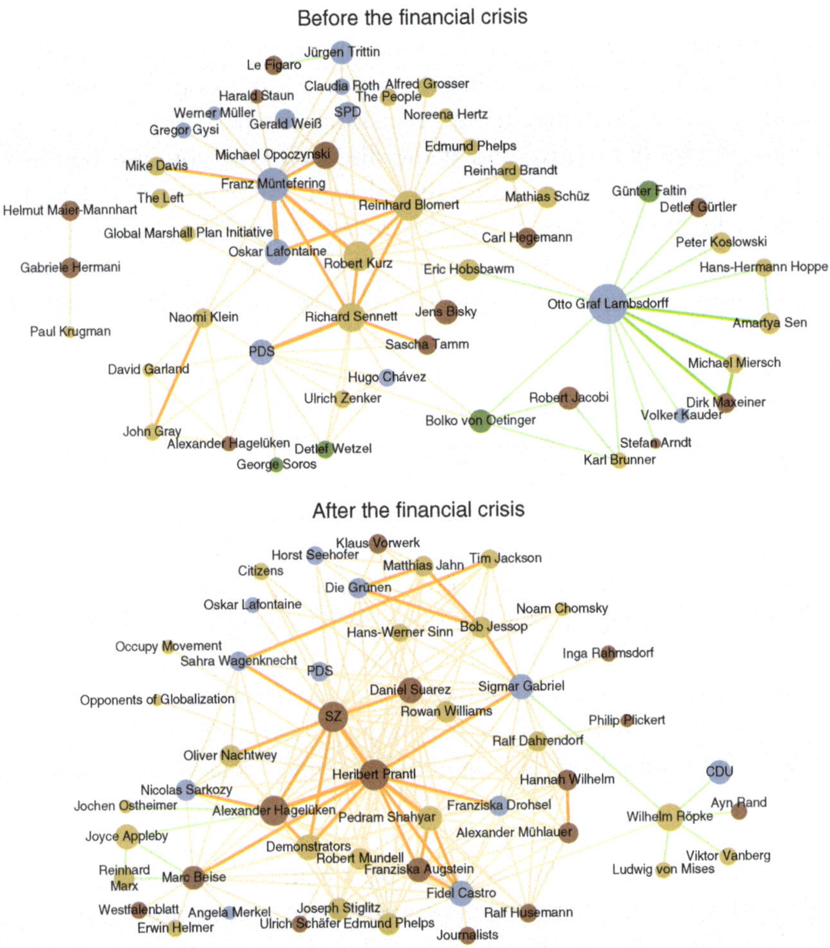

Fig. 7.8 Germany, discourse coalitions pre-/post-financial crisis, 2-slice

whose members shared at least two legitimation criteria in the respective period. For example, before the financial crisis, Oskar Lafontaine and Robert Kurz both criticized capitalism using the legitimation criteria 'personal virtues' and 'democratic stability'. They are therefore connected by an edge with the edge weight 2.

In the period before the financial crisis, two clearly distinct camps can be observed: a legitimating discourse coalition around FDP politician Otto Graf Lambsdorff and a delegitimating discourse coalition comprising several subgroups of politicians from the SPD, the Greens and the Leftist Party together with a number of intellectuals and journalists. Individual economic actors also participate in the debate, both legitimating and delegitimating the economic regime.

Since the financial crisis, the discourse coalitions have changed significantly. Although the actor networks before and after the financial crisis include approximately the same number of actors connected through shared arguments (52 before and 50 after the financial crisis), it should be noted that the earlier network is the result of an aggregation of discourse data over ten years (1998–2007) while the second network aggregates statements from only four years (2008–11).

Changes between the networks before and after the financial crisis are expressed in the significant increase of network density (measured as average degree centrality of the nodes) from 21.76 to 30.88.[6] In the post-crisis observation period, much stronger discursive links between actors can be observed, with more actors in the delegitimating discourse coalition sharing a higher number of legitimation criteria.

A very important change with regard to discourse participants has also taken place since the financial crisis: Politicians are no longer at the centre of the close-knit delegitimating discourse coalition, but journalists and intellectuals, especially Heribert Prantl and Alexander Hagelüken from the *Süddeutsche Zeitung*. At the same time, the legitimating discourse coalition has become fragmented and no longer includes political actors. Only the Christian-Democratic Union (CDU) and Social Democrat Sigmar Gabriel appear as being ambivalent (legitimating and delegitimating), therefore bridging the two actor coalitions. Economic actors have completely vanished from the much more critical debate.

The colour intensity of the edges in Fig. 7.8 reflects the number of shared legitimation criteria through which actors are connected. Lightly coloured edges represent two shared legitimation criteria, while dark-coloured edges indicate more than two shared criteria. Taking into account this information about tie strength, we can identify cores of strongly connected actors for both periods. In Germany, there are three strongly connected discourse coalitions before the financial crisis: two delegitimating coalitions with nine and two members, respectively, and a legitimating discourse coalition consisting of five actors. In the period after the financial crisis, the legitimating coalition disappears and one strongly connected delegitimating discourse coalition with 18 actors emerges.[7] In this relatively large sub-network, journalists from the *Süddeutsche Zeitung* occupy the most central positions.

The development in the United Kingdom (Fig. 7.9) is similar, although a strongly connected legitimating discourse coalition does not exist either before or after the financial crisis; the actor network grows from 24 to 37 actors and density goes up from 13.35 to 20.16. Before the financial crisis, the larger one of the two strongly connected delegitimating discourse coalitions comprises only five actors; afterwards, the sub-network of strongly connected actors has grown to 15 in the United Kingdom. Even more conspicuously than in Germany, journalists are at the centre of the actor network, whereas politicians play only a marginal role.

Thus, both in Germany and the United Kingdom, the most vocal critics of the economic regime – especially after the financial crisis – are journalists and intellectuals. Only a small number of politicians participate in the debate. Economic actors are only marginally involved since they apparently see no need to defend the legitimacy of capitalism against its critics. What is striking is the absence of representatives of large social interest groups, especially of trade unions, which would have been obvious candidates for critical evaluations of the capitalist economic regime in a time of crisis. While unions did participate in the public debate about economic policy during the crisis, they limited their criticism to the policy level without questioning the legitimacy of the capitalist economic regime as such, even against the backdrop of the collapse of the financial sector and of entire economies (Bieling 2013: 434–41). Moreover, civil society actors usually

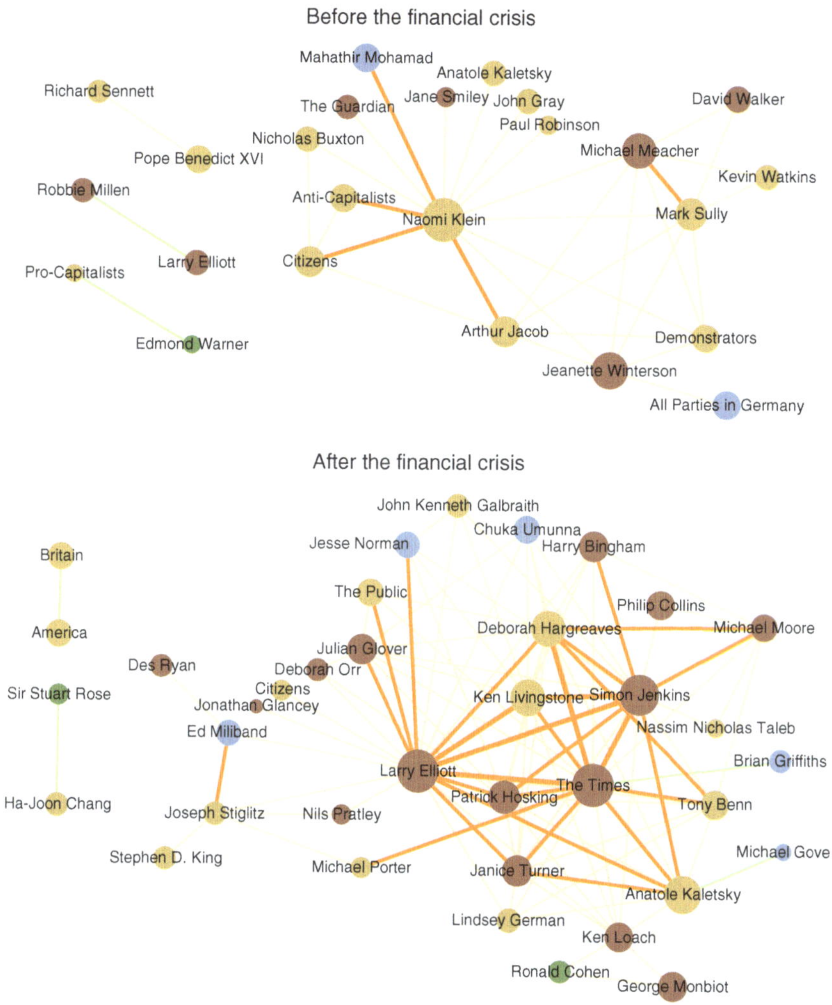

Fig. 7.9 United Kingdom, discourse coalitions pre-/post-financial crisis, 2-slice

speak as individual intellectuals and not as representatives of member organizations or NGOs in our material. The structure of the legitimation discourse in Germany and the United Kingdom thus corresponds to the only sporadic and weak protest mobilizations in these countries during the crisis (della Porta 2015).

To sum up, after the financial crisis, there are no strongly connected discourse coalitions delegitimating the economic regime in the United States and Switzerland. In contrast, in Germany and the United Kingdom, we clearly observe the emergence of strongly connected discourse coalitions criticizing the economic regime. Compared to the period before the financial crisis, the cohesion of critical assessments of the economic regime increases, but at the same time the social diversity of the anti-capitalist discourse coalition remains very low (the United Kingdom) or even decreases in comparison to the pre-crisis period (Germany). Members of the delegitimating discourse coalition are predominantly recruited from the media, culture and academia. In the post-crisis observation period, intellectual critics of capitalism and the market economy rise to speak, but the debate rarely extends beyond these intellectual circles and finds little echo and manifest support in the broader society.

The analysis of the actor networks helps to explain why even in the two countries with the most intense debate, Germany and the United Kingdom, the initial impulse of the legitimation crisis dissolved without leaving fundamental traces in the economic regime. In the wake of the financial crisis, an integrated political discourse about the legitimacy of the capitalist market economy has emerged, but it is supported neither by powerful individual actors nor by a broad coalition of societal actors. Therefore, the weak presence of economic actors should be interpreted as discursive restraint rather than as marginalization: Apparently, protagonists of the economic regime have so far not found it necessary to intervene in the debate in order to defend the capitalist market economy against its critics.

Thus, in the wake of the financial crisis, a discourse coalition consisting of key actors from the media, science and culture has emerged and developed a strongly connected discourse delegitimating the economic regime. However, this discourse is not picked up by politicians, unions or a broad coalition of social actors nor does it develop sufficient strength to force members of the business elite to respond and to defend the economic regime against its critics. In sum, after the financial crisis, the discourse has remained limited to the feature pages of the quality press and has failed to create bridges to political debates and mobilization efforts elsewhere in society.

Conclusion

Discourse network analysis provides a detailed picture of legitimation statements on the economic regime in German, Swiss, UK and US quality newspapers between 1998 and 2011. It allows us to judge the dynamics and the scope of the post-2008 legitimation crisis of the capitalist market economy. And it enables us to understand why, in the four countries examined, the critical juncture of the financial crisis and the ensuing delegitimation of the capitalist market economy did not lead to a fundamental transformation of the regime. Overall, three aspects characterize the development of public debates about the legitimacy of the economic regime in the context of the financial crisis.

Firstly, the financial crisis has left its mark in all four countries, both materially and discursively. The intensity of debates and the connectedness of arguments about the legitimacy of the capitalist economic regime have increased in all four countries. However, in the United States, the country in which the financial crisis originated, both the intensity of the debate and the density of the discourse networks have remained the lowest. Here, the regime was not seriously challenged in the public either before or after the financial crisis, and the anticapitalist discourse coalition never comprised more than a handful of actors. At the same time, statements by individual actors remained scattered and links between the arguments of different actors are observed only occasionally. Even in Switzerland, a country that was only mildly impacted by the financial crisis, a more strongly connected discourse about the legitimacy of the economic regime has developed, although it was sustained to a large degree by only a small group of journalists. As a consequence, a broad political discourse about the legitimacy of the regime did not emerge in Switzerland, neither before nor after the financial crisis. Overall, our data indicate that in Switzerland and the United States, despite the increase of critical statements, the situation remains close to the a-legitimacy scenario, where the economic regime's core principles are broadly accepted and its legitimacy is, therefore, not even explicitly discussed.

In Germany and the United Kingdom, the discourse network analysis presents a different picture, with a strongly connected and predominantly critical discourse emerging between 2008 and 2011. Tightly integrated political discourse about the capitalist market economy develops and, because of its predominantly negative tone and the high number of actors involved, a development from legitimation crisis to institutional change of the regime seems possible at first. Nevertheless, the other results help to understand why this transformative impulse has quickly disappeared.

Secondly, the analysis of discursive connections between individual legitimation criteria does not point to a strongly connected and integrated discourse. Even in the two countries with the most intense debates, sets of arguments are only seldom shared by different speakers. Aggregated over the whole crisis period, a larger repertoire of arguments emerges that may well form the basis for a critical discourse coalition. Disaggregated by year, however, two actors almost never share more than two criteria to delegitimate the capitalist market economy. This observation points to a marked weakness of the regime's critics: They are unable to develop an overarching master frame that might bridge the perspectives of different actor groups.

Thirdly, in Germany and the United Kingdom, the two countries in which relatively large discourse coalitions are visible, their emergence has been accompanied by a decrease in the social diversity of discourse participants. In both countries, anticapitalist discourse since the financial crisis has been dominated by journalists, artists and academics. In the core networks, politicians participate only at the periphery, with economic actors as well as representatives of large civil society groups and unions completely absent; pronounced journalistic dominance can be found in both countries. The network analysis thus shows the emergence of critical discourse with a not very strongly connected argumentative core which is dominated by actors from the cultural sector and whose criticism does not reverberate beyond the media sphere. The actors of the delegitimating discourse coalition tend to come from the cultural sector and do not update their artistic critique focusing on alienation, disenchantment and the suppression of individual expression and creativity, which is characteristic of the new social movements (Boltanski and Chiapello 2007: 170). Instead, we see the emergence of a discourse that combines criticism of the collapse of the capitalist market economy's operating principles with discontent about the lack of virtues of the system and its economic leaders. This combination of elements from a classical critique drawing on free market and growth-centred legitimation criteria with culture-centred arguments focusing on the lack of personal virtues and greed fails to resonate beyond the cultural sphere. The framing falls short of bridging the artistic critique of the new social movements and the social critique of the unions and social democrats. It lacks a clear injustice frame and downplays democracy-centred criticism.

As a consequence, critical discourse in both Germany and the United Kingdom is not accompanied by significant protest mobilization addressing the societal consequences of the financial crisis. Anticapitalist criticism does not extend beyond the cultural sector and thus remains smoke without fire – visible in national public spheres but largely without material consequences.

Notes

1. More technically speaking, an affiliation network G^{aff} connects the actors a_1, $a_2, \ldots, a_m$ with the legitimation criteria $lc_1, lc_2, \ldots, lc_n$. If the data contain – as in our case – information about legitimation statements at different points of time, then there is an affiliation network G_t^{aff} for any time t. The projection of the original bipartite network is the result of multiplication of the (non-symmetric) affiliation matrix X with its transposed matrix X^T. The result of the projection is a symmetric co-occurrence matrix, which – depending on the order of the multiplicands – represents either the actor network or the concept network (of connected legitimation criteria). Accounting for the positive (legitimating) and negative (delegitimating) use of the legitimation criteria, the image networks are actually multiplex matrices: The projection for the positive and negative use of the criteria is done separately.
2. What is considered 'large enough' cannot be determined *a priori*. Obviously, an anticapitalist discourse coalition consisting of only ten actors should not be interpreted as a sign for the serious delegitimation of the economic regime even if the legitimating coalition is still smaller.

3. Since discourse networks are bipartite networks, degree centrality reflects only the number of statements each actor makes or the number of times a concept is mentioned by an actor. In the literature, various centrality measures for bipartite networks have been discussed (Borgatti and Everett 1997). A particularly suitable centrality measure is hub or authority centrality (Kleinberg 1999; Brandes and Wagner 2004), which takes into account, with decreasing weight, the degree centrality of all other (indirectly) connected nodes.
4. In an exploratory network analysis, basic structures of the network are often easier to detect by considering the strongly connected cores rather than the complete networks. Network cores are maximal sub-networks where nodes have at least a certain number of connections (n-cores) or where all edges are above a certain weight, thus representing stronger connections between adjacent nodes (m-slices). An n-core refers to the maximal sub-network in which all nodes have at least a degree centrality of n, an m-slice is the maximal sub-network in which all edges have at least a weight of m (de Nooy et al. 2005: 70, 109).
5. Hub centrality values are normalized and can take values between 1 and 0 where the node with the maximal hub centrality in each network has always a hub centrality value of 1.
6. The simple density measure that calculates the proportion of existing ties in relation to the maximum possible number of ties strongly depends on the size of the network and cannot be compared between networks of different sizes. I therefore measure the density of the network as the average degree centrality of all nodes, as suggested by de Nooy et al. (2011: 75).
7. The second strongly connected network, consisting of the *Süddeutsche Zeitung* journalists Hannah Wilhelm and Alexander Mühlauer, is the result of one jointly written article, and is thus more an artefact of the coding procedure than a meaningful core discourse coalition.

References

Banks, Andrew, Sami Hamroush, Ciaren Taylor and Michael Hardie. 2014. *An International Perspective on the UK – Gross Domestic Product.* London: Office for National Statistics, http://www.ons.gov.uk/ons/dcp171766_360847.pdf (last accessed September 15, 2016).

Benford, Robert D. and David A. Snow. 2000. 'Framing Processes and Social Movements: An Overview and Assessment'. *Annual Review of Sociology* 26(1): 611–39.

Bieling, Hans-Jürgen. 2013. 'Gewerkschaftspolitische Strategien in der Eurokrise: Zwischen Krisenkorporatismus und sozialem Widerstand'. In *Arbeitsbeziehungen im Prozess der Globalisierung und Europäischen Integration*, Baden-Baden: Nomos, 427–46.

Blyth, Mark. 2002. *Great Transformations. Economic Ideas and Institutional Change in the Twentieth Century*. Cambridge: Cambridge University Press.

Boltanski, Luc and Ève Chiapello. 2007. *The New Spirit of Capitalism*. London: Verso.

Borgatti, Stephen P. and Martin G. Everett. 1997. 'Network Analysis of 2-Mode Data'. *Social Networks* 19(3): 243–69.

Brandes, Ulrik and Dorothea Wagner. 2004. 'Netzwerkvisualisierung'. *it – Information Technology* 46(3): 129–34.

Della Porta, Donatella. 2015. *Social Movements in Times of Austerity*. Cambridge: Polity Press.

de Nooy, Wouter, Andrej Mrvar and Vladimir Batagelj. 2005. *Exploratory Social Network Analysis with Pajek*. Cambridge: Cambridge University Press.

de Nooy, Wouter, Andrej Mrvar and Vladimir Batagelj. 2011. *Exploratory Social Network Analysis with Pajek*. Revised and Expanded Second Edition. Cambridge: Cambridge University Press.

Drezner, Daniel W. 2014. 'The System Worked: Global Economic Governance During the Great Recession'. *World Politics* 66(1): 123–64.

Hajer, Maarten A. 1993. 'Discourse Coalitions and the Institutionalization of Practice: The Case of Acid Rain in Britain'. In *The Argumentative Turn in Policy Analysis and Planning*, eds. Frank Fischer and John Forester. Durham, NC: Duke University Press, 43–76.

Hajer, Maarten A. 1995. *The Politics of Environmental Discourse. Ecological Modernization and the Policy Process*. Oxford: Oxford University Press.

Hajer, Maarten A. 2002. 'Discourse Analysis and the Study of Policy Making'. *European Political Science* 2(1): 61–5.

Hennig, Marina, Ulrik Brandes, Jürgen Pfeffer and Ines Mergel. 2012. *Studying Social Networks. A Guide to Empirical Research*. Frankfurt am Main: Campus.

Jansen, Dorothea. 2006. *Einführung in die Netzwerkanalyse*. Third, Expanded Edition. Wiesbaden: VS.

Kleinberg, Jon M. 1999. 'Authoritative Sources in a Hyperlinked Environment'. *Journal of the Association for Computing Machinery* 46(5): 604–32.

Korpi, Walter. 1985. 'Power Resources Approach vs. Action and Conflict: On Causal and Intentional Explanations in the Study of Power'. *Sociological Theory* 3(2): 31–45.

Kriesi, Hanspeter. 2004. 'Political Context and Opportunity'. In *The Blackwell Companion to Social Movements*, eds. David A. Snow, Sarah A. Soule and Hanspeter Kriesi. Malden: Blackwell, 67–90.

Leifeld, Philip. 2013. 'Reconceptualizing Major Policy Change in the Advocacy Coalition Framework: A Discourse Network Analysis of German Pension Politics'. *Policy Studies Journal* 41(1): 169–98.

Leifeld, Philip and Sebastian Haunss. 2012. 'Political Discourse Networks and the Conflict over Software Patents in Europe'. *European Journal of Political Research* 51(3): 382–409.

McClurg, Scott D. and Joseph K. Young. 2011. 'Political Networks'. *PS: Political Science & Politics* 44(1): 39–43.

Mirowski, Philip. 2013. *Never Let a Serious Crisis Go to Waste. How Neoliberalism Survived the Financial Meltdown*. London: Verso.

Rhodes, R.A.W. 2008. 'Policy Network Analysis'. In *Oxford Handbook of Public Policy*, eds. Michael Moran, Martin Rein and Robert E. Goodin. New York: Oxford University Press, 425–47.

Sabatier, Paul A. and Christopher M. Weible. 2007. 'The Advocacy Coalition Framework: Innovations and Clarifications'. In *Theories of the Policy Process*, ed. Paul A. Sabatier. Boulder: Westview Press, 189–220.

Schneider, Volker, Frank Janning, Philip Leifeld and Thomas Malang, eds. 2009. *Politiknetzwerke. Modelle, Anwendungen und Visualisierungen.* Wiesbaden: VS.

Snow, David A., R. Burke Rochford, Jr., Steven K. Worden and Robert D. Benford. 1986. 'Frame Alignment Processes, Micromobilization, and Movement Participation'. *American Sociological Review* 51(4): 464–81.

Cited Newspaper Articles

Frankfurter Allgemeine Zeitung 4 April 1998. 'Der Bürger entscheidet selbst'.

Frankfurter Allgemeine Zeitung 10 October 2000. 'Standpunkte: Otto Graf Lambsdorff'.

Süddeutsche Zeitung 14 April 2005. 'Balsam für die linke Seele'.

8

Capitalism's Resilience after the Financial Crisis: A Discursive Explanation

Jennifer Gronau and Sebastian Haunss

The financial crisis has left deep marks in societies on both sides of the Atlantic. In the Southern European countries, unemployment rates have reached historical peaks with values between 27.5 per cent in Greece and 12.7 per cent in Italy. Between more than one-third (Portugal) and more than half (Greece, Spain) of the 15–24 year olds are without jobs (OECD 2016a, 2016b). The financial and economic crisis even affected the labour markets of the advanced economies considered in this volume (Germany, Switzerland, the United Kingdom and the United States). Unemployment rates more than doubled from 4.8 to 9.9 per cent in the

J. Gronau (✉)
Centre for Global Cooperation Research (Käte-Hamburger-Kolleg), Duisburg, Germany
e-mail: jgronau@uni-bremen.de

S. Haunss
Research Centre on Inequality and Social Policy (SOCIUM), University of Bremen, Bremen, Germany
e-mail: sebastian.haunss@uni-bremen.de

S. Schneider et al. (eds.), *Capitalism and Its Legitimacy in Times of Crisis*, Transformations of the State,
DOI 10.1007/978-3-319-53765-8_8

United States; they rose from 5.3 to 8.3 per cent in the United Kingdom and from 3.4 to 5.1 per cent in Switzerland. In Germany, the labour market effect of the crisis remained weakest due to the extensive use of a corporatist short-term work programme, with only a slight increase of unemployment from 7.1 to 7.8 per cent (Schelkle 2012; OECD 2016a).

Growing unemployment rates and the expansion of short-term work with reduced income are negative effects of the crisis that are immediately felt by a country's population. It would therefore not have come as a surprise if the capitalist market economy had plunged into a severe legitimation crisis and if alternative economic ideas had replaced the current orthodoxy, laying the foundations for substantial institutional transformation (Chapter 1; see also Blyth 2002: 50).

But this structural change has not taken place. Despite unprecedented state intervention, including rescue measures for failing banks, the EU's concerted action plans (Quaglia et al. 2009) and internationally coordinated measures, for instance, regarding youth employment (OECD and ILO 2011), the economic regime has weathered the storm of the Great Recession largely unscathed. Fiscal stimulus packages and tax cuts were introduced in the United States and most European countries to varying degrees (Bermeo and Pontusson 2012; Mayntz 2012). But these measures were short-lived and did not radically transform the economic regime (for a detailed discussion, see Cameron 2012). Whether the moderate adaptation of economic policies should be interpreted as evidence that the 'system worked' (Drezner 2014) or as indicating the incapacity of a dying system to change (Streeck 2014) is hotly debated among supporters and critics of the capitalist market economy. However, both sides agree that the crisis did not result in substantial changes of the ideas upon which the current economic regime rests (Crouch 2011). Hence, 'with few exceptions, the Great Recession did not cause striking changes in people's political perceptions and behavior' (Bermeo and Bartels 2014: 8), support for redistributive policies did not significantly grow in the wake of the crisis (Soroka and Wlezien 2014: 111) and support for the euro did not decline (Hobolt and Leblond 2014).

This is not to say that the economic crisis did not have severe political consequences. In many countries, governing coalitions lost large shares of their voters or were voted out of office (van Gent et al. 2013; Kriesi 2014). New parties on the left emerged in Spain (*Podemos*), Italy (*Movimento 5 Stelle*) and Greece (*Syriza*), with double digit results in national elections.[1] The rise of right-wing populist parties in many European countries can be partially attributed to the economic crisis as well (Kriesi and Pappas 2015). At the supranational level, the Eurozone witnessed a reform of its economic and financial governance architecture. The European Stabilization Fund and the European Stability Mechanism were created in 2010 and 2011. For the first time in its history, the European Union is not expanding but losing one of its member states. While the 'Brexit' was certainly not a direct consequence of the financial crisis, Eurobarometer data indicate that in the United Kingdom the crisis significantly affected citizens' trust in the EU (Caporaso and Rhodes 2016).[2] Thus, in many respects, the consequences of the crisis for *political* systems have been more severe than the impact on the economic regime.

The stability of the economic regime in its most severe crisis since the 1930s has puzzled many observers. Some scholars argue that the remarkable absence of substantial change is due to the fact that the Great Depression was simply more dramatic and lasted longer than the Great Recession (Drezner 2014: 131). Others contest the general applicability of this argument. They show that the diagnosis is only true for some countries (among them the United States and the United Kingdom), while for others (e.g. Ireland and Greece) the current crisis was actually much more severe (Bermeo and Bartels 2014: 6).

A Discursive Explanation of Capitalism's Resilience

This volume explains the lack of transformative institutional change by analysing the dynamics of mediated legitimation discourse instead of considering economic indicators or the (in-)effectiveness of (inter-)national policy coordination. We argue that one has to begin with an analysis of public debates about the merits and shortcomings of the capitalist market economy and its alternatives to explain why the financial crisis did not lead to structural change.

Institutional or structural change of an economic regime – as long as it does not amount to outright disintegration – is invariably based on a set of arguments and ideas that convincingly challenge established legitimating ideas. A convincing challenge is one that is capable of mobilizing the support of more than a handful of critics, and hence is backed by a large and powerful coalition whose voice cannot be ignored.

The five empirical chapters of this volume contribute to explaining why such a convincing challenge did not emerge. Here, we integrate their threads to solve the puzzle raised in Chapter 1: Why was the opportunity provided by the critical juncture in the wake of the financial crisis in 2008 not seized more forcefully by critics of capitalism to challenge the economic regime in ways that would have led to institutional change? Our answer starts from a counterfactual: How would such an effective challenge look like? It would have to rest on a set of causal and normative ideas that can convince others to question the value of the current economic regime and to demand substantial change. But it is *a priori* unclear which frames might be suitable for such a task, apart from some general insights into the rhetorical power of injustice frames (Gamson 2013).

What we do know from research about the framing strategies of social movements (Snow and Benford 1988; Snow et al. 2014) is that successful collective action framing has to accomplish three tasks: It has to provide convincing diagnostic, prognostic and motivational frames. A successful collective action framing has to present a convincing *diagnosis* of the problem at hand, a *prognosis* (a prescriptive outline of things that should be done to solve the diagnosed problem) and, finally, a rationale for *mobilization* – an urgent call to action. Moreover, it has to offer access points or bridges for various actors to connect their individual framing to the broader collective action frame. A similar point is made in Blyth's work on the crucial role of ideas for institutional change. His sequential model (Blyth 2002: 34–5) consists of (1) the problem diagnosis, which helps to reduce the uncertainty that comes with an open-ended critical juncture, (2) the delegitimation of the underlying ideas of the status quo (diagnosis and prognosis), (3) the development of institutional blueprints (prognosis), and (4) the mobilization of powerful coalitions. Following this line of reasoning, we discuss how the results of the previous chapters can help to understand why a convincing collective action framing did not develop in the four countries examined in this book.

Findings

The contributions to this volume all share a constructivist research perspective and are based on the same original corpus of newspaper articles in which the economic regime is criticized or supported. The five empirical chapters address individual but related research questions and apply different methods of qualitative and quantitative text analysis, highlighting different facets of legitimation discourse before and after the financial crisis in 2008. Various aspects of discourse, including responsibility attributions, metaphors, narratives and discourse coalitions, were examined to identify discursive conditions that prevented a more vivid public discussion about radical institutional change or the mobilization of support for it after 2008. The following sections trace these discourse dynamics and identify the missing elements of successful collective action framing with regard to diagnosis, prognosis and mobilization.

Diagnosis

Did diagnoses of the normative merits and shortcomings of the capitalist market economy change between the pre-crisis and the post-crisis period? Who or what was identified as the cause of the financial crisis? Which (normative) deficits of the capitalist market economy were addressed in media discourse?

In their statistical analysis, Henning Schmidtke and Steffen Schneider (Chapter 3) not only show that in all four countries the legitimacy of the economic regime was discussed more vividly after the financial crisis, but also that the tone of legitimacy evaluations became significantly more negative. Hence, they diagnose a *legitimation crisis* of the economic regime in the quality press. The growing intensity of the debate and the growing predominance of negative evaluations after the financial crisis marked a *critical juncture*, that is, an open-ended turning point with high levels of uncertainty about the future of the regime. But the analysis also shows that the scope of this legitimation crisis was limited: While the overall levels of criticism rose, many of the negative legitimacy assessments were directed at varieties of the capitalist market economy and economic actors rather than the capitalist market economy as a whole; managers and bankers – not the regime – were the main target.

This is not only evident when we look at legitimacy evaluations. It is also a key characteristic of responsibility attributions. According to Falk Lenke's and Henning Schmidtke's analysis of responsibility discourse (Chapter 4), the perceived 'troublemaker' that caused the financial crisis was not the capitalist market economy as such, but merely a segment of its elites. This finding is corroborated by Dominika Biegoń's analysis of legitimating narratives on the capitalist market economy (Chapter 6). She shows that market-friendly narratives remained intact despite the increase of public criticism after the financial crisis. Over the whole period of observation, Biegoń identifies two relatively stable narratives in defence of the capitalist market economy – the freedom and the wealth narrative. Only the wealth narrative changed after the crisis in two important aspects. Firstly, the neoliberal indictment of the state was replaced by a re-evaluation of the state as a helper correcting some malfunctions of the capitalist market economy. Secondly, the welfare state figured no longer as the main opponent and villain, a role now assigned to bankers and managers.

The legitimating narratives thus essentially externalize criticism by distancing the economic regime as a whole from the groups of economic actors held responsible for the crisis in critical discourse. This displacement strategy was facilitated by an overall shift to personalized criticism, which is also indicated by the dominance of personalizing metaphors (Jennifer Gronau, Chapter 5) and the growing centrality of personal virtues as a normative criterion in anticapitalist statements after 2008 (Sebastian Haunss, Chapter 7).

Gronau argues that personifications and other frequently used metaphors – animal, machine, human body and gambling – entail diagnoses with limited scope. These metaphors are mostly related to three normative criteria highlighted by Adam Smith and other classical economic theorists, namely the contribution of the capitalist market economy to economic stability, the self-regulative capacity of the market and the personal virtues that characterize the businessperson as a benefactor of society. The crisis diagnoses entailed in personifying metaphors highlight the lack of personal virtues in economic affairs while animal and machine metaphors are used to lament over capitalism's inability to overcome its instincts, and to criticize its inability to ensure economic stability. These metaphorical representations of the capitalist market economy are characterized by a highly selective form of diagnosis. Personal misbehaviour can be corrected, wild animals can be tamed, malfunctioning machines can be repaired and diseases can be cured. As a result, there is no need for a Great Transformation of the economic regime. Other metaphors used in anticapitalist statements also suggest the adequacy of minor reforms rather than a need for fundamental change, as shown in the next section.

But there is evidence of more far-reaching diagnoses in post-crisis legitimation discourse as well. Schmidtke and Schneider show, for instance, that crucial legitimation resources of the capitalist market economy such as the legitimation criteria of economic stability and efficiency have become weaker sources of legitimation. Haunss's discourse network analysis even suggests that – at least in the United Kingdom and Germany – these former legitimation resources have been integrated as core elements into a delegitimating discursive repertoire that goes beyond personalizing criticism of bankers and managers.

Overall, the empirical analyses point to a diagnostic framing of the crisis in which personalization is very prominent, but which also addresses the ideational and functional core of the capitalist market economy, its ability to generate wealth and economic stability, its efficiency in allocating resources and its capacity of self-regulation. This shift in terms of prominent legitimation criteria indicates that speakers who argue that capitalism is no longer able to fulfil its core functions have become more prominent in public discourse after the financial crisis. What is conspicuously missing is a strong injustice frame; the criterion of distributive justice has even become more marginal after the crisis.

At the level of diagnosis, we thus discern factors that enhance the likelihood of institutional change and others that reduce it: The publicly perceived incapacity of today's capitalism to even meet classical expectations such as guaranteeing economic stability would appear to make a paradigmatic shift in economic ideas and regime change urgent. However, the critique is too focused on economic actors and specific varieties of the capitalist market economy while the capitalist market economy as a whole fades into the background. The blaming of banks, bankers and managers in combination with the absence of an injustice frame further limits the transformative potential of the legitimation crisis.

Prognosis

The prognostic dimension points to possible solutions for the diagnosed crisis in terms of institutional change and in terms of actors held responsible for solving the crisis. A convincing prognosis has to address who should solve the financial crisis and what future route capitalism should take. While diagnoses have to develop a consistent interpretation of the causes and culprits of the crisis, prognoses have to provide a way out of it. They may either be ideas about the restoration of the *status quo* or about alternatives that go beyond the existing regime. In any case, normative and causal ideas have to provide blueprints for institutional change. The more adaptable these blueprints are and the less uncertainty about future developments and outcomes they entail, the more likely they are to be translated into political action.

The responsibility to solve the crisis was largely directed at international and national political decision-makers (Chapter 4). While *blame* for the emergence of the financial crisis was primarily directed at bankers and banks, political elites featured most prominently among the actors expected to provide a *solution* for the financial crisis. Despite such positive attributions of responsibility to the political sphere, national political actors were nevertheless frequently criticized for their management of the crisis; some discourse participants saw a change of mind of economic actors as a necessary condition for solving the crisis.

Chapters 3 and 5 suggest that the capitalist market economy was diagnosed to be unable to correct its own failures. Hence, the responsibility for solving the crisis was mostly shifted away from the economic regime and its actor groups towards governments and intergovernmental organizations. This is reflected in Biegoń's analysis (Chapter 6), which indicates that after the financial crisis, the wealth narrative assigned a helper role to the state and highlighted the 'ordering hand' of governments in the reorganization of financial markets. However, Biegoń also highlights the temporary nature of the idea that the state has crisis-solving capacity. She concludes that the greater significance of the state as helper did not imply a defence of far-reaching state intervention in economic processes. Hence, a shift towards legitimation narratives that advocate an economic regime more strongly regulated by the state did not take place. Instead, legitimation narratives highlight the overall malleability and adaptability of the capitalist market economy. The economic regime is assumed to stabilize itself once the dysfunctional aspects of the financial sector are solved. These findings reveal countervailing tendencies in legitimation discourse. On the one hand, discourse provides the communicative ground for intervention by political elites, making a radical institutional shift at least conceivable. On the other hand, the debate restricts the scope of possible interventions.

Yet another discursive limitation regarding the likelihood of institutional transformation results from the absence of blueprints for alternatives to the current economic regime in the long run. The *diagnosis* information from the responsibility discourse (Chapter 4) suggests that political decision-makers' solutions to the crisis should focus on banking and manager regulation rather than critically reviewing the whole economic regime. Since economic actors can be substituted or 're-educated' without transforming the entire regime, the blaming of banks and bankers did not have the potential to destabilize the capitalist market economy as a whole. The focus on business elites instead of systemic failures made institutional solutions within the capitalist market economy appear much more plausible than political demand for a radical transformation. Hence, the discourse on responsibility for solving the crisis suggests that the economic regime as such just needs some regulation to correct the wrongdoings of economic actors.

This prognosis becomes even more evident in Chapter 5, in which the transformative potential in anticapitalist discourse is scrutinized. Gronau concludes that metaphors used to criticize the capitalist market economy clearly limit thinking about alternatives to the current economic regime. Some of the delegitimating metaphors at least entail plausible regulatory ideas such as throttling the engine of capitalism, therapies for its diseased body and containing the lack of virtues or animal instincts built into it. However, even after 2008, metaphors that portray the economic regime as manufactured and hence susceptible to human intervention are relegated to the sidelines by metaphors that entail little or no such potential; delegitimating discourse is suffused with the notion that human beings cannot seriously transform the regime and therefore have to limit themselves to regulatory reform.

It is exactly this regulative framing that follows from the above-mentioned diagnosis. Since bankers' and managers' immoral and irresponsible behaviour caused the financial crisis, these actors and *not* the economic regime as a whole need to be regulated by political decision-makers in order to prevent further damage and to enable the capitalist market economy to recover its self-regulative power.

In sum, politicians rather than economic actors were expected to deal with the crisis. At first glance, this appears to provide an opening for radical change of the capitalist market economy. Yet, the focus of criticism on only one part of the regime and the lack of an institutional blueprint for encompassing reform limit the transformative potential of this constellation, suggesting piecemeal reform and tinkering instead.

Mobilization

Finally, a convincing diagnosis of the crisis and a prognosis that opens up avenues for reform or even fundamental transformation have to be combined with a resonating call for action, a rationale for mobilization that embeds the statements made by individual actors in a broader social process from which political pressure for change may result. Only when a proposed diagnosis of the problem and the solution offered by one set of actors resonate with other actors does institutional change become likely. An effective challenge to the legitimacy of the economic regime thus has to come from a discourse coalition sharing a set of arguments and comprising actors from several social sectors. The literature on political and discursive opportunity structures (Koopmans and Statham 1999; Kriesi 2004) suggests that a narrow discourse coalition including only a limited set of actors with limited political clout will rarely be in a position to impose new interpretations and new ideational foundations on a given society. Instead, a discourse coalition ideally has to be large in membership and broad in terms of actor types, and it must comprise members of the political elite.

In the *mobilization* dimension, our analysis shows most clearly why the 2008 financial crisis did not result in far-reaching institutional change in the four democracies examined. The overall trends reported in Chapter 3 suggest a relatively weak resonance of delegitimation discourse. Firstly, while the overall trend after 2008 is a shift towards the legitimation crisis scenario, the intensity and tone of legitimation discourse nevertheless continue to fluctuate in all four countries. Secondly, political elites retain much more positive evaluations of the economic regime than civil society actors. Thirdly, journalists increasingly dominate. So there is no steadily growing discontent with an increasingly broad social base.

Chapter 4 offers a partial explanation for the relatively weak coherence of discourse coalitions criticizing the capitalist regime by showing that different groups of speakers did not arrive at the same problem diagnosis. Civil society speakers mainly blamed bankers and banks for the crisis, while domestic politicians primarily accused their colleagues to have caused the financial crisis. Together, civil society speakers and national political elites could indeed have formed a powerful discourse coalition, but they did not agree in their attributions of responsibility for the causes of the financial crisis and directed their criticism only at specific aspects or actor groups rather than questioning the regime as a whole.

Chapter 7 shows that in two of our four countries (the United States and Switzerland) densely connected discourse coalitions of more than a handful of actors did not form after the financial crisis. In Germany and the United Kingdom, sizeable critical discourse coalitions were visible and they grew after the crisis. But their diversity in terms of actor types decreased at the same time. While – at least in Germany – politicians held central network positions in delegitimating discourse coalitions before the crisis, after the crisis politicians occupied only marginal positions in German and British discourse coalitions. In both countries, actors from the cultural and educational sector – journalists, authors and academics – formed the core of delegitimating discourse coalitions. Instead of gaining more prominent and diverse support, delegitimating discourse coalitions narrowed down their social base and lost elite support. In addition, unions were suspiciously absent from these coalitions.

For three of the four countries analysed in this volume, the findings about the missing societal resonance of critique are in line with the results of studies about protest mobilization triggered by the financial crisis. Several European countries experienced intense protests as a result of the crisis (della Porta 2015), but Switzerland, the United Kingdom and Germany were not among them and saw only very limited protests. The somewhat puzzling exception is the United States, where the Occupy Movement mobilized strong protests and received a lot of publicity. Here, our results indirectly confirm Todd Gitlin's (2013: 8) claim that Occupy Wall Street did not manage to garner lasting support outside its activist core despite the fact that its main thrust was supported by the majority of US citizens.

The Closing Window of Opportunity

Why did the 2008 financial crisis not lead to structural change of the economic regime? We base our answer to this question on a multifaceted analysis of legitimation discourse about the capitalist market economy in the quality press. The strongly growing intensity of discourse and its more negative tone indicate that the financial crisis did indeed result in a legitimation crisis of the regime. A critical juncture opened up. But only by taking additional information on the discursive dynamics into account are we able to understand why the regime persisted instead of experiencing fundamental institutional change. Discursive dynamics are crucial for explaining this development because ideas about the capitalist market economy and regime alternatives are causally prior to institutional change. Collective action for change rests on shared perceptions and evaluations of the capitalist market economy. The discursive construction of the financial crisis and of solutions thus has an impact on the breadth and depth of institutional responses.

Findings on the basis of quantitative text analysis as well as responsibility, metaphor, narrative and discourse network analysis corroborate our argument about the enabling or limiting effects of diagnostic, prognostic and motivational framing. We conclude that in order to explain the moderate reforms that resulted from the financial crisis, we do not need to resort to deprivation theories that implicitly inform the claim that the magnitude of the 2008 financial crisis was not big enough to trigger a Great Transformation (Drezner 2014). Even a deeper financial crisis with yet more painful consequences would not have 'guaranteed' structural change of the economic regime. The explanatory link between the financial crisis and institutional change is located at the discursive level. Substantial change has not occurred because legitimation discourse has not provided convincing diagnostic, prognostic and motivational frames. Crisis diagnoses limited the scope of possible consequences. Their personalizing thrust was not conducive to more radical interpretations of systemic failure. In addition, the critique that capitalism does not live up to its own standards did not translate into convincing alternative ideational and institutional blueprints. The critique of capitalism voiced predominantly by actors from the cultural sector did not resonate in the wider society. The actors who were visible in the public debate did not build discursive bridges that would have allowed other actor groups to connect to the existing delegitimation discourse. As a result, the window of opportunity offered by the financial crisis closed again before a convincing challenge to the capitalist market economy could develop and a relevant level of oppositional mobilization was reached.

Admittedly, it is an open question whether a different development at the level of discursive legitimation would have resulted in fundamental change of the economic regime. For instance, discourse about the legitimation of capitalism in Greece certainly differed significantly from discourse in Germany. It brought a radical left, explicitly anticapitalist party into government, only to see it forced to follow a policy of austerity and privatization in line with the pre-crisis ideology of the superiority of private markets. Thus, our claim is not that a convincing discursive challenge to the economic regime would have been sufficient to trigger far-reaching institutional change, but that it is a necessary condition for such change.

By highlighting the communicative grounds of institutional change, we demonstrated the value of empirical legitimation research on the capitalist market economy and offered empirical insights into the discursive consequences of the financial crisis. The volume contributes to historical-institutionalist research as it offers and corroborates an argument about the link between discursive dynamics and the institutional outcomes of critical junctures.

Political Consequences of the Financial Crisis

In hindsight, the financial crisis had a paradoxical outcome. The very structures and principles of the economic regime that caused the crisis have survived it. The challenge to the legitimation of the regime has not brought about substantial change, but the repercussions of the crisis in the political system are still present. The rise of right-wing populism, growing nationalism and far-reaching alterations in national political systems could already be observed before the crisis. But they gained momentum after it, and in some cases – such as the 'Brexit' referendum – the crisis may even have provided a tipping point. The nation state and national political institutions experienced a comeback as entities to which responsibility for solving the crisis was assigned. This call for the nation state in times of crisis confirms findings according to which the legitimacy of the democratic nation state has remained remarkably stable even under conditions of globalization (Schneider et al. 2010: 183; Genschel and Zangl 2014: 348). Yet, national politicians were reluctant to consider a radical change of the structures and institutions of the economic regime. Thus, the crisis has not increased the agency of national governments vis-à-vis the economy. On the contrary, especially in the countries hardest hit by the crisis, the developments rather showed the limits of agency and national sovereignty. As in the Greek case, governments had to submit to harsh austerity measures dictated by international institutions and by other, more powerful nation states.

The developments we observe in the current crisis have some parallels to the Great Depression. The political consequences of the Great Depression – the transformation of democracies into fascist regimes – proved to be more radical and more consequential than the establishment of Keynesian economic policies. While the spectre of fascism does not seem to be an imminent threat today, further political consequences of the Great Recession are currently much more likely than change of the economic regime.

The findings presented in this volume show that the stability of the economic regime is – despite more intense criticism and growing public visibility of anticapitalist voices – directly related to the absence of an integrated set of alternative ideas shared by more than a handful of actors. We thus conclude that the stability of the regime is not necessarily a result of its economic performance but the consequence of the inability of anticapitalist actors to develop a master frame that would resonate beyond the cultural sphere.

Notes

1. While Syriza was originally founded in 2004 as a coalition of oppositional leftist groups and thus predates the crisis, it became a formal party in 2012.
2. Before the crisis, more people trusted the European Union than distrusted it. From 2010 to the most recent Eurobarometer wave in May 2016, the percentage of people distrusting the EU exceeded those claiming that they trusted the European Union, http://ec.europa.eu/COMMFrontOffice/PublicOpinion/index.cfm/Chart/getChart/chartType/lineChart//themeKy/18/groupKy/97/savFile/37 (last accessed 29 August 2016).

References

Bermeo, Nancy and Larry M. Bartels. 2014. 'Mass Politics in Tough Times'. In *Mass Politics in Tough Times. Opinions, Votes, and Protest in the Great Recession*, eds. Nancy Bermeo and Larry M. Bartels. Oxford: Oxford University Press, 1–39.

Bermeo, Nancy and Jonas Pontusson, eds. 2012. *Coping with Crisis. Government Reactions to the Great Recession*. New York: Russell Sage Foundation.

Blyth, Mark. 2002. *Great Transformations. Economic Ideas and Institutional Change in the Twentieth Century*. Cambridge: Cambridge University Press.

Cameron, David R. 2012. 'European Fiscal Responses to the Great Recession'. In *Coping with Crisis. Government Reactions to the Great Recession*, eds. Nancy Bermeo and Jonas Pontusson. New York: Russell Sage Foundation, 91–129.

Caporaso, James A. and Martin Rhodes. 2016. *Political and Economic Dynamics of the Eurozone Crisis*. Oxford: Oxford University Press.

Crouch, Colin. 2011. *The Strange Non-Death of Neo-Liberalism*. Cambridge: Polity Press.

della Porta, Donatella. 2015. *Social Movements in Times of Austerity*. Cambridge: Polity Press.

Drezner, Daniel W. 2014. 'The System Worked: Global Economic Governance during the Great Recession'. *World Politics* 66(1): 123–64.

Gamson, William A. 2013. 'Injustice Frames'. In *The Wiley-Blackwell Encyclopedia of Social and Political Movements*, eds. David A. Snow, Donatella della Porta, Bert Klandermans and Doug McAdam. Oxford: Wiley-Blackwell.

Genschel, Philipp and Bernhard Zangl. 2014. 'State Transformations in OECD Countries'. *Annual Review of Political Science* 17: 337–54.

Gitlin, Todd. 2013. 'Occupy's Predicament: The Moment and the Prospects for the Movement'. *British Journal of Sociology* 64(1): 3–25.

Hobolt, Sara B. and Patrick Leblond. 2014. 'Economic Insecurity and Public Support for the Euro Before and During the Financial Crisis'. In *Mass Politics in Tough Times. Opinions, Votes, and Protest in the Great Recession*, eds. Nancy Bermeo and Larry M. Bartels. Oxford: Oxford University Press, 128–47.

Koopmans, Ruud and Paul Statham. 1999. 'Political Claims Analysis: Integrating Protest Event and Political Discourse Approaches'. *Mobilization* 4(2): 203–21.

Kriesi, Hanspeter. 2004. 'Political Context and Opportunity'. In *Blackwell Companion to Social Movements*, eds. David A. Snow, Sarah A. Soule and Hanspeter Kriesi. Malden: Blackwell, 67–90.

Kriesi, Hanspeter. 2014. 'The Political Consequences of the Economic Crisis in Europe: Electoral Punishment and Popular Protest'. In *Mass Politics in Tough Times. Opinions, Votes, and Protest in the Great Recession*, eds. Nancy Bermeo and Larry M. Bartels. Oxford: Oxford University Press, 297–333.

Kriesi, Hanspeter and Takis S. Pappas, eds. 2015. *European Populism in the Shadow of the Great Recession*. Colchester: ECPR Press.

Mayntz, Renate, ed. 2012. *Crisis and Control. Institutional Change in Financial Market Regulation*. Frankfurt am Main: Campus.

OECD. 2016a. *Harmonised Unemployment Rate (HUR)*. DOI: 10.1787/52570002-en (last accessed August 17, 2016).

OECD. 2016b. *Youth Unemployment Rate*. DOI: 10.1787/c3634df7-en (last accessed August 17, 2016).

OECD and ILO. 2011. *Giving Youth a Better Start. A Policy Note for the G20 Meeting of Labour and Employment Ministers Paris, 26–27 September 2011*. Paris and Geneva: OECD and ILO, http://www.oecd.org/g20/topics/employment-and-social-policy/48732154.pdf (last accessed August 17, 2016).

Quaglia, Lucia, Robert Eastwood and Peter Holmes. 2009. 'The Financial Turmoil and EU Policy Co-operation in 2008'. *Journal of Common Market Studies* 47(S1): 63–87.

Schelkle, Waltraud. 2012. 'Policymaking in Hard Times: French and German Responses to the Eurozone Crisis'. In *Coping with Crisis. Government Reactions to the Great Recession*, eds. Nancy Bermeo and Jonas Pontusson. New York: Russell Sage Foundation, 130–61.

Schneider, Steffen, Achim Hurrelmann, Zuzana Krell-Laluhová, Frank Nullmeier and Achim Wiesner. 2010. *Democracy's Deep Roots. Why the Nation State Remains Legitimate*. Basingstoke: Palgrave Macmillan.

Snow, David A. and Robert D. Benford. 1988. 'Ideology, Frame Resonance, and Participant Mobilization'. In *From Structure to Action. Comparing Social Movement Research Across Cultures*, eds. Bert Klandermans, Hanspeter Kriesi and Sidney Tarrow. Greenwich: JAI Press, 197–217.

Snow, David A., Robert Benford, Holly McCammon, Lyndi Hewitt and Scott Fitzgerald. 2014. 'The Emergence, Development, and Future of the Framing Perspective: 25+ Years Since "Frame Alignment"'. *Mobilization: An International Quarterly* 19(1): 23–46.

Soroka, Stuart N. and Christopher Wlezien. 2014. 'Economic Crisis and Support for Redistribution in the UK'. In *Mass Politics in Tough Times. Opinions, Votes, and Protest in the Great Recession*, eds. Nancy Bermeo and Larry M. Bartels. Oxford: Oxford University Press, 105–27.

Streeck, Wolfgang. 2014. 'How Will Capitalism End?' *New Left Review* 87: 35–64.

van Gent, W.P.C., V.D. Mamadouh and H.H. van der Wusten. 2013. 'Political Reactions to the Euro Crisis: Cross-national Variations and Rescaling Issues in Elections and Popular Protests'. *Eurasian Geography and Economics* 54(2): 135–61.

Index

S. Schneider et al. (eds.), *Capitalism and Its Legitimacy in Times of Crisis*, Transformations of the State,
DOI 10.1007/978-3-319-53765-8

The manufacturer's authorised representative in the EU is Springer Nature Customer Service Centre GmbH, Europaplatz 3, 69115 Heidelberg, Germany. If you have any concerns regarding our products, please contact ProductSafety@springernature.com

Printed and bound by CPI Group (UK) Ltd, Croydon, CR0 4YY
25/09/2026
02222894-0001